Struggling Upward

Harvard East Asian Monographs 393

Struggling Upward

Worldly Success and the Japanese Novel

Timothy J. Van Compernolle

Published by the Harvard University Asia Center
Distributed by Harvard University Press
Cambridge (Massachusetts) and London 2016

Printed in the United States of America

The Harvard University Asia Center publishes a monograph series and, in coordination with the Fairbank Center for Chinese Studies, the Korea Institute, the Reischauer Institute of Japanese Studies, and other facilities and institutes, administers research projects designed to further scholarly understanding of China, Japan, Vietnam, Korea, and other Asian countries. The Center also sponsors projects addressing multidisciplinary and regional issues in Asia.

Library of Congress Cataloging-in-Publication Data

Van Compernolle, Timothy J., 1968–
Struggling upward : worldly success and the Japanese novel / Timothy J. Van Compernolle.
pages cm — (Harvard East Asian monographs ; 393)
Includes bibliographical references and index.
ISBN 978-0-674-65979-7 (hardcover : alk. paper) 1. Japanese fiction—Meiji period, 1868–1912—History and criticism. 2. Naturalism in literature. 3. Japanese fiction—European influences. 4. Social mobility in literature. 5. Ambition in literature. 6. Success in literature. 7. Social change in literature. 8. Literature and society—Japan—History—19th century. I. Title. II. Title: Worldly success and the Japanese novel. III. Series.
PL747.63.N29V36 2016
895.63'42—dc23

2015022032

Index by the author

♾ Printed on acid-free paper

Last figure below indicates year of this printing
25 24 23 22 21 20 19 18 17 16

For Isadora and Chloe

Contents

Preface

At the main gate of the West Cemetery in Amherst, Massachusetts, is a sign alerting visitors to two names, Emily Dickinson (1830–1886) and William Smith Clark (1826–1886). They were almost exact contemporaries. Dickinson is surely the most famous person to have ever lived in Amherst. There are usually a number of visitors to the cemetery on any given day, and most are there to see her grave. Clark does not have such fame, not even in his native state of Massachusetts. Apart from historically minded people at Amherst College, from which Clark graduated in 1848 and where he taught chemistry from 1852 to 1867, and at the University of Massachusetts' flagship campus, over which he presided as its third president for over a decade beginning in 1867, when the institution was still an agricultural college, his name is not widely recognized. His gravestone features the following words: "In memory of William Smith Clark, whose Life as a teacher, soldier, and citizen was Devoted to the service of God and His fellow man, Died March 9, 1886, aged 60." There is no mention of his connection to Japan. In an eventful life that included service in the American Civil War in addition to teaching and leadership positions at two institutions of higher education, the brief time he spent in what was once called the Far East was probably not especially significant to his kin. Although Dickinson is also admired in Japan, with many books, academic groups, and even fan clubs devoted to her work, it may be the one place in the world in which the name of William Smith Clark is equally, if not better known than that of the poet.

As part of a larger project of building a modern educational infrastructure, the still inexperienced Meiji officialdom hired Clark in 1876 to advise them in their effort to establish an agricultural school in the archipelago. His innovations at what was to become the University of Massachusetts had given him an international reputation, and the Japanese government was eager to tap his expertise. Clark was on the country's northernmost island for less than a year, where he helped found Sapporo Agricultural College, the forerunner of today's Hokkaidō University. Before departing from Japan on April 6, 1877, to return to his duties in Massachusetts, he addressed a gathering of students of the new Japanese school, uttering, or so it is reported, the following immortal words: "Boys, be ambitious!" This exhortation is known in the original English to almost every college-educated Japanese I have ever met, and most also know the name of the man who spoke it. The words are inscribed in stone on the statue of Clark that stands in Sapporo to this day.

Clark's admonition takes its place amidst a host of canonical utterances on worldly success that appeared in speech and in print throughout the 1870s. Nakamura Masanao's (1832–1891) translation of Samuel Smiles's worldwide bestseller *Self-Help* (1859) as *Saikoku risshi hen* (Stories of Lofty Purpose in the West, 1871) opens with words known to most Japanese even today: "Ten wa mizukara tasukuru mono o tasuku." More than a few even know Smiles's original English: "Heaven helps those who help themselves." Within a year of its release, Fukuzawa Yukichi (1834–1901) began publishing *Gakumon no susume* (An Encouragement of Learning, 1872–1876), which would eventually amount to seventeen pamphlets. Its opening sentence can still be recited by most Japanese: "Ten wa hito no ue ni hito o tsukurazu, hito no shita ni hito o tsukurazu to ieri" (It is said Heaven makes no man above another and no man below another). Clark advocates ambition. Nakamura (translating the ideas of Smiles) urges self-reliance. Fukuzawa lays a claim for universal equality with regard to both education and opportunity. Together, the three can be taken as signifying different facets of a new discourse on social mobility, which became vital beginning in the second half of the nineteenth century and supported Japan's modernization well into the twentieth century. Its vestiges can still be felt today, well over a century later.

The name for this discourse is *risshin shusse* (立身出世). This is a compound of two pairs of evocative ideographs formed from the common phrases *mi o tateru* (身を立てる to establish oneself), abbreviated to *ris-*

shin (立身), and *yo ni deru* (世に出る to go out into the world), abbreviated to *shusse* (出世). I will have occasion to detail the nuances of these terms later, but I would like to emphasize at the outset that *risshin shusse* is, despite the etymology of the term itself, a Japanese variant of a globally circulating discourse about social mobility and worldly success that was common in all the industrialized and industrializing countries around the world during the late nineteenth and early twentieth centuries.

The ways in which this discourse intersects with modern Japanese literature is the subject of this book. I hope to show that *risshin shusse* and new ideas about social mobility, both of which are fundamentally linked to an emergent capitalist modernity, played a major role in shaping the modern Japanese novel as it emerged in the 1870s by mimicking features of European fiction, then grew to encompass a set of wide-ranging themes, and reached maturity at the turn of the twentieth century. But to see the influence of a social discourse on narrative form is to tell only half the story. Though more difficult to demonstrate, I also show the influence of literature on developing notions of worldly success so as to make the case that the novel is a bearer of ideas and takes part in the broader social debate within print capitalism and the public sphere regarding the meaning of social mobility, social boundaries, and the place of individual ambition within the larger polity. My book, then, is about the intertwining of social discourse and narrative form in the Meiji period (1868–1912), with lines of influence moving in both directions.

The claim that such narratives are preoccupied with social mobility is not itself a new one. Indeed, as I enumerate in the introduction, studies of Meiji fiction can hardly do without some acknowledgment of the novel's upwardly aspiring characters, a theme that would continue well beyond the Meiji era and even extend to cinema and other narrative art forms. Though *risshin shusse* has been the topic of a number of essays and book-length historical and sociological studies, both in Japanese and English, the way worldly success is imbricated with the modern novel has not been treated in a monograph in any language, and there is no developed conceptual framework for understanding its role in shaping the fiction of modern Japan. This book does not pretend to offer either a complete conceptual vocabulary or a comprehensive survey of the topic. Its ambitions are rather more modest. Although *Struggling Upward* brings the Meiji period as a whole into its purview, it is concerned with creating a detailed picture of the variety of literature written in the final decade of that era. Within this body of writing, I focus on the way *risshin shusse* helps create the spatial imagination of the modern novel. I believe this topic takes us to the heart of the way social mobility and the modern novel are intertwined, and late Meiji fiction explores the implications in rich and complex ways that deserve and require full explication.

The distinctiveness of the modern novel compared to the fiction that came before it is a point that I stress throughout *Struggling Upward.* One of the greatest challenges in the study of Meiji fiction is the double vision required to see both the influence of earlier domestic genres of fiction, especially those of the Tokugawa period (1600–1868), and the immense and undeniable influence of European literature, especially that of England, France, and Russia. It was common in the past to see a fairly decisive break between modern literature and what came before it. More recent studies have tended to stress the continuity between Edo and Meiji literature. My earlier work on Higuchi Ichiyō led me to place the emphasis on the influence of the past, whereas my research into the literature of worldly success will stress difference over continuity, and, drawing on historical and geographical studies, I will show that the spatial imagination of the modern novel is quite distinct from that of the literature of earlier eras. This conclusion does not invalidate studies that stress the afterlife of Edo or earlier Japanese literature in the Meiji era; rather, it simply acknowledges the complexity of the literary culture of this period of immense change and accepts the seeming paradox that whether one stresses continuity or difference depends very much on the vantage point from which one looks.

This book has been a long time in the making, and it is a pleasure to acknowledge at last those who contributed to its development. Its roots go all the way back to my discussions of Natsume Sōseki's *Mon* (The Gate) with Komori Yōichi at the University of Tokyo, where I was a graduate student researching my doctoral dissertation on Higuchi Ichiyō at the end of the 1990s. I had delved into the literature on *risshin shusse* in my study of Ichiyō, but the immersion in *Mon*, and in Sōseki's oeuvre more generally, was my first intimation of the centrality of the topic to modern Japanese literature as a whole rather than being just a local theme that engaged a handful of canonical writers. Since then, I have come to see *risshin shusse* as having significant implications for literary form, but many of the ideas about theme I developed during those discussions with Professor

Komori underlie this book in fundamental ways, most visibly in the third chapter and parts of the fifth.

I carried out the bulk of the literary research for the project during the 2007–2008 academic year at Waseda University, spending countless hours at its incomparable Central Library, which houses one of the finest collections of Meiji-era books and periodicals in the world. I was originally inspired to look closely at advertising for the second chapter because Waseda had much of the fiction and nonfiction being promoted in the advertisements, thereby allowing one to reconstruct a media field. The staff of the Central Library and that of the library at Waseda's School of Education were invaluable in helping me gather obscure materials. Special thanks go to Richi Sakakibara, who hosted my stay at Waseda and who also commented on the first draft of the introduction. I had the privilege of doing research on Meiji intellectual history at rival Keiō University during the same period. I thank Professor Komuro Masamichi, then head of the Fukuzawa Research Center, for his time and generosity in hosting me. Examining the original pamphlets of *Gakumon no susume* and other texts, with Professor Komuro as my guide, was an unforgettable experience.

I carried out the remaining research during the autumn of 2009 at Dōshisha University in Kyoto. Here I made my first foray into a still relatively new frontier of research by making use of searchable electronic databases of periodicals. The fourth chapter would have been nearly impossible (or at least would have taken far longer) without this resource. I thank the library staff for their patience with a beginner. I hope I did not disappoint them too much, when, after locating articles in the database, I went to the stacks to find the original, in their fine collection of Meiji periodicals, rather than print them from the computer. For those who spend much of their time in library stacks, there is something reassuring about tactile contact with the original material. My stay at Dōshisha was made possible by Shindō Masahiro and facilitated by the staff of the Faculty of Literature there. Professor Shindō made all the resources of the institution available to me and generously welcomed me in his graduate seminar.

Academic books are made with two fundamental luxuries: time and money. Nine months of research in Tokyo during the 2007–2008 academic year was made possible by a Fulbright Scholars grant, which I gratefully acknowledge. Amherst College, an institution that truly understands that teaching and research are intertwined, has been enormously generous ever since my arrival in the autumn of 2007. A semester leave in Japan in 2009 allowed me to finish the research for the book, and a full year of sabbatical leave under the Senior Sabbatical Fellowship program during the 2011–2012 academic year allowed me to complete the manuscript. I also received funding from Amherst for those periodic (and increasingly expensive) short trips to Japan, which are absolutely necessary for pinning down the unexpected details that proliferate during writing. The Center for Japanese Studies at the University of Michigan, where I was a graduate student some years ago, provided a timely long-term research grant to use Michigan's superlative Japanese collection when I unexpectedly found myself needing to learn about literary sketching for the first and fifth chapters.

I wrote the entire book surrounded by wonderful colleagues, friends, and students at Amherst and the Five Colleges Consortium, but I especially want to single out my compatriots on the Japan side of the Department of Asian Languages and Civilizations—Trent Maxey, Samuel C. Morse, and Wako Tawa—for stimulating conversations over the years. Each of the chapters herein benefited from scrutiny and penetrating questions when they were given as talks at a variety of venues: as panel presentations in Atlanta, Philadelphia, and Wellesley College for the national and, for the last venue, regional meetings of the Association for Asian Studies; and as longer lectures at Keiō University, the Fulbright office in Tokyo, Yale University, the University of Maryland, and the University of Massachusetts, Amherst. I especially want to thank Ellen Shattschneider (Brandeis University), Keith Vincent (Boston University), and Tomiko Yoda (Harvard University) for inviting me, a neophyte in colonial studies, to present the fifth chapter at the Modern Japanese Literature and Culture Study Group at the Reischauer Institute at Harvard, where I was spoiled by a lively hour-and-a-half discussion of my work among twenty or so people, each of whom had read the draft chapter in advance. I thank Marnie Anderson, Alex Bates, Ken Ito, Trent Maxey, Richi Sakakibara, Amanda Seaman, Kristina Vassil, and Abbie Yamamoto for reading individual chapters and offering valuable comments for improvement. I am grateful to Sara Brenneis, my friend and colleague at Amherst, for making sure my most fundamental ideas made sense to those outside the field of Japanese literature. I thank the two anonymous referees for their incisive and immensely helpful remarks and the editors at the Harvard University Asia Center for helping see this work through to publication. Despite all the generous assistance and wise counsel I have received in making this book, there are no doubt errors and infelicities. They are entirely my own responsibility.

Material for chapter 2 first appeared in an article entitled "A Utopia of Self-Help: Imagining Rural Japan in the Meiji-Era Novels of Ambition," *Harvard Journal of Asiatic Studies* 70, no. 1 (2010): 61–103, and is reprinted here with permission of the editors. I thank the Mead Art Museum at Amherst College for permission to use the images on the book jacket and the frontispiece.

Finally, a brief note on conventions: All names are given in Japanese style, surname first, given name last, and I refer to most people by their family name. Most Meiji-era authors, however, used pen names, and I follow convention in referring to authors by those pen names (for example, Tayama Katai is referred to as Katai, Natsume Sōseki as Sōseki). In the notes, however, I use the family name (thus, Tayama, Natsume) because the bibliography is alphabetically arranged by family name. I use macrons to indicate long vowels in Japanese, except for well-known place names, such as Tokyo or Osaka. Finally, all translations from the Japanese are mine unless otherwise noted.

May 2015
Amherst, Massachusetts

Detail, Utagawa Kunimasa IV, Japanese (1848–1920). Brocade picture of the "Pavilion above the Clouds" Sugoroku (Ryounkaku kikai sugoroku). Woodblock print with collage elements on medium thick laid paper, 1890 (Meiji 23), sheet: 28¾ in x 9¾ in; 73.0 cm × 24.8 cm. Mead Art Museum, Amherst College, Museum Purchase Accession Number: AC 2008.48

INTRODUCTION

> A revolution that does not produce a new space has not realized its full potential.
>
> —Henri Lefebvre, *The Production of Space*

Made in 1890, the image reproduced on the jacket of this book consists of two *ōbon*-size woodblock prints mounted vertically, giving it a height of seventy-three centimeters.[1] It depicts the Ryōunkaku, or "Pavilion above the Clouds," designed by the Scotsman William K. Burton and completed in 1890, the same year the print was created. Located in Asakusa, a religious and entertainment district in northeastern Tokyo, the tower was colloquially known as the Asakusa Jūnikai—the Asakusa Twelve-Story. These twelve floors rose sixty-nine meters in the air, making it the tallest building in Tokyo for a while. Featuring an elevator and electric lighting, in addition to its formidable height, it was the marvel of the metropolis in its day and was depicted in countless prints and photographs between 1890 and 1923, when the Great Kantō Earthquake irreparably damaged it.

But there is more to this image, as is suggested by the title, *Ryōunkaku kikai sugoroku* (Mechanism Sugoroku of the "Pavilion above the Clouds"), with *kikai* (mechanism; machine) referring to its internal workings. The image is not just a print, but a board for the game *sugoroku*, in which players would have rolled dice and advanced up the structure to the top. The central part of this large image has flaps that open up to reveal the inside of the Ryōunkaku, a detail of which is reproduced as the frontispiece to this book. The second through seventh floors housed a variety of shops, the eighth a lounge, the ninth an exhibition space, and the top three observation decks. In the print, flaps on all the floors from the first to the eleventh open to reveal these features of the structure. There are additional flaps on the third and seventh floors, which open to reveal the elevator. Not only would players roll dice and proceed up the structure, but they would also open the flaps at each stage and learn about the "Twelve-Story."

Players would vicariously experience this modern wonder as they moved through the space, opening and closing flaps, but another striking feature of this print is its insistent verticality. This is uncommon among *sugoroku* boards. Regardless of the theme depicted, game boards typically feature a layout that moves the players in some kind of spiral pattern, often from the edge of the board to its center. Kunimasa's print moves the characters continually upward; to reach the top is to win the game. In addition to signifying a vicarious modernity and consumerism, Kunimasa's board is the perfect metaphor for upward mobility in an era when the discourse was new and in a society being remade into vertically stratified classes under capitalism. Verticality was rapidly becoming a prominent metaphor in Meiji Japan, which even impacted conceptions of the archipelago's geography: Tokyo was the apex and everything else was "below" it, regardless of cardinal direction or height above sea level.

The foundation of this new vertically oriented society is *risshin shusse*.[2] In some decades the term took on quite narrow meanings of personal (or at best, familial) social advancement. Certainly to present-day Japanese ears, the phrase has an archaic ring and, to some, connotations of self-interest as the sole guide to action. However, my research on this topic has led me to consider *risshin shusse* in relation to a larger literary, social, political, and economic nexus and to see it as one of the most powerful ideologies of modernity. This is certainly a greater claim than is usually made for *risshin shusse*, and I will elaborate on and defend this more expansive view in the chapters that follow. At a fundamental level, *risshin shusse* is concerned with the achievement of individual ambitions and the attainment of worldly success. However, this is only one facet of a larger problematic, for "going out into the world and establishing oneself" is inseparable from the neighboring discourses of individualism and self-fashioning.

This book, *Struggling Upward: Worldly Success and the Japanese Novel*, explores the intersection of these facets of the modern experience with the prose narrative in the Meiji period (1868–1912). It does this through a focused examination of the relationship between the discourse on upward mobility and the Japanese novel during the final decade of that era. Its starting point is the observation that the formation of the novel, the consolidation of the nation-state, and the emergence of the discourse on worldly success all occur at the same historical moment in Japan. The methodology is historicist, utilized with an eye toward putting the institution of literature in contact with the intellectual ferment and social dislocations of modern Japan. My thesis is that the modern novel developed as an artistic form to represent an upwardly mobile national subject negotiating the space of the emerging capitalist nation-state and, by the end of the Meiji era, an emerging empire in East Asia.

In their quest for a suitably grand theme in the new age, novelists, in particular, eagerly took up the problem of the gap between what one is and what one wishes to become in order to stage dramatic, conflict-filled encounters between the upwardly mobile individual and the ever-shifting social boundaries of a modernizing nation. There has been little in-depth exploration of the relationship between *risshin shusse* and the modern novel, despite the fact that most studies of Meiji literature are unable to do without some discussion of it, even if the focus of such monographs lies elsewhere.[3] The fact that upward mobility is a mandatory reference point for examinations of such widely varying topics, themes, and genres should suggest at the very least that *risshin shusse* is important to the study of the modern novel in Japan. I will argue here that it is indispensable. I will move beyond focus on schools or movements or genres to show that *risshin shusse* is a form-giving discourse for the modern novel as a whole and thus that it structures narrative and crosses boundaries between genres. *Struggling Upward* places the discourse on worldly success at the center of the study of the novel's emergence and maturation in Japan.

Modern fiction took up a set of issues surrounding upward mobility that emerged in the public sphere at the very beginning of the Meiji period, a set of issues that, like so much else in modernity, had roots in the preceding Tokugawa period (1600–1868). In that era, *risshin* and *shusse* had somewhat different connotations due to the separate ethico-linguistic worlds from which the terms originated: the provenance of the former lay in Confucian thought, whereas the latter emerged from popular Buddhism. Each term traveled its own route away from its origins to arrive at its respective meaning in the nineteenth century. By that time *risshin* was closely associated with samurai ideals of using knowledge and talent as measures of social status, and *shusse* had become joined to the commoner ideal of increasing one's prosperity and social prominence.[4] The commonality between them can be found in their regard for the collective bodies that nurture individual efforts, for *risshin* was also marked by a desire to strengthen the larger warrior house, whereas *shusse* was meant to benefit the extended family lineage.

The joining together of these two strands of thought into one idea—the elevation of those of education and demonstrated talent to positions of social eminence and material advantage—originated with the class of low-ranking but highly educated samurai in the mid-nineteenth century. Their championing of social mobility is one expression of their discontent with the status quo at the end of the era of Tokugawa rule, by which time the sinecures of patronage and the system of inherited rank left little room for ambitious samurai to move up the hierarchy to a spot befitting their education and talents. The dissatisfaction among such low-ranking, impoverished samurai with the ossified social system of late Tokugawa suggests that the nascent ideology of *risshin shusse* played an underexamined role in toppling the shogunate in 1868.[5] Ultimately, however, *risshin shusse*, as two formerly distinct but related discourses cobbled together into one, was bound to the project of modernization, for it was yoked to the new socioeconomic system emerging in the wake of the Restoration. By the turn of the century, capitalism, industrialization, and urbanization were working profound and irreversible changes on the island nation, which required ambitious, upwardly mobile subjects for its needs. The Meiji state quickly realized the advantage of harnessing this energy for the long-term project of modernization and "catching up" with the West.

The strength of the modern capitalist nation-state would thenceforth rest on the individual desire for social advancement, for in a country confronting crisis, ambition was supposed to be an energy put in the service of securing the new polity rather than be reduced to mere self-interest. To accomplish the mission of liberating individual ambition and simultaneously coaxing the individual to put his energies to use for the benefit of the nation, proponents of *risshin shusse* had to simultaneously borrow from and defeat an entrenched opponent in the form of the *kinsei mibun seido*, the early-modern status system of the Tokugawa era. Rooted in a stark divide between samurai and the rest of the population, this was a system that valued social actors based on their utility to the maintenance of warrior society and sorted subjects into particular status categories determined by the occupation and residence of each.[6] As David Howell has argued, the status categories set the terms of social identity in early-modern Japan, but did so in broad strokes so as to ensure that the state was not involved in everyday life or in the realm of individual interest.[7] As long as communities fulfilled their status obligations, both material and symbolic, the Tokugawa authorities kept clear of relations within communities and did not much concern themselves with whether or not individual subjects identified with the political order. (How different this is from the modern nation-state, which is obsessed with whether or not its citizens identify with the larger national body and which pursues this concern even into the psyche of its citizen-subjects.) In the early-modern system, the needs of the collective had priority; the household, not the individual, was the smallest meaningful unit of production and social calculus; and mobility, though it existed, was not valorized. From the perspective of a dynamic, vigorous, and full-blown capitalist socioeconomic system, the status system of the earlier era, in spite of having loosened considerably over the two and a half centuries of Tokugawa rule, was still far too rigid to meet the requirements of the new age. Indeed, as Fukaya Katsumi has argued, the early-modern status system represented an effort by the warrior-ruled state to fix human beings in place within the social system, though it could not ultimately suppress a desire for social advancement.[8] The hold of this earlier mode of social organization extended for several decades into the new Meiji era, but by the end of the nineteenth century, this lingering opponent from an earlier age had been largely subdued, and the new ideology of social mobility spread throughout the archipelago from the defunct samurai class to the new national subjects of Imperial Japan.[9] Obligation to the collective in the earlier form of social organization was transformed in modernity into a nationalist concern for the country's welfare within a dangerous, imperialist world dominated by Great Power rivalries.

In its initial skirmishes with the early-modern status system, *risshin shusse* had formidable spokesmen, as I suggested in the preface. The overturning of the prioritization of the collective over the individual with the aim of granting wide scope for the exercise of agency to the latter are goals shared by the two foundational texts of the new ideology. *Saikoku risshi hen*, Nakamura Masanao's translation of Samuel Smiles's worldwide bestseller, *Self-Help*, is the first. This book's siren song was powerful: with only slight exaggeration, Hirakawa Sukehiro calls it "the volume that created Meiji Japan" and notes that sales of the hefty and expensive tome had reached a million by the time of the Meiji emperor's death in 1912.[10] The number of readers was several times this figure, and the number of people exposed to its ideas through school primers was greater still. Fukuzawa Yukichi's *Gakumon no susume* (An Encouragement of Learning) is the second book. When the seventeen individual pamphlets were to be published in a single volume in 1876, Fukuzawa ruminated on the social penetration of his treatise; he estimated that each of the seventeen pamphlets sold about 200,000 copies, resulting in total sales of 3.4 million copies for the entire work.[11] Even given Fukuzawa's propensity for self-promotion through exaggeration (the later installments, for example, did not sell nearly as well as the earlier ones), we must surely expand Hirokawa's statement and say that there were two volumes that defined Meiji Japan.

There are important differences between these texts, which should not be overlooked. The Christian convert, Nakamura, was translating the Victorian ideal of rugged individualism promoted in Smiles's book, which places emphasis on work and labor over educational attainment and valorizes worldliness and invention. In contrast, Fukuzawa's collection of essays, as the title suggests, places overwhelming emphasis on educating the nation's citizens to be innovators. The similarities between the two projects, however, are ultimately more important than the differences in a larger historical context; and it should come as no surprise that these two treatises were penned by men who had been low-ranking samurai in the ancien régime—that is, exactly those men of education and talent who were frustrated by the lack of opportunity and the social rigidity of the early-modern status system. This goes a long way toward explaining the quickness of their embrace of new ideas from overseas. Both Nakamura (by ventriloquizing Smiles) and Fukuzawa argue for the reversal of the collective's authority over the individual while retaining the ideal of service to the larger community so that the nation's subjects can, through their own unhindered initiative, creativity, sense of purpose, and desire for social advancement, help elevate Japan's status in the world and remove it from the purgatory of the unequal treaties. Each author places a high value on individualism and promotes the notion that those with initiative, ambition, and good ideas deserve more shares of society's wealth and honors, irrespective of their social origins. In Takeuchi Yō's succinct phrase, these two texts inaugurate "the liberation of ambition" (*yashin no kaihō*) in modernity.[12] I agree with the inherited wisdom in seeing these ideas as revolutionary. Worldly success reorganizes the relationship between the individual and the collective, invests the human life cycle with new meanings, and creates a social contract of sorts in which those who cultivate ambition are promised success and achievement.

If we are to view this liberated ambition as a form-giving discourse for the Meiji novel, what we need after the recognition of the centrality of *risshin shusse* to modernity are tools to theorize the way upward mobility, as a form of desire, was made available for literary exploration beyond mere theme. Nancy Armstrong's study of the English novel in *How Novels Think* provides a powerful apparatus for thinking about how desire can mediate between society and literature. The focus of her study is on what might be called the novel's pedagogical function: as she argues, the British novel "came into being, I believe, as writers sought to formulate a kind of subject that had not yet existed in writing. Once formulated in fiction, however, this subject proved uniquely capable of reproducing itself."[13] This subject is the individual. The novel takes over from philosophical discourse on individualism to show (rather than tell) what it means to fulfill one's desires in a world defined by inequality. This is accomplished through a specific technique: the novel, in Armstrong's view, features protagonists confronting a gap between what they are and what they could be or wish to be; the novel thus inscribes the desire to close this gap as a "rhetorical additive" or, in deconstructive terms, a "supplement." The protagonist may begin by being poor, or disenfranchised because of gender, or face discrimination due to race, but, through the inscription of desire, is launched on his or her mission of closing that gap between unequal social positions through the unfolding of the plot. Armstrong is less interested in the perennially popular question of the origins of the novel than in exploring the way that the energy of individualism is encouraged, subverted, or contained within literary works in different historical periods. In trying to reach a different state in the social hierarchy, the individual will inevitably confront barriers and resistance to the desire to transcend the social circumstances in which he or she is initially located by birth, all of which are historically contingent.

Such barriers were particularly complex in Meiji Japan, for they were entangled in shifting social boundaries, changing attitudes toward tradition, and new patterns of socialization. First, any discussion of worldly success involves both the singular and the plural in society, for the social hierarchy is a collective construction that is being constantly contested and modified as society itself changes, making social boundaries, as well as the perspective from which one views individual striving, highly unstable. Regardless of how personally and intimately ambition and the fruition of subjective desires may be experienced, the individual would be unable to define and savor success or lament failure without the collective, for all yardsticks for measuring one's place in the social order are socially produced. *Risshin shusse* also became entangled with shifting notions of tradition and modernity, in which transgressions of inherited social norms by those conversant in the upstart new discourses of success were viewed with suspicion. This collision between the ambitious individual seeking to rise in the world and the shifting social boundaries of an era implies, too, a story of socialization or its failure. Narrative can be seen as devoted at least in part to exploring the possibilities and limitations of the integration of the individual and his or her desires into society. Armstrong argues that in some periods narrative symbolically conditions individuals to accept the boundaries in place in a particular era, while in others it celebrates an individualism that challenges and exceeds those boundaries.

Ambition, then, propels the individual on a course of attempting to move up the social hierarchy and to close the gap between what one is and what one wishes to become, all while negotiating changing social norms. Narrative inscribes this desire in a protagonist in the form of a "supplement" or "rhetorical additive." We will need to add one element that does not receive as much attention in Armstrong's framework: a consideration of space. Ambition sets the protagonist of a novel on his (or sometimes her) course of attempting to close a social gap by traversing a spatial hierarchy, most emblematically by moving from the provinces to Tokyo. Given that educational and economic opportunities are unevenly distributed within a spatial hierarchy, the path of success would normally lead from one's native home in the provinces, which is where the vast majority of the population lived in the mid-nineteenth century (possibly as much as 80 percent), to Tokyo, the nation's capital and the center of learning. "Going up to the capital" (*jōkyō suru*) is indeed one of the major tropes of modern Japan and is not confined to literature. In addition to acknowledging Tokyo as the emperor's capital, with "up" referencing the ruler's exalted place, the phrase names the vertical path (the second meaning of "up") linking the ancestral home to the metropolis, the humble life of anonymous toil in the country to the dream of a successful life in the capital. Movement up the social hierarchy and through the narrative thus entails motion across a literarily constructed space, for the village, the provincial capital, and the metropolis, among other communities, were differentially coded in relation to *risshin shusse*. The discourse on ambition has a cartographic dimension, mapping onto physical territory and charging different locales from the most remote provinces to the nation's capital with valences as diverse as longing, fulfillment, anxiety, and discontent.

With Japan as an example, I follow Henri Lefebvre, in the epigraph to this introduction, in arguing that the revolution of *risshin shusse* does indeed produce a new space.[14] Considered at the broadest level, *risshin shusse* was a mechanism created by industrial capitalism to facilitate the movement of a mostly rural population to the cities, where capital, industry, and educational opportunities were concentrated. It accomplished this by inscribing within the individual the desire known as ambition and by creating the social and institutional infrastructure that allowed for and even encouraged social mobility and self-fashioning. Such an infrastructure centered on credentialing in the educational system during the years of childhood and adolescence, and thereby acquiring an educational capital that could be converted to upward mobility as one advanced into the world of work and adult responsibility. There is, thus, also a temporality of success.

These considerations suggest that the study of literature's engagement with *risshin shusse* can be enriched and deepened by drawing on a theoretical framework that allows one to link the representation of space and time. The chronotope, "time-space," is a neologism created by the Russian literary and cultural critic Mikhail Bakhtin in the context of his work on the European novel. It names the way in which the representations of space and time are inextricably linked and take on expressive functions in narrative. In characteristically metaphorical language, Bakhtin writes: "Time, as it were, thickens, takes on flesh, becomes artistically visible; likewise, space becomes charged and responsive to the movements of time, plot and history. This intersection of axes and fusion of indicators characterizes the artistic chronotope."[15] What we have in the chronotope is the plasticity of time and space, with the "thickening" and "charging" referring to the artistic molding of both through narrative construction and selective, concentrated description. Furthermore, Bakhtin notes that "temporal and spatial determinations are inseparable from one another" and that they are "always colored by emotions and values," thus indicating the way space and time are invested with varying desires and ideological values.[16] The chronotope, then, helps us see that the representation of time and space bears meaning, functioning as more than just reference points for the presentation of narrative information.

The concept of the chronotope is surely the most enigmatic and least theorized of Bakhtin's many fecund ideas. Moreover, since he himself tended to elaborate on the term within the context of a discussion of a typology of European genres, its utility outside of that framework was lessened.[17] Attempting to untangle the contradictory and circular aspects of Bakhtin's formulation in order to provide the chronotope with more analytical utility, Jay Ladin has shown that an individual "space-time-event cluster" becomes visible in the reading process only when related to a different cluster.[18] There may be a dominant chronotope, but it can never be singular. The implication is that "we must abandon Bakhtin's tempting vision of a complete taxonomy of chronotopes, a list of distinct space-times with specific generic, historical, and ontological implications."[19] Ladin instead reorients conceptualization of the chronotope around the portrayal of character in fiction and with the way authors, narrators, and readers relate to that character. "Thus," Ladin concludes, "any representation of time and space implies a synthesizing consciousness (whether a character's, a narrator's, an author's, or our own)."[20] This accords well with the centrality of the protagonist in Armstrong's formulation of the novel: narrative inscribes desire in the hero or heroine as a rhetorical additive and follows his or her effort to close a gap between that desire and the circumstances of birth. In literary study, then, the chronotope is most productively utilized in an analysis of the protagonist's subjective experience of his or her world and of the techniques the narrator and author use to make that experience available to readers. In this book, that subjective experience can only be understood in relation to another, dominant chronotope.

I would argue that the discourse on *risshin shusse* creates this new, dominant chronotope for Japanese literature, one that is able to best represent the experience of modernity in terms of social mobility and self-fashioning and one that cannot be confined to genre. I will call it the chronotope of success. In terms of the axis of time, ambition defines the significance of a human being's life in new narrative terms. *Risshin shusse* creates a new conception of the proper shape of the socially significant life in modernity. This new desire called ambition propels the individual subject from childhood to the attainment of success, after which the life course can be considered completed and fulfilled—the end of the story, if not of the individual's actual life span. *Risshin shusse* is a way of conceiving a life as having a definite, socially significant shape with a distinct, well-defined telos. The other axis of the chronotope is space. The temporal dimension of a *risshin shusse* narrative does not unfold against the backdrop of an empty, homogeneous space, but against spaces that had come to be invested with social meaning. *Risshin shusse* contributes to the reorganization of space in the cultural imaginary into hierarchical concentric circles stretching from the center of Tokyo (the imperial seat and the home of the first, and for a short time the only, imperial university) to the far corners of the nation. This also maps onto a heterogeneous topography of industrial development and modernization, with the highest concentration of capital and educational opportunities found in Tokyo and other major urban areas, then extending outward to the provincial capitals, and finally reaching, with a time lag, to the rural areas of the nation. After Japan embarks on its project of imperial expansion toward the end of the nineteenth century, its colonial possessions—Taiwan, the Korean peninsula, and especially Manchuria—became inscribed in the spatial imagination as a new periphery.

As we will discover, most literary texts do not feature protagonists who experience this idealized route to success. Rather, the chronotope of success is a kind of ground against which the texts project competing chronotopes. They may offer an alternative temporal or spatial axis; in extreme cases, they may even offer an oppositional chronotope. Yet authors cannot ignore the idealized chronotope of success. The construction of artistic chronotopes centers on the protagonist of a work of fiction and his or her subjective experience of the dominant ideology of worldly success. *Risshin shusse* impacts literary form by inscribing desire in the protagonist as a rhetorical additive and linking this desire to the representation of time and space. The result of such a complex negotiation is a narrative in which the protagonist traverses a spatial hierarchy in an effort to close the gap between circumstances and desire in order to achieve success. This yields a life story that shares some of the characteristics of the European *bildungsroman*.[21]

The novelistic spaces connected in the circuit of success necessarily involve metropolis and countryside, center and periphery. These spaces may be hierarchically related to each other, but they are ultimately mutually dependent for their meanings. The study of literature's engagement with the city has shed light on the urban experience from a variety of disciplinary perspectives, and chapters 3 and 4 in this book have profited enormously from this interdisciplinary work. The countryside has received less attention, perhaps because we are still prone to consider it the site of unchanging tradition. It is perfectly understandable that studies of modernity tend to focus on the city; after all, the metropolis is the first to see the material culture of the new era—the streetlights, the new architecture, new forms of consumerism, novel forms of entertainment, and so forth. Still, one of the important lessons from these studies is that the city depends upon the country for its meaning, just as the periphery lacks meaning without a center. Another goal of this book is to deconstruct this binary of country and city while acknowledging that the tension between them has a real, material basis. Indeed, a study of upward mobility in the novel can help us understand the ways in which a differential and heterogeneous rural landscape became unified under a national and imperial banner and how Tokyo came to exert the pull it did. This will require more detailed elaboration in subsequent chapters, but we can simply note here that urbanization deeply impacted the countryside in a number of ways, most obviously by siphoning off much of its population, who moved to the nation's urban centers seeking new opportunities. It took less than a century for Japan to shift from an overwhelmingly rural population to a majority urban population. Every modernizing society has had to struggle with this phenomenon, but there is nothing natural or inevitable about the outcome.

Equally important, there is a modernizing nation in the background of these tales of individual striving, and the nation functions as a "third term" that prevents a simple analysis of competing dichotomies of country and city. The upwardly mobile subject travels not through a literary set piece, but through a nation-state in the making, nor through a decorative rural or metropolitan backdrop but within a national collective on the move. In the same way that social boundaries within this collective body are unstable and constantly shifting, the space of the nation-state is also neither stable nor homogeneous, not in the wake of the Restoration during early Meiji and certainly not during the subsequent era of imperial expansion, which began in fits and starts after Japan's victory in the

Sino-Japanese War of 1894–1895 and became a policy of opportunism after the Russo-Japanese War of 1904–1905.

Uncovering the relationship between narratives and nations has been one of the most productive avenues within recent novel studies. We have learned that the novel is best conceived as a socially symbolic form that helps produce and sustain the nation conceived as an "imagined community," to use Benedict Anderson's now canonical phrase.[22] Timothy Brennan has described this most admirably:

> It was the *novel* that historically accompanied the rise of nations by objectifying the "one, yet many" of national life, and by mimicking the structure of the nation, a clearly bordered jumble of languages and styles. Socially, the novel joined the newspaper as the major vehicle of the national print media, helping to standardize language, encourage literacy and remove mutual incomprehensibility. But it did more than that. Its manner of presentation allowed people to imagine the special community that was the nation.[23]

Much of my analysis in subsequent chapters will connect the two forms Brennan and Anderson highlight by taking up novels serialized in newspapers and magazines. But to relate Brennan's ideas to the current discussion, not only must we consider social mobility in a Japanese context to be a form-giving discourse for the modern novel; we must also see the novel as giving form to the nation. It thus satisfies a longing for the individual to be part of a larger collective body and helps members of that body forge imaginative connections to people within the nation's borders.

The greatest challenge is to cultivate the double vision required to see the complex relationship involved in the era when novels made nations and nations produced novels. Though taking up a much earlier time period, Timothy Hampton's gloss on Brennan's discussion is instructive in this regard. From one perspective, the novel seems to follow in the wake of the emerging nation-state and to take that political formation as its object. Viewed from another perspective, however, the novel precedes the nation-state and, together with other forms of print capitalism, actively produces the political body within the cultural imaginary. Ultimately the only approach that can succeed in conceptualizing the relationship between novel and nation, as Hampton explains, is one that views it as a dialectical relationship, with the novel simultaneously objectifying and producing the nation through its spatial imagination. Hampton approaches the problem through the idea of genre mixing:

> I shall show that the interplay of space, social identity, and narrative form . . . results in a much more complex dynamic than anything suggested by such well-worn phrases as "epic to novel" or "the rise of the novel." Rather, I will show, it is precisely through their *mixing* of genres that . . . writers . . . attempt to confront the social transformations that accompany the emergence of modern nationhood. And, conversely, that very generic complexity constructs a spatial regime that gives expression to the inclusive volume of the nation-state.[24]

This is a way of conceiving the novel as a socially symbolic act that both produces and is produced by the "imagined community" of a nation in the making. It is also an instructive effort to concretely link nation-building and narrative form. Hampton ultimately sees a writer's mixing and transformation of inherited genres as a sign of that writer's effort to take the measure of an existing nationhood and produce the nation as such.

I have found such ideas insightful and productive, but in the pages that follow, I will seek a solution to the problem of double vision along different lines than genre mixing, which, though immensely productive in Hampton's study of France, is not the crux of the issue in Meiji Japan, which witnesses the consolidation and hegemony of a single genre, the novel. In order to show that Japanese novels both follow and objectify the nation but also precede and produce the polity, I will kick those novels into the fray of the broader social debate on modernity. Every thinker and writer in Meiji Japan had to confront the complex entanglement of foreign and domestic ideas and to find some sort of resolution between individual striving to better one's lot in life and social mores or barriers. The participation of literature in larger social debates in the age of modern print media will be the focus of the conclusion to this book, where I will connect print culture to the public sphere. The chapters in between will provide the evidence and tools. In preparation, we can note that as literature engages with larger debates in society, albeit through narrative construction rather than exposition, it seeks to persuade readers of its view and also inculcates a particular imagination of the space of the nation. At the same time, such novels posit themselves against other views in the public sphere. They not only constitute themselves as alternatives, they take those other views and other imaginative visions as rejoinders and respond to them. They do this most visibly by proffering alternative chronotopes to the time-space of success. This way of viewing literature underlies my decision to juxtapose literary texts with other texts from different culturally demarcated zones and to pursue a historicist mode of literary criticism.

In order to show that the novel is a participant in a national debate over the fate of the nation, my study is synchronic. All of the works I discuss were written during the same historical moment: the final decade of the Meiji era. By narrowing my focus to a ten-year period, I do not wish to imply that *risshin shusse* was important only at the end of Meiji. I have chosen to concentrate this study on novels written within a few years of each other in order to demonstrate that novelists proffer a range of solutions to national dilemmas and, in important ways, "talk" to each other, even if indirectly. Additionally, late Meiji is an era when a range of important issues related to social mobility and national space come to the fore. First and foremost, it is the era of the Russo-Japanese War, which brings to the surface a number of underlying tensions in a rapidly modernizing country. Far from being a moment of national unity and celebration during a time of conflict and victory, the war and its aftermath witnessed an astounding diversity of reaction and opinion, ranging from a virulent, chauvinistic nationalism to a steadfast pacifism and internationalism, as well as everything in between. The war also revealed a fractured society and a public sphere engaged in tense, ambivalent, and ever-shifting relations with the state, none of which could be covered over by a stupendous military victory over a Western power.[25] The Russo-Japanese War brought the nation-state itself into focus as an object of intense scrutiny and engendered debate about which part of the national space might best represent ideal cultural values. Furthermore, in the years leading up to and following the conflict—which was the first sizable international conflict of the twentieth century and an early example of an industrial war in Asia—capitalism came into its own in the archipelago, while industrialization and urbanization were creating enormous tensions between the countryside and the expanding urban areas, as well as tensions between both these and the state itself. The final years of the Meiji era are strategically useful; social mobility, individualism, the welfare of the collective, nationalism, the country, and the city all came under intense debate in the public sphere and thus became the subjects of persistent thematic exploration in novels of the era, which constitute a narrative form that had reached maturity.

By organizing my book in this way—tracing a broad range of representations of space and social mobility at a particular historical moment—I hope to achieve a number of related goals. First, regardless of the agenda of a particular text, a confrontation with the tension among individual desires, social boundaries, and the nation is unavoidable, and each novel must negotiate a position among them. Second, by juxtaposing both heavily studied texts, such as the novels of Natsume Sōseki (1867–1916), with such noncanonical works as the popular fare of Horiuchi Shinsen (1873–?), a forgotten author writing at exactly the same time, I wish to put in contact the venerated works of the modern canon and the generally ignored lineage of the popular novel in order to demonstrate their engagement with each other. What does it mean, for example, that Sōseki's novel *Mon* (The Gate, 1910) specifically mentions the magazine *Seikō* (Success) in which Shinsen's genre staples were serialized? This is merely one example of the larger dialogue I hope to evoke through this kind of juxtaposition of texts that occupy various places on a continuum of canonicity and that sometimes obliquely reference each other. Limiting one's purview to canonical works or, alternatively, to the emerging mass fiction of the Meiji era yields a skewed understanding of how the novel engages with a social discourse; indeed, such a circumscribed approach limits the claims that can be made for the novel as a whole. Third, I hope to show that the novels herein engage in a struggle over representation, a struggle that centers on, but is not limited to, a conception of national space and a distinct representation of the human life cycle created by *risshin shusse*. In particular, they share an engagement with the dominant chronotope of success and its representational system. These three goals will ultimately allow the book to make a contribution to our understanding of the novel as a literary form, through a focused study of its representation of physical, social, and national space.

This book partakes of the larger trend within novel studies to historicize the dominant literary form of modernity. However, I am not aware of other scholarly work that shows how the novel and social mobility are mutually constitutive. It is my hope that *Struggling Upward* will suggest avenues and approaches for those studying the novel in other periods and places. I also hope that this monograph can cast new light on familiar topics in Japanese literary studies, whether in relation to specific "schools" (such as naturalism), forms (serial novels, for example), theoretical approaches (especially historicist criticism), larger historical contexts (colonialism), or specific authors (Natsume Sōseki, for one). After all, each of these schools, forms, approaches, contexts, and authors appears in a new light when viewed from the perspective of worldly success.

Given that *Struggling Upward* is synchronic in conception and takes up the mature Meiji novel, it is worth glancing at some major signposts marking the intersection of worldly success and the prose narrative in early Meiji so as to provide some context for the discussions in subsequent chapters. Following Komori Yōichi's basic narrative connecting *risshin shusse* and the literature of the 1870s and 1880s,[26] I supplement it with the work of other scholars, especially that of Maeda Ai, and then develop a framework that can encompass the Meiji novel as a whole. Oda (or Niwa) Jun'ichirō's (1851–1919) *Karyū shunwa* (Romantic Stories of Blossoms, 1879) is an abridged translation and adaptation of a minor British novel and its sequel, *Ernest Maltravers* (1837) and *Alice* (1838), penned by Edward Bulwer-Lytton (1803–1873). The Englishman's current status as a lesser novelist unknown to any but specialists, should not deter us from recognizing how important his work was for the history of modern Japanese literature, on both linguistic and thematic levels. Oda helped raise the stature of prose fiction by rendering the hackneyed phrases of Bulwer-Lytton into an elevated Sino-Japanese rhetoric.[27] Oda's novel also thematizes the intertwining of love and success within a single narrative. The main characters are joined in a story of love gone astray at first then triumphantly consummated, as the man attains his success in the world of politics, and the woman attains her own kind of success by marrying him, thereby making a stupendous move up the social ladder. It is the quintessential story of "the man of talent and the beautiful woman" (*saishi kajin*), in which the gendered nature of *risshin shusse* is already evident. *Sero nikki* (Diary of a Life Journey, 1884) by Kikutei Kōsui (1855–1942) is the transposition of this basic form into a work written by a Japanese. In its thematization of the man of talent and the beautiful woman, Kikutei's novel stays fairly close to the pattern established in *Karyū shunwa*. The novel makes use of retarding devices and suspense, but the hero and heroine, Hisamatsu Kikuo and Matsue Take, ultimately find their way into each other's arms. Equally important is the novel's adherence to the quintessential route to success, which, in the era in which the work was written, necessarily centers on going to Tokyo and finding one's way into the wider world with a beautiful woman at one's side.

With the basic paradigm set by *Karyū shunwa* and *Sero nikki*, we next witness the gradual enrichment of the new form, with some writers continuing elements of the original model and others broadening its thematic range. Many political novels, such as Suehiro Tetchō's (1849–1896) *Setchūbai* (Plum Blossoms in the Snow, 1886) and its sequel, *Kakan'ō* (Warbler amidst the Blossoms, 1887), took up and developed into elaborate narratives the story of the "talented youth," who attains worldly success by reaching the pinnacle of the political system with the aid of a "beautiful woman" and the dowry she supplies. But the political inflection of *risshin shusse* was short-lived, partly because of the concerted efforts of other novelists to rid the template supplied by these early novels of their overtly political dimension. While harkening back to the complexities of both early-modern Japanese theater and heavily plotted British fiction in its tale of mistaken identity and recovered social status, Tsubouchi Shōyō's (1859–1935) *Tōsei shosei katagi* (The Character of Modern Students, 1885–1886) is, like its predecessors, a story of failure and success among the student crowd, but one that divests the *shōsetsu* of its political themes. Shōyō's novel retains the love story by joining the protagonist Komachida Sanji and the geisha Tanoji (though their marriage is not depicted in the novel) and reorients its valorized success around the politically neutral student and scholar. The critical acclaim that greeted Futabatei Shimei's (1864–1909) *Ukigumo* (Drifting Clouds, 1887–1889), with its portrait of the disaffected intellectual who neither succeeds in life nor gets the girl, provided the basic template for the serious novels that would emerge in the twentieth century. The qualification of being "serious" meant avoiding the happy ending in preference for critical distance and a generally pessimistic portrait of the embattled individual. Corresponding to the larger bifurcation during the turn of the last century between serious and popular fiction, the novels that make up the canon of modern Japanese literature would treat the discourses on ambition and success with skepticism, while the celebratory treatments of upward mobility retreated to the popular lineage of the novel.

Success stories of the kind that were common in the first half of the 1880s would look naive to major writers a decade later. In addition to

Ukigumo, Mori Ōgai's (1862–1922) "Maihime" (The Dancing Girl, 1890) is exemplary of the skeptical tradition of modern fiction. This rich short story has been analyzed from any number of perspectives, but is perhaps most fruitfully discussed through the lens of *risshin shusse*. The protagonist, Ōta Toyotarō, is sent by the Japanese government to Berlin to study law, but ends up becoming engrossed in the literary and art scene in the German capital. He also falls in love with a lower-class German dancing girl, Elise, ultimately getting her pregnant. This story pits *risshin shusse* against love, thereby providing the impetus for the protagonist's probing self-analysis, which calls into question the conformity bred by the ideology of upward mobility. When, after being derailed from the standard course of success, the protagonist is offered a lifeline back to Japan, he takes it, thus choosing success and conformity over love, a choice he regrets for the rest of his life.

Maeda Ai links the divestment of politics from the narrative fiction of the late 1880s to the disillusionment with politics among serious writers after the failure of the Freedom and People's Rights movement to found real democracy in the new Japan. But Maeda also locates another large-scale historical "cycle" (in his words), in which this disillusionment with an earlier form of *risshin shusse* is linked to a growing valorization of the countryside, as exemplified in Miyazaki Koshoshi's (1864–1922) *Kisei* (The Return, 1890).[28] This short novel recounts the narrator-protagonist's return to his provincial home for the anniversary of his father's death, but much of that narration is preoccupied with the way the natal home provokes anxiety and doubt about the metropolitan-based life course laid out for youth within the ideology of *risshin shusse*. Although it is appealing to see Miyazaki's popular novel as the end of a cycle of works about success, I would prefer to view it as a contribution to the continuing enrichment of the links between worldly success and the novel, for even while it is true that politics was divested from such narratives, politics narrowly conceived was replaced by more sustained exploration of the links among city, countryside, and nation after 1890.

An excellent illustration of this trend is Tokutomi Roka's (1868–1927) semi-autobiographical *Omoide no ki* (A Record of Memories), published by Min'yūsha in 1901.[29] This organization was headed by Roka's older brother, Tokutomi Sohō (1863–1957), and had published *Kisei* eleven years earlier. The two novels share much in common, especially a valorization of the countryside, but Roka navigates a far more complex ideological terrain in his sprawling novel. The tale begins with childhood in the provinces and ends with graduation, marriage, and fame in the capital. Exemplifying the celebratory lineage of modern fiction, in contrast to *Ukigumo* and "Maihime," it is that rare, perfect literary example of the chronotope of success, in that the narrative moves its protagonist, Kikuchi Shintarō, from rural Kyūshū to Tokyo and from childhood struggle to worldly success in early adulthood. The spark of ambition is lit early on in a scene in which Shintarō's mother drags her son to the grave of his deceased father, brandishes a knife, and demands that the boy restore the family, which has fallen into abject poverty. Here is the exact moment when desire is inscribed in the protagonist as a rhetorical additive. The narrative completes its arc eighteen years later, when Shintarō achieves success as a man of letters and revisits his father's grave, his mother's words still seared in his mind. But the provincial home remains a soothing memory, for, true to the tenets of *risshin shusse*, Shintarō marries and makes his home in Tokyo. Shintarō's age is never explicitly stated, but through internal evidence it is clear that he, like his creator Roka, was born in 1868, meaning that his birth coincides with that of the new Japan. His personal success thus implicates the nation in addition to the family; and, given that his family was of samurai blood, his personal achievement is also a symbolic story of the samurai class's successful transition to the modern era.

Roka also juggles politics and institutional religion, especially Christianity, and shows his protagonist to be infatuated with both during the era in which Meiji youth in general were exploring them with passion. However, politics and religion are largely pushed to the wayside by Shintarō's abandonment of them (though he remains faithful to his personal view of Christianity). Instead, we have an exploration of the way the successful individual and the provincial home that formed his core values contribute to the welfare of the nation, as Shintarō chooses journalism as a career, thus keeping a watchful eye out for government abuses in the new Meiji polity. As Roka's popular novel pointedly illustrates, by the turn of the century political success was largely divested from the novel, as others have noted, but what took its place was something that has not been thoroughly analyzed in previous scholarship: a complex topography in which the nation-state was inserted as a mediating term between city and countryside.[30] This is why the study of space is so crucial to understanding the intertwining of worldly success and narrative fiction.

Struggling Upward continues this story into the final years of the Meiji era. The rich novels taken up in subsequent chapters offer differing agendas and thematic concerns and thus require different itineraries through their fictional worlds. Each chapter will center on a major novel, supplemented with discussions of other literary and nonliterary works. Chapter 1 focuses on Japanese naturalism, with particular emphasis on the fiction of Tayama Katai (1872–1930). Beginning with a discussion of Katai's novella, *Jūemon no saigo* (The End of Jūemon, 1902), and continuing with his highly regarded but infrequently discussed novel, *Inaka kyōshi* (A Country Teacher, 1909), I show how the provincial naturalist text utilizes tropes of personification and revelation in order to rhetorically separate a homogeneous countryside into nature and provincial community. As a textual and rhetorical maneuver, this unmasking and bifurcation of rural Japan allows the natural world to function as a compensatory object for ambitions that must be perpetually deferred due to social inequality as the protagonist languishes in the countryside, longing for the city and the receding promise of success.

Chapter 2 shifts to almost completely unexplored terrain in Japanese literary studies, a genre of fiction called *risshi shōsetsu* (novels of ambition), associated primarily with Horiuchi Shinsen and popular during the decade after the Russo-Japanese War. Through a close reading of Shinsen's iconic novel of ambition, the pungently titled *Ase no kachi* (The Value of Sweat, 1910–1911), I show how the work is part of a larger advertising network of the magazine *Seikō*, which not only helps sell the fiction but also helps sell success, and how the explicit didactic points in the novel reinforce and are reinforced by similar points being made across the magazine in such a way as to constitute a particular media network. However, I also demonstrate that the representational level of the text partakes of other social discourses and that the novel ends up providing a vision of success in a rapidly industrializing Japan that is a meaningful alternative to the dominant view. By then casting a wider net, I show how the novels that constitute the genre appropriate *risshin shusse* to effect a symbolic, utopian rebuilding of a beleaguered countryside threatened by the twin forces of urbanization and industrialization.

Chapter 3 turns to Natsume Sōseki's first loose "trilogy," *Sanshirō* (Sanshiro, 1908), *Sore kara* (And Then, 1909), and *Mon* (The Gate, 1910). Drawing on the concepts of gift and commodity from anthropology, this chapter shows how Sōseki utilizes the circulation and exchange of objects and money in order to structure the narrative and map out novelistic relations among characters. In tracing these connections in the middle novel of the trilogy, I argue that *Sore kara* explores the ways in which social relations are instrumentalized by *risshin shusse,* while also cumulatively offering up a portrait of the individual's growing distance from society as a result of his resistance to the ideology of success, especially in its common Darwinian inflection. The alienation of the protagonist from society ultimately implicates the experience of the metropolis, and I show that Sōseki paints a portrait of the city as a space of ennui.

Chapter 4 asks a seemingly simple question that turns out to have a complex answer: Is there a *risshin shusse* for women in Meiji Japan? As I show, the very question was apt to generate anxiety about the unsettling of gender norms with the appearance of educated and upwardly mobile women in the nation's capital. The chapter brings together Kosugi Tengai's (1865–1952) melodramatic blockbuster, *Makaze koikaze* (Demonic Winds, Passionate Winds, 1903), and the contemporaneous scandal journalism about degenerate schoolgirls in order to illustrate how these fictional and nonfictional narratives stage dramas of compromised female virtue as a way to generate and then master social anxiety about the city as a site of female self-fashioning. Such an approach helps us understand the difference between reactions to the upwardly mobile man and his female counterpart and helps explain why female success was ultimately reduced from its original universal promise to become merely marriage to a successful man.

Chapter 5 takes up Japanese-language works about the colonies in order to position the territories acquired through imperial expansion in relation to *risshin shusse.* One of the striking, if unsurprising, elements in Japanese fiction at the turn of the last century is the prevalence of an emerging Japanese empire at its margins. The narrative function of colonial Asia is with few exceptions that of a dumping ground for problematic characters. Drawing on contemporary discourses on emigration, I provide a framework for understanding such marginal characters by showing how colonial Korea and semicolonial Manchuria are coded as the destination for failures in the home islands. After uncovering the basic character types who light out for the colonies in works by Shimazaki Tōson (1872–1943), Natsume Sōseki, and Nakamura Seiko (1884–1974), I turn to a work by Takahama Kyoshi (1874–1959), his impressionistic novel *Chōsen* (Korea, 1911–1912), written at the very end of the Meiji period, in which the colonies move from the margins of the novel to the main stage of its action. I argue that when viewed from the perspective of the national subject negotiating colonial space, the colonial settler is rendered as a representative, even pioneering national subject, but when the novel is viewed through the lens of *risshin shusse*, the Japanese expatriate functions as the Other of the upwardly mobile national subject in the home islands.

Compensation, utopia, alienation, anxiety, and adventure: these are the major themes that will emerge from our examination of late-Meiji narratives, including heavily studied canonical novels, popular melodramas, and forgotten potboilers. Some offer celebratory portraits of social mobility, just as other novels will savage the very notion of success as a delusion. Most take a critical stance as they explore the collision between the energetic, upwardly mobile subject and the shifting social boundaries that both empower and constrain the individual. For all of their differences, the novels share an engagement with a particular imagining of space: a developing capitalist nation-state and an emerging empire that consists of hierarchical concentric circles stretching from the capital to the colonies, all shaped by the ideology of social mobility.

In this introduction, I have highlighted the way the modern novel can be conceptualized as a literary form subtended by two primary thematic concerns relating to *risshin shusse*: the exploration of the relationship between the individual and the collective and the portrayal of the individual's negotiation of national and colonial space in his (and sometimes her) effort to move up the social ladder and close the gap between circumstances and desire. If the sketch remains tentative in its details for now, I hope that it makes clear the importance of the discourse on social mobility for the understanding of modern Japan and the modern novel. Another goal is theoretical, directed at a larger audience than just scholars working in Japanese studies: to expand the problematic of desire in modernity to include ambition, success, and self-fashioning. We will begin our exploration in the rural provinces north of Tokyo, the favored venue of the naturalist school of writers.

CHAPTER 1

Desire and Deferral: Japanese Naturalism in the Countryside

> Nature is nature. It is neither good nor evil, neither beautiful nor ugly. It is simply that a particular people in a particular country in a particular era, understanding only a small part of nature, decide to declare it good, evil, beautiful, or ugly.
>
> —Kosugi Tengai, preface to *Hayari-uta* (1902)

In the village of Shioyama, nestled in the mountains of Nagano Prefecture, a forty-something man—his head topped with a crown of disheveled hair, stout legs protruding from his tattered kimono—has been covertly setting fires to houses with the help of an equally wild local woman many years his junior. Pretending to assist the victims, the man even brazenly shows his face during these cataclysms. This stirs the ire of the locals, but having never caught him in the act, they cannot prove he is the culprit; and the local representative of the law seems none too eager to make an arrest without irrefutable evidence. The pariah drinks excessively one night, growing increasingly bellicose and confrontational, whereupon a group of local youths forcefully drags him away. What happens next is something of a mystery, although there is the suggestion of an execution. The youths, however, claim that in his drunkenness, the hotheaded older man stumbled into a pond and drowned; no one believes them, but no one challenges the story either, for all are grateful that life will return to normal in this once peaceful village. But an even greater calamity soon strikes: in a fearsome act of revenge, the wild woman sets ablaze the entire village and dies in the flames herself, although it is not clear if she was caught in the inferno by accident or whether it was an intentional suicide committed by a woman who could not live without her mate.

Tayama Katai (1872–1930) recounts this macabre little tale in his novella, *Jūemon no saigo* (The End of Jūemon, 1902). It is based on the lynching of the real-life Fujita Jūemon (1862–1893), the details of which Katai heard when he was traveling in Nagano in the summer of 1894, almost a decade before the composition of the work.[1] It is said that Katai even saw the place where the lynching occurred. At the time of the novella's publication, the author was an editor in the publishing house Hakubunkan, doing work he found unfulfilling. Katai had gained some notice as a promising writer, first of travel pieces, then of lyrical stories and critical essays, but he was not yet the literary superstar he would be a few years later, after he published *Futon* (The Quilt) in 1907 and almost single-handedly changed the course of modern Japanese fiction. *Jūemon* garnered more attention than anything Katai had previously written, partly due to the sensational subject matter and partly because the novella marked something new in his writing. The work reveals the tutelage of European realists, especially Émile Zola (1840–1902), whom Katai first encountered in English translation in the 1890s, and Ivan Turgenev (1818–1883), widely known among Japanese literati since the 1880s.

In the story-within-a-story framework of *Jūemon*, which, incidentally, is a structure often used by Turgenev, the narrator of and witness to the inner tale of arson—a man named Tomiyama—is part of a group discussing different facets of Russian literature in the novella's bookend sections. At the end of the opening chapter, Tomiyama remarks, "This talk about Turgenev has reminded me that I once met a character [*jinbutsu*] out in the provinces who could have come right out of *Sketches from a Hunter's Album*. It was very moving."[2] He then launches into his extended tale of Jūemon, the ostensible Japanese counterpart to a provincial in Turgenev.[3] This ostentatious name-dropping is best interpreted as a struggling writer's effort to affiliate his novella with the new style of writing about the countryside pioneered in the Japanese translations of Turgenev done by Futabatei Shimei (1864–1909) in the 1880s and later utilized with remarkable effectiveness by Katai's good friend, Kunikida Doppo (1871–1908), at the end of the 1890s, a few years before *Jūemon*'s publication.

Additionally, at one point Tomiyama wonders to himself while contemplating the motive of the mercurial Jūemon, "Was it the character he'd inherited, or did it arise out of his environment" (*Sententeki seishitsu ka, soretomo kyōgū kara okotta koto ka*, 349)? This is, to be sure, a heavy-handed gesture toward Zola's creed of naturalism, especially his calculus of the shaping power of heredity and environment. Katai's desire to link his work to the prestigious tradition of European literature heavily marks all his writings. More to the point, the direct reference to Zola's mantra is the effort of a young and opportunistic writer to ride the crest of the "Zola boom," which exploded briefly in the Japanese literary firmament at the turn of the century. It spawned obvious imitations of the French master, such as the rewriting of Zola's marvelously outrageous *Nana* (1880) by Kosugi Tengai (1865–1952) in his *Hatsu sugata* (New Year's Finery, 1901).

In *Jūemon no saigo*, Katai is genuinely interested in the question of how Zola's keywords, "character" and "environment," shape a violent, irrepressible figure such as Jūemon, though in practice the terms tend to be cast as "nature" and "culture." Katai was so interested in this question, in fact, that he heavily embellished the story of the real-life Fujita Jūemon he had heard nearly a decade earlier, turning a strange tale of village retribution into a sensational, violent, even mythic story.[4] The village, the locus of human civilization in the novella, is a space carved out of nature and tamed so as to produce riches for the benefit of the inhabitants. The village may seem to exist in harmony with a beautiful, bountiful natural world, but nature sometimes shows a fiercer side. Jūemon and his nameless female counterpart could be read as representing a nature that refuses to be tamed and that can strike back with remorseless unpredictability. Jūemon is the inscrutable and ultimately unfathomable child of nature, whose motives are never made clear.

And yet, this reading is complicated by additional points: the inner story unfolds in separate places of action—part in Tokyo, part in Shioyama—widely separated in time. Tomiyama visits Shioyama in order to get reacquainted with friends he met in Tokyo during his student days, five years after their first encounter in the capital and seven years before the actual narration of those events in the novella's bookend sections. The men named Nemoto, Yamagata, and Sugiyama left provincial Shioyama with the desire to rise in the world and ended up at the same school in Tokyo as Tomiyama. Each was embarked on the path of *risshin shusse*: leave one's natal home for the educational opportunities in Tokyo and then become a great man, wealthy and respected in society. The three young men from Shioyama, however, are among the failures: Yamagata's family could not afford his tuition, so the boy was forced to return to the village and become a local country teacher, one of the most common professions in Meiji literature for signifying unfulfilled ambitions; Nemoto was ordered back to his natal home by his family in order to take over its ailing provincial business; Sugiyama succumbs to the enticements of Tokyo's prostitution districts and returns home broke (he is eventually drafted and sent to the front in China). Another theme in Katai's novella, then, is the circulation of young men of ambition between the country and the city.

This has important implications for how we think about the role of nature in the text. During his student days, Tomiyama hears much about Shioyama and the surrounding countryside from his new friends. Yamagata, for example, paints a picture in words of Shioyama in his Chinese poetry (313), recounts stories of the beauties that can be found there in abundance (317), and shows Tomiyama an evocative if amateurish sketch of his provincial home (313). In other words, before Tomiyama sets foot in the village, it exists for him as an idealized space: "My imagination began to run free. How I wanted to visit, if only once, their peaceful mountain village" (314). We can even push this observation one step further: as Tomiyama sighs, "what magnificent poetry I could make there" (314), we realize that there is a metafictional aspect to Shioyama and that this rural paradise is fundamentally a space of the *literary* imagination—a bucolic setting constructed through words and fantasies.

When Tomiyama finally visits this idyllic space, expectations and reality coincide at first. The descriptions of the provinces are beautiful, and the countryside even has a therapeutic effect on him: "I breathed my fill of the clean mountain air. For ten years I had been surrounded by the dust of the city and unable to take in such pure air" (319). Part of Shioyama's appeal is that it is steeped in the rhythms of the natural world, the antithesis of the noisy life in the crowded capital. Nature is a balm that can relieve the stress of the rat race for success in Tokyo. This representation turns out to be pure irony, for this "peaceful mountain village" is being racked by an endless, seemingly unstoppable series of destructive acts, which threaten the very existence of the community. Katai has set up expectations of a rural paradise only to abruptly turn those expectations upside down.

A strange thing happens, though, as the story of Jūemon's crimes unfold: nature itself continues to be portrayed in idyllic terms, despite the increasing chaos that rages in its midst. This is true even as the violence reaches its apogee; the narrator describes the place where Jūemon's body is found thus:

> The moon cast its bright light upon the pond, and the faint ripples around the drowned man's floating hair sparkled beautifully in its light. In a clump of grass a few feet away bell and pine crickets sang a joyful, heedless song to this beautiful night. And the dark forms of the mountains—they seemed completely unmoved that there could be such tragedy in the world of men. (379)

Evocative it may be, but nature is serenely indifferent to the human tragedies that play out in its midst. Nature is here anthropomorphized and represented as a distinct entity, completely separate from and unconnected to everything else in the novella.

This complicates the easy association of Jūemon with the natural world, for his "pathetic corpse" (379) is also distinct from nature. The wild, unruly Jūemon is better interpreted not as nature as such, but as that which society must suppress in order to bring about its laws. This would make Jūemon an embodiment of the return of the repressed, an interpretation that takes on additional weight when we consider that much of his behavior is "explained" by his deformity: greatly enlarged testicles. A reading that places emphasis on Jūemon as a metaphor for a dangerous and irrepressible reproductive energy, whose full power must be curtailed for society to develop into a rule-bound human community, links this text to a larger problematic within Katai's oeuvre and to the Japanese naturalist project more generally: desire and sexuality as "natural laws" that are somehow incommensurate with "nature."

This chapter seeks to uncover the status of nature within naturalism. It will detail the literary maneuvers by which nature is separated from the world of human community, history, provincial life, and even natural law. I will argue that the representation of nature is inseparable from the thematization of *risshin shusse* by showing that nature functions as a compensatory object for deferred ambition. This will allow us to make sense of several recurring binaries within Japanese naturalism: the country and the city; nature and culture; sexual desire and its repression; success and failure. The oeuvre of Tayama Katai, the quintessential naturalist, will be our focus, especially his most sophisticated novel, *Inaka kyōshi* (A Country Teacher, 1909). By pursuing in this work what is not fully developed in *Jūemon* and carefully examining Katai's 1909 novel in conjunction with his contemporaries' writings on the topic of literary sketching, one of the pillars of naturalist representation, I hope to make a contribution to Japanese literary studies and develop some important terms and concepts for the argument of this book. In the first instance, I wish to pursue the implications of the rhetorical separation of nature from the country, which will yield a new perspective on literary naturalism in Japan. I also want to connect this rhetorical maneuver to the way in which worldly success helps produce space in modernity, especially that of the provinces.

Naturalism and the Novel of the Countryside

Naturalism has an ambiguous place in the history of Japanese literature. Called *shizenshugi* (a literal rendition of the English and French terms), it is sometimes seen as a derivative, short-lived movement (1906 and 1911 are the most common bookend dates assigned to the movement's high-water mark) that either misread or only selectively applied the principles of the European movement on which it was modeled. Other voices stress that, despite its brief hegemony, literary naturalism occupies a crucial place in the Japanese appropriation of European techniques of realist narration. Even with these differing assessments of *shizenshugi*, there is a consensus that the Japanese advocates of naturalism conceived of themselves as part of a relatively coherent, international movement that generated in a short span of time a large number of theoretical and critical pieces, many of which came to shape the development of the novel in Japan.[5] My assumption here—by no means original—is that fidelity is an unproductive framework and that we should instead privilege the point of reception, concentrating on the localization of naturalism in a Japanese context.[6]

Yet the difficulties do not end by simply accepting this assumption. As in Europe and the United States, there is no shortage of formulations about naturalism in Japan. The narrowest definition would highlight what we have already discussed in relation to *Jūemon*: a kind of novelistic scale that weighs the shaping power of heredity and environment on the individual.[7] As reductive as this may be for the characterization of an entire literary movement, even a short-lived one, it is this Zola-esque brand of naturalism that first seduced Japanese writers at the beginning of the twentieth century. I mentioned Kosugi Tengai's rewriting of Zola's *Nana* in his 1901 *Hatsu-sugata*; Tengai's *Hayari-uta* (A Popular Song, 1902) is reminiscent of Zola's *Thérèse Raquin* (1867) in the way it links the innate sexual excess of the heroine and her subsequent decline into degeneracy in a narrative of cause and effect.

More broadly, Japanese naturalism can be conceived as a movement that draws upon a society-wide preoccupation with new scientific and quasi-scientific ideas so that themes of degeneration, atavism, sexual desire, and natural law can be explored through a detached, objective gaze, or at least a gaze that is represented as such. In this view—an extension of Zola's ideas—naturalism is an exploratory laboratory, producing imaginative worlds that stage a fraught fictional situation in order to dissect a particular social phenomenon through the motifs supplied by science and without the overt intervention or commentary by the narrator.[8] In Katai's "Shōjobyō" (The Girl Watcher), written in 1907, the voyeuristic protagonist of the story, Sugita Kojō, cannot reconcile society's moral prescriptions with his own fetish for young women; he dies in a train accident as he strains to get a better look at the perfect girl, and the drab, dusty cityscape he inhabits connects environment and psychopathology. Early naturalism in Japan tended to produce works of this kind, in which an individual racked by dark drives and needs faces off against a society that can harbor no tolerance for such eccentric personalities, and crafted fatalistic narratives in which the protagonist typically meets a bitter end. This corpus of fiction, which trawled the bottom of society as a way to highlight the shortcomings of modernization, caused a good deal of dismay on the part of the authorities and much hand-wringing among the bourgeois reading public, leading to many cases of censorship.[9] Indeed, it is worth underscoring that for Japanese at the time, naturalism was most associated with scandalous depictions of incorrigibles inhabiting the nether regions of society, often conjoined with what was considered at the time to be shocking portrayals of adultery and loose sexuality—a situation not so different from the reaction to naturalism in other countries.

After the midpoint of the first decade of the twentieth century, literary naturalism, with its dogged pursuit of truth, often featured a third-person omniscient narrator conveying the life and thoughts of a protagonist who was closely modeled on the author himself. After all, if truth is the goal, what better material does the author have than his own life? Katai's *Futon* (The Quilt, 1907) is often said to have irrevocably lured Japanese naturalism onto an autobiographical and confessional course, which eventually led to its metamorphosis into the *shishōsetsu* (the I-novel; the personal novel) in the Taishō era.[10] Shimazaki Tōson (1872–1943), Tokuda Shūsei (1871–1943), Masamune Hakuchō (1879–1962), Katai himself, and several others wrote autobiographical works in the third person. With characteristic acuity, Mori Ōgai (1862–1922) saw into the very heart of the new literature when he penned his novel *Vita sekusuarisu* (Vita Sexualis, 1910), after the naturalist movement had veered onto its autobiographical course. Ōgai's sexual *bildungsroman* is most persuasively read as a parody of the naturalist writer's seemingly interminable need to confess to carnal desire.

The frank portraits of desire in these more subjective, autobiographical texts of late naturalism link them to the treatment of adultery and illegitimate sexuality in the more objective, fictional works of early naturalism. Tomi Suzuki is one of the few to grapple in detail with the status of "truth" in Japanese naturalism. By using *Futon* to reconsider naturalism's most important keyword, her work has been instrumental in clearing away the critical cobwebs that have gathered over Katai's writings, in particular. Drawing on Foucault's work, Suzuki highlights the way truth and sexuality become intertwined, and indeed inseparable, in naturalist discourse: "In works published after *Futon* it was truth or desire for truth that served as a medium for the sudden manifestations of sexual consciousness and for the desire to narrate about sex."[11] Although I would certainly take issue with her suggestion that naturalist works before *Futon* were not preoccupied with sex (as we have seen, most were), the basic point still holds: literary naturalism seeks to more realistically represent human nature, to plumb its dark secrets and explain them in terms of natural law; and the more the human subject is seen as being ruled by desire, the more the representational project of naturalism will turn on an exploration of sex. The naturalist preoccupation with truth is surely behind the autobiographical turn in the movement, but in Suzuki's formulation it does not much matter whether the protagonist is based on the author's own life or is a purely fictional creation. In both cases, the desire to ascertain the hidden truth of human nature is the quest to discover the true nature of desire itself.

Each of these attempts to grapple with naturalism in Japan highlights something important about the body of literature produced in its name. "Zola fever" provided an undeniable impetus to the movement, yet works written under the naturalist banner were never exclusively concerned with the determining influences of heredity and environment. As Eric Carl Link has discussed in the context of American literary naturalism, Zola's polemical theories often do not carry over into his own fiction, much less that of authors from other countries claiming him as an influence.[12] Many naturalist writers in Japan did advocate an objective narrative voice and a positivistic diegesis in which the elements of plot were materially and causally linked by what was represented as natural law. Nonetheless, naturalist fiction still includes episodes, such as Segawa Ushimatsu's hearing the voice of his dead father in *Hakai* (Broken Commandment, 1906) and the storm raging at the end of *Futon*, that link these works to romanticism, where, in what would be incongruous in a European context, most Japanese naturalists had their literary roots.[13] The naturalist writers did move toward incorporating autobiographical elements into their fictional worlds, yet reading such works as confessional tends to downplay the ironies that create distance between writer and protagonist, an effect we see even in the supposedly autobiographical *Futon*, as Suzuki demonstrates.[14] What even her own astute reading overlooks, however, is that naturalist fiction is preoccupied with multiple kinds of desire: sexuality, to be sure, but also ambition, which we might categorize as biological and social drives respectively.

All of these impulses outlined here fed the movement, but none exhausts it, nor can any of these formulations exhaust the literary output of any single writer. Like so many of the European literary movements that washed onto Japanese shores in rapid succession after 1868, naturalism was a hybrid, and writers who embraced its principles at some point in their careers were invoking the names of a whole host of European realist authors. Such invocations are inextricably bound up with a larger generational struggle over control of the domestic literary scene (the *bundan*). Thus, there are more than literary principles at work here. A more sociological view makes clear that Japanese naturalists affiliated themselves with a foreign literary movement as a rather unfilial show of cultural capital in the faces of their domestic predecessors—who were deemed to have only a superficial relationship with Western literature—while writing works that tended to cluster around a privileged set of themes, only some of which resonated with the foreign works that served as models.

Three central themes that have received too little attention will be of central concern here: nature, the countryside, and success.[15] In its attempt to break from the conventions of depicting nature and in its vigorous treatment of rural society, naturalism can be seen as the provinces writing back to the metropolis. The first three decades of Meiji literature were ruled by Tokyoites such as Ozaki Kōyō (1867–1903) and his Ken'yūsha compatriots, who represented a distinctly urban sensibility. In their wake followed other latter-day *Edokko* (children of Edo, the city's name before it became Tokyo) such as Nagai Kafū (1879–1959), who flirted with Zola early in his career, but who then became the seer of old Edo. In contrast, the writers who thought of themselves as representing the naturalist movement in Japan were really the first modern literary group to consistently set entire works in the countryside and to take seriously the lives that unfolded outside the major urban areas.[16] To be sure, many naturalist works are set in the city, but a large portion of canonical naturalist fiction—novels such as Shimazaki Tōson's *Hakai* (1906), Mayama Seika's *Minami Koizumi-mura* (The Village Minami Koizumi, 1907), much of Tokuda Shūsei's *Arakure* (Rough Living, 1915), and Tayama Katai's own *Inaka kyōshi*—is set in the provinces.

There is undoubtedly an autobiographical element in the widespread preoccupation with rural society among the naturalists and in their obsession with the new ideologies of ambition and success. These new discourses, together with the new educational system, had successfully spread to the far corners of the nation within a few decades, though not without meeting some resistance.[17] Many naturalist writers were shaped by these new ideologies and even shared a common trajectory: they were born in the provinces, often in the prefectures surrounding Tokyo and, seized by the promise of *risshin shusse* while in the new rural schools, eventually made their way to the capital, seeking to further their education and make names for themselves. Kunikida Doppo was born in Chōshi, in present-day Chiba Prefecture, and spent much of his early life moving with his father's administrative work throughout Yamaguchi and Hiroshima Prefectures. He lived for a time in Saeki, on the island of Kyūshū, as a country teacher and made long trips to various northern areas, including Hokkaidō.[18] Shimazaki Tōson lived until the age of eight in Magome, Nagano Prefecture, born to a family that had the hereditary duty of giving lodging to traveling officials. Tōson and his brothers went to Tokyo at an early age to continue their education, sent by a father who had high hopes for his boys' futures. Later, Tōson lived in Komoro, also in Nagano Prefecture, for seven years and worked as a country teacher before returning to Tokyo to secure his reputation as a novelist.[19] Katai, who was friends with both Tōson and Doppo, was born in the village of Tatebayashi, then in Tochigi Prefecture, now in Gunma. He moved to Tokyo to get an education, moved back to his natal home, and finally returned to the capital fired with ambition to become a man of letters.[20] These are just three examples, but almost every writer who called himself a naturalist hailed from the provinces; these men formed the second generation of Meiji writers and, in opposition to the urbane writings of the Ken'yūsha, found ways to move back and forth in their fictional worlds between the city and the country, producing nuanced portraits of both and of the provincial youth who were seized by the desire to rise in the world. Thus, I would call naturalism a literature *from* the provinces, meaning that its fictional worlds were filtered through the critical eyes of those born outside the major urban centers, even as the writers needed to establish themselves in Tokyo to succeed in their craft.

The imperative of social advancement joins the country and the city, and the naturalist canon is preoccupied with exploring both the routes connecting these spaces and the psychology of social mobility. Katai's *Inaka kyōshi* is particularly useful in this regard, for not only does it engage each of these themes, it reprises all the concerns of naturalism in its Japanese incarnation. The novel stages a pessimistic encounter between the individual and the social order, whereby the young Hayashi Seizō, his dreams of success having come to naught, is cast aside by an indifferent society. In its treatment of Hayashi's fatalistic affair with a prostitute and his eventual death by tuberculosis, which can easily be read as a stand-in for syphilis, *Inaka kyōshi* reveals the same preoccupation with the causal lines between sexuality and degeneracy that so marks the movement. Katai's novel also features a narrator who is sympathetic to the protagonist and who relates the shifting fortunes of his hero with a precision and a patience that would have pleased those naturalist practitioners who valorized the European tradition of realism.[21] But the text also exhibits the naturalist glee in revealing the underbelly of society, with its descriptions of the misery and sexual scandals hidden behind the tranquil surface beauty of the countryside. Consider, too, that Katai's interest in a fictional treatment of the real-life tragedy of Kobayashi Shūzō (1884–1904), whose diary he had read, likely stems from the fact that the boy's story resonated with Katai's own experience as a youth and that Kobayashi's story unfolded in an area close to Katai's own native home.[22] Thus, one can glimpse both the documentary and the autobiographical impulses of naturalism in Katai's adaptation of a thwarted youth's diary.

This pessimistic novel is ultimately a psychological portrait of the effects of failure on the individual, for the protagonist is an ambitious young man who is unable to advance in society.[23] Katai's text thematizes a gap between dreams of success and the ability to fulfill those dreams, thus creating a tale of social inertia. The results are unhappiness, self-recrimination, and angst. Hayashi Seizō's setbacks seem temporary in the first half, but a sense of resignation, even despair, settles over the second. The novel is unambiguous about the cause of Seizō's inability to rise in the world: the father's small clothing shop has failed, and, facing the specter of a hand-to-mouth existence, the family is unable to provide the tuition money needed by their son to proceed to the higher reaches of the educational system and to eventual success. Having finished only middle school, he must put his incomplete education to use by taking a teaching position at an undistinguished country schoolhouse in the backwater of Saitama Prefecture and help stave off the family's inexorable decline.

The path of success would normally lead from one's native home in the provinces to Tokyo, and this would suggest an idealized representation of Tokyo as an object of longing, but the novel's treatment is more complicated. The metropolis is described only once, when Seizō travels there to take the entrance exam to the Tokyo Music Academy. Realizing he has likely done poorly on the lengthy, grueling test, he ventures out onto the hillside of the southern end of Ueno Park:

> Below him spread the vast metropolis. One tiled roof followed another, and Seizō could see fearsome black smoke rising from the chimneys. The many sounds merged into a single great din, which Seizō felt was the fervent cry of the city. There would be crime and commerce, fame and fortune, hunger and despair. The many scandals, about which he read each day in the papers, rose in his mind's eye. Coming down from the hill, he could see the Hirokōji market fan out before him. Carriages and trolleys followed

> one after the other in an endless procession. The waterman picked his way nimbly through the traffic. The rickshaw pullers ran about with loud shouts.[24]

This is a clear-eyed portrait of the metropolis as a complex, living entity, filled with extremes of wealth and poverty. And while one might argue that the emphasis on dark imagery is an expressive touch meant to reflect Seizō's hostility to the city,[25] this ambivalent depiction of the metropolis is more persuasively interpreted, in my view, as a space of complexity, noise, destitution, and stimulation together, in which can be found in microcosm the full range of human experience, the darkness together with the light, the wealth along with the poverty. For those with ambition, it is a space of energy and danger in which one can test one's mettle, even at the risk of failure and the possibility of plummeting to the bottom rungs of society. The lack of opportunity to embrace the challenge is the real tragedy depicted in the novel.

At one time in his life, Tokyo was a space of hope (*kibō*) for Seizō, but as he realizes that a life there is beyond his reach, the capital becomes a cruel symbol of its opposite (*shitsubō*). And, indeed, as Seizō gazes upon the metropolis, he is "caught between his earlier hope and his present despair" (191) in a state of liminality. Paralleling Seizō's increasing hopelessness, the narrative is punctuated throughout its second half with references to the development of a train line connecting the nation's capital to the provinces to its north. This keeps Tokyo visible on the horizon of the possible while casting ironic light on the protagonist's desires.

If the metropolis is treated as a complex symbolic space, we encounter an even more complicated portrait of the countryside in *Inaka kyōshi*. The text begins in medias res and in motion, with Seizō hitching a ride on the long four-*ri* route (just shy of ten miles, with one *ri* equal to 2.44 miles) from his parents' home in Gyōda to Miroku and to the school where he will take up his new duties. He gazes out over the countryside from his moving berth:

> A new life was spread out before Seizō. He felt that there was significance and hope in any new beginning in life. Each morning for the past five years he had awoken early, donned his school uniform, and taken the three-*ri* road from Gyōda to Kumagaya. But that life was now in the past. (5)

This passage perfectly captures Seizō's ambivalence toward the provinces. The reference to a student life now irrecoverably in the past suggests hopes for the future now on hold for economic reasons. This is echoed later on that page, when the narrator alerts us that Seizō "gradually came to realize how different his life now was from the life he had glimpsed from the school window" (5). And yet, even as the country inevitably possesses a negative hue, what is emphasized here on the opening page is the hopeful quality that accompanies any new stage in life. This awareness finds its echo in a subsequent chapter when Seizō, ready to write about his first day as a provincial teacher, begins the new entry in his diary immediately after the old, but, realizing that "today was the first day of the beginning of a new life," erases the entry and symbolically begins it again on a new page (17).

Although the novel begins after Seizō has graduated from middle school, we learn that his early education took place in the regional center of Ashikaga, in Tochigi Prefecture, where his father had his shop. With the failure of that business, the family moved across the Tone River to the smaller Kumagaya, in Saitama Prefecture, where Seizō continued his education in middle school while his family tried to reestablish its business. As the novel opens, the family is facing dire straits, having moved to the town of Gyōda, also in Saitama. Seizō leaves Gyōda for the even smaller town of Hanyū, where he rents a room and treks daily to Miroku, a tiny community with little more than the school itself. As Seizō's life progresses, then, he moves from a regional city to successively smaller communities, thus penetrating farther into the hinterland—meaning that on a symbolic and psychological level (though not necessarily in a strictly geographical sense), he moves ever farther from Tokyo. Seizō is acutely aware of the significance of this life course: "Kumagaya to Gyōda, Gyōda to Hanyū, Hanyū to Miroku: He felt that his energy had dissipated little by little with each move, and he now traveled the long road with a feeling of sadness" (75). This life course is an inversion of the chronotope of success, for one was supposed to move from local town to regional city to the capital as one continued one's education. Seizō and his family instead embark on what can only be called a route of failure, and we can characterize its spatial and temporal axes as a chronotope of inertia. It is also a trail of death, for the narrator takes pains to note that the family has left a grave with each move: the grandfather's is in Ashikaga (228), the grandmother's in Kumagaya (228), the brother's in Gyōda (61), and, by the end of the novel, Seizō's remains rest in Hanyū (263). What is more, with Seizō gone, the family lineage will likely be extinguished, meaning that the story of individual failure is quietly subtended by a family's inexorable decline and extinction.

Katai extends his critique to encompass the hero's alienation from the social bonds that had once sustained him by giving us portraits of a number of Seizō's friends, who in their diverse backgrounds constitute a microcosm of the provincial male community. A few examples will suffice to outline this character system. Ikuji, Seizō's closest friend as the novel opens, is the son of a local school superintendent, and by the end of the novel, having been betrothed to one of the local girls and having moved on to ever higher reaches of the educational system, he is poised to gain everything promised by *risshin shusse*. Similarly, Obata, the son of another local administrator, also seems assured of a respectable life as he enters a normal school in Tokyo, presumably to become a teacher higher up in the system than Seizō, thus giving him greater pay and prestige. Sakurai is the son of an old samurai family and his inherited wealth is stressed throughout the novel; this wealth supports him as he enters the Tokyo Institute of Technology, presumably to become an engineer. We learn little about Ishikawa, but he seems to have lived out one of the great fears of the age: having gone to Tokyo and been seduced by a life of hedonistic pleasure, he is recalled to the country to marry and to begin a humdrum life in his ancestral home. Finally, there is Ōgyū, an unambitious youth who, content with an ordinary provincial life, decides to work in the local post office.

Utilizing this character system, Katai produces a detailed picture of male homosocial bonds across time and portrays the effects on these ties of widely varying levels of achievement. Male friendships are forged within the lower reaches of the educational system and are held together by the mutual belief in society's promise of upward mobility. Such bonds can be maintained only if each of the youth advances more or less evenly through the educational system. But in *Inaka kyōshi*, Katai is interested in what happens to these bonds in the face of inertia and failure. As the life courses of members of the community begin to diverge through unequal levels of education and achievement, the homosocial bonds sustained by shared beliefs dissolve over time. Consequently, Seizō comes to see the discourse on *risshin shusse* with eyes that grow increasingly cynical and finds himself estranged from his former friends, eventually becoming a virtual stranger to all but the unassuming Ōgyū.

Given its status as a painful symbol of social inertia, familial extinction, and alienation from friends, the negative side of the representation of the provinces comes as no surprise. Eventually overpowering the hopeful depiction of the protagonist's new life, the novel's portrait of the countryside evokes a quite predictable, even stereotypical world of narrow-mindedness and contentment with the status quo. Indeed, one of the most common words to describe the provinces within the pages of the novel is *semai*, meaning "narrow" or "cramped." This central metaphor is mobilized to indicate the country's frightful capacity to stifle social mobility and its inability to embrace the ideals of the new era. The critical representation of the country can be found on almost any page, but grows more pronounced in the second half of the novel, echoing the protagonist's deepening resignation.

By examining the connections among the country, the city, and the desire for success, we have arrived via an atypical route at the most typical—and, I would add, unavoidable—reading of *Inaka kyōshi*, which would highlight the way the text constructs a subjective, ambivalent portrait of society even as it attempts to fulfill the naturalist goal of objective social analysis.[26] This reading, however, leaves unanswered many questions that arise because of the great variety of themes that emerge in the pages of a novel that is deceptively placid and static on the surface. We are still left with the problem of explaining exactly how the text can harbor competing representations of the country. Is this difficulty best left to the term "ambivalence"? More to the point, why is there intensely detailed, even loving attention devoted to the natural world that surrounds the constricting, provincial world of town and village? A host of other questions that are at first glance unrelated to the novel's main concerns also rear their heads. How do we interpret Seizō's short-lived fling with a prostitute about halfway through the novel? Why are Seizō's illness and death exactly synchronized with the Russo-Japanese War? Why are the arts so strenuously thematized throughout a text ostensibly about the quest for worldly success? To answer these questions, I rely on the keywords of "desire," "deferral," and "compensation." I will show that many of the seemingly extraneous elements that appear in the novel function as compensatory objects for desires that must be interminably deferred because of the economic decline of the protagonist's family.

As we saw in the introduction, *risshin shusse* inscribes within the individual that particular form of desire called ambition and creates a social contract of sorts in which those who cultivate this drive are promised success and achievement as they advance from the provinces to the capital. Success hinges on the newly constructed educational system, which provides an arena for competition and for the acquisition of an educational capital that can be transformed into social mobility. To this mix we need to add the naturalist preoccupation with sexuality. The social drive of success is linked to the biological drive of sexuality through the family; sexual desire can be sanctioned only when it takes the socially legitimated form of marriage within a mandatory heterosexuality. In a society in which the preferred sexual partners are married couples and in which a good marriage can only take place once the future of the new household seems assured, we see the deferral of marriage, sexuality, and family until a point in life is reached whereby success can be reliably predicted, a point often marked by the completion of one's schooling and the acceptance of a prestigious salaried position.

Seizō, who is trapped in a state of social inertia as a country teacher despite his ambitions, defers marriage and sexual relations until he completes enough education to make his prospects of success likely. Hence, we are given Seizō's deflections of all attempts to find a wife for him, especially as his life becomes a downward spiral and success proves elusive. When Seizō's mother remarks that the family has "a good prospect" for him, her son balks: "I'm barely able to feed myself right now," he complains. When his mother presses him, Seizō changes strategies and retorts, "I still have ambitions. I'm thinking of studying for the license to be a middle school teacher. I can't get married right now" (183–84). The mother's priorities lie in reproducing the family lineage; Seizō, as a youth of the new era, is preoccupied with individual social mobility over the continuity of the household. Not only is he unwilling to pursue any marriage prospect prior to achieving a certain level of stability and success, he also feels that being encumbered with more mouths to feed before that time would foreclose future advancement.

In a gesture that seems to hearken back to Katai's roots in romanticism, the novel proffers the former pupil Hideko, among the few female characters in the novel, as an ideal partner, if only Seizō could somehow get back on the path of success. This, of course, is impossible, because his inertia is the result of economics not a failure of willpower, and the novel consistently foregrounds this through its thematization of debt and money problems. Seizō is constantly deferring his desires, both large and small, because his family is always pestering him for money. Nonetheless, given that none of the female characters has more than two dimensions in this thoroughly male-dominated novel, such potential partners as Hideko are little more than novelistic devices for evoking sympathy for the protagonist in an ostensibly objective work.

I would read the presence of the prostitute, Shizue, with reference to this framework, as well. In a story of how social inertia leads to the continuing deferral of sexuality, the prostitute figures as a return of the repressed (a favorite naturalist theme)—that is, as a biological drive that stubbornly refuses to be subdued or to wait until one reaches an ideal level of social stability. The brothel in *Inaka kyōshi* functions partly as a site in which the imperatives of the biological drive can be temporarily abetted while the liminal state of social inertia continues. There is, of course, the risk in frequent visits to a brothel, and Seizō comes perilously close to social ostracism and financial ruin. At the same time, frequenting a brothel becomes for Seizō a kind of revenge on a society that promises success to the ambitious but that ultimately reneges on that compact by failing to provide opportunities for advancement. The prostitution district is represented as both dark and alluring, which captures its dual function in the novel as a space that is a threat to the upwardly mobile as well as a site that enables moral revenge on a society that is unable to fulfill its end of the social contract. Katai thus uses prostitution to treat the discrepancy between ideals and opportunities within the discourse on *risshin shusse*.

If we reframe this slightly as the problematic of appearance versus reality, we discover a major theme in Katai's novel that has so far gone unnoticed in critical discussions of *Inaka kyōshi*. Provincial life, though not inspiring for a man of ambition, nonetheless gives every appearance of being a pastoral paradise quietly nestled in the arms of a beautiful and bounteous nature. And yet, at roughly the midway point of the novel, the trope of appearance versus reality takes center stage, and the seemingly bucolic if unambitious lives lived out in rural society are unmasked as illusions. The process begins with Seizō losing some of his egocentric preoccupations and gaining increased understanding of the reality of the lives of quiet desperation in the hinterland:

> The more stories he heard, the more he became aware of the lives of hardship and sadness in this village he assumed was so peaceful. There was the perpetual conflict between the landowner and the tenant farmer, the rich and the poor, for one. Seizō gradually came to understand that the country, which seemed to enfold within its bosom a quiet, idyllic life, was in fact a world of passion and struggle. (157–58)

Seizō encounters numerous stories, including harrowing accounts of thefts by those with no options left and tragic tales of suicide committed in desperation (157). He develops sympathy for those who lead a "hard life" (the word is borrowed from English in the novel, 157) and realizes the gulf separating the hopes and dreams of the relatively privileged consumed by ambition and those who eke out an existence around them. Seizō's discovery has a particular side effect: there emerges a sharp critical distance between protagonist and the provincial society in which he was born.

The farther Seizō moves into the hinterland—to less populous and more obscure corners of the region—the more his newfound critical eyesight alights on the turbulence and despair behind the facade of the presumed pastoral idyll, and the harsher, more subjective the narrator's voice becomes in order to reflect this:

> Seizō came to realize that the country was a place of licentiousness, false fronts, and filth. Such things could be gleaned from the gossip around him. So-and-so's daughter had done this. Some woman had done something scandalous with some man. So-and-so was keeping a mistress on the sly. A husband and wife were bickering over another woman. The stories were endless. He even saw unequivocal proof in some cases, leading him to recognize that these stories were not empty rumors. (158)

Behind the facade of peaceful tranquility and harmony lies a very different reality of crime, passion, and immorality, and, in keeping with naturalist fetishes, the emphasis has shifted quickly and noticeably from class tensions to sexual transgressions. Tellingly, Seizō learns of the licensed prostitution district in nearby Nakada, across the river in Ibaraki Prefecture, shortly after these discoveries and begins his regular visits.[27] Having traversed a route of failure, penetrated the hinterland, and been corrupted, Seizō has discovered the "truth" of the provinces. Much as he does in *Jūemon no saigo*, Katai rewrites an idyllic, romanticized countryside into a pessimistic naturalist environment, adding to the confining portrait of the provinces the image of rural society as a space hiding dark secrets, especially sexual secrets.

This rewriting process utilizes a rhetoric of unmasking and revelation, with the naturalist preoccupations with immorality and dark eroticism prominently foregrounded. Nature plays an important role here. It is the charming sheen that covers up the harsh reality of rural community, a curtain that needs to be pushed aside in order to see the truth. Yet revelation does not impact the representation of nature itself, which continues to receive detailed, loving attention, even after the tables have been turned on our expectations of a world of pastoral repose. Katai relies on the preexisting distinction between the city and the country,[28] but the complexity extends beyond this in that the country itself cannot be considered a singular entity. From start to finish, nature is unchanging, beautiful, and completely distinct from the countryside conceived in social terms, just as it was in *Jūemon*. But Katai has shifted from the personification of nature in the 1902 novella to the rhetoric of unmasking in the 1909 novel so as to more actively separate the country into two distinct entities, nature and rural society, the sphere of natural beauty and the ugly world of human intercourse; the latter comes to be represented negatively as a space of narrowness, moral bankruptcy, and the endless deferral of desire, while the former can then be held up as a consolation for social inertia, a balm for unrealized dreams, and perhaps even a sublimation of repressed sexual desire. In effect, the text makes an effort to rescue nature from the countryside, a recuperation that fulfills a deep psychological need on the part of the protagonist, for the rhetorical separation of one entity into two parts allows the country, in which Seizo is compelled to live, to be the source of both pain and pleasure simultaneously; it is both cage and consolation.

Sketching between Nature and Society

A chronotope of inertia, then, features a subjectively experienced constriction of space and opportunity in the provinces, typically, as in Katai, by featuring a protagonist traversing a route of failure. Such a chronotope also features the perpetual deferral of desire in time, with the protagonist unable to close the gap between what he is and what he wishes to be. Katai's narrator provides extensive excerpts from the protagonist's diary, which allows the reader direct contact with his subjective experience. The diary recounts a wide range of Seizō's reactions: the fear of failure ("Will I finally be buried in the country as a local teacher?" 46); anxiety about social inertia ("Seizō couldn't help but think how things had changed when he compared his diary entries now to those from last winter," 112); self-exhortation ("Following one's fate is the mark of courage," 197); and resignation ("I will throw away my previous ambition and make my success a peaceful life with my parents," 199). Even more, the diary has the capacity to provide solace: "by keeping a diary he could console himself" (145). His diary is not the only medium that provides such assuagement: as Seizō also records, art, poetry, and music, among other pursuits are "things that can quiet a heart in turmoil" (midaruru kokoro o shizumuru, 143). In individual psychological terms, then, diary keeping and the arts are displacement activities, together functioning as compensation for social inertia. I want to pursue the full implications of this observation by turning to a specific example of the larger phenomenon of compensation: the treatment of literature in Katai's novel.

In the early chapters, Seizō and his friends are embarked on a grand project of launching a regional literary magazine, with an eye toward creating a cutting-edge journal like those produced in Tokyo. In order to showcase the literary talent in the provinces, the new publication will take its name from the town in which several characters have roots and be titled *Gyōda bungaku* (Gyōda Literature). The frequent discussion of literature early on and the explicit mention of scores of individual authors and titles are narratively motivated because the characters themselves are budding writers and poets trying to get the attention of their metropolitan heroes. They will be writing what they know: the provincial world converging on the Tone River—namely, the abutting corners of Saitama, Ibaraki, Tochigi, and Gunma Prefectures—which defines the spatial boundaries of the novel, Seizō's trip to Tokyo being the sole exception. *Gyōda bungaku* fails miserably. The first issue comes out with great excitement (84) but ceases with the fourth issue (116). Part of the reason is that the countryside lacks the infrastructure to support a vibrant literary magazine, but it is also clear that, despite the early enthusiasm for the project among the young compatriots, the interests of most eventually shift to pragmatic endeavors that are more lucrative than writing stories and poems. Literature may intoxicate some early on and may even help maintain male homosocial bonds for a time, but the respective paths of the youth ultimately diverge. This suggests that literature is a metaphor for many things—idealism, youthful ambition, and such—but the rapid folding of the journal is unmistakably meant to foreshadow the foreclosed path to success and Seizō's resignation to the life of an obscure country teacher.

Even acknowledging that literary name-dropping is narratively motivated, the text foregrounds literature to an extent that can be rivaled by few other novels of the era. An astonishing number of works and magazines are explicitly referenced as the novel unfolds, covering virtually the entire range of literary expression in Meiji Japan: the Ken'yūsha group; the school of Romanticism centered on the journal *Bungakkai* (Literary World); the "idealist" school of poetry represented by the journal *Myōjō* (Bright Star; Venus); the neoclassicism of Kōda Rohan (1867–1947) and Higuchi Ichiyō (1872–96); premodern Japanese literature; the Chinese classics; and foreign works.[29] More than any of these, however, emphasis falls on the emerging canonical works of literary naturalism, especially on the writings of Shimazaki Tōson and Kunikida Doppo, and the narrator mentions many titles by these two writers by name, including the pastoral sketches and lyrical poems of Tōson and Doppo's impressionistic rural stories.

In the early chapters, Seizō is infatuated with the fresh winds blowing through the world of the traditional poetic forms, the tanka and the haiku. Afterward, "the new trends of the Myōjō school washed over Seizō's breast like a stream of fresh spring water" (40). "The Myōjō school" refers to the group of poets gathered around the journal of the same name, especially Yosano Tekkan (1873–1935) and his wife, Akiko (1878–1942). It also included other new-style poets of traditional forms, and what appeals to Seizō is the sensual lyricism of the group. This enthusiasm is replaced by Seizō's discovery of the poetry of the young men involved in the journal *Bungakkai* (Literary World), which represents the main current of Japanese romanticism. Seizō's infatuation with the *Bungakkai* writers leads him to sketching, a prominent literary technique at the turn of the century. Through his shifting artistic interests and disappointing life experiences, Seizō eventually comes to the well-nigh Zola-esque conclusion that "human beings are creatures of their circumstances" (137). Seizō's literary trajectory enacts a journey from fin-de-siècle lyricism through romanticism to arrive, via sketching, at an incipient naturalism. At the same time that Katai constructs a chronotope of inertia, he shows Seizō traversing a path traveled by almost every writer who called himself a naturalist, though our hero does not in the end become a writer.

This extensive name-dropping is the focus of Fujimori Kiyoshi's stimulating reading of the novel in his book on modern narrative, representation, and visuality. Fujimori has isolated the portrayal of nature in *Inaka kyōshi* and linked it to a larger intertextual dialogue that takes place through literature in Katai's novel. Fujimori demonstrates that *Inaka kyōshi* rehearses in miniature the entire naturalist project of representation, which is certainly convincing enough given the protagonist's literary and intellectual trajectory. Fujimori concludes that what the narrative depicts as the protagonist's discovery of nature and the hard life of the country is essentially a reflection of the unshakable hold of Tōson and Doppo on Katai.[30] Fujimori ultimately uses this observation to pronounce Katai's novel "conservative" (*hoshūteki*), and by implication unoriginal, at least compared to the path opened by his fellow naturalist writers. This pronouncement is dubious, however, for, as Fujimori himself notes, the representation of nature among these writers can itself be traced back to Futabatei Shimei and his translations of Turgenev. Origins and originality are not the most productive frameworks for understanding such intertextual and international webs. We can instead follow through on Fujimori's suggestive lead that on a metafictional level *Inaka kyōshi* foregrounds a particular technique of writing nature—sketching (*shasei*)—that was common within and beyond naturalism and uses it for a very different purpose: to further draw out the themes of representation and compensation.

Shasei (literally, "copying life"), also sometimes referred to using the English loanwords *suketchi* (sketch) or *sutadi* (study), is the technique of sketching from nature in order to capture as fully and realistically as possible the minute details one sees in the world. *Shasei* lies at the intersection of three larger literary discourses in the Meiji era: the emphasis on representing the world "just as it is" (*ari no mama* or *aru ga mama*); the development of a vernacular writing style; and the imperative of freeing the representation of nature from the hold of classical literature. *Ari no mama* discourse is best viewed as the translation into the Japanese literary context of the West's post-romantic ideals of realistic representation.

A major goal of the advocates of this new verisimilitude was the creation of an objective narrative discourse that could dispassionately recount the events of the story as a way to overthrow the continuing influence of the didactic narratives of an earlier age. Part of this larger project was creating a new literary discourse, *genbun itchi* (literally, the unification of the written and spoken words), as a counter to the classical rhetoric of early-modern fiction and to the moral perspective that is inherent in its linguistic universe.[31] A third current underscored this felt need to free Japanese literature from the hold of the past by exploring new ways of seeing the landscape unencumbered by the millennium-long tradition of poetic composition.[32] As the influence of novelists such as Turgenev makes plain, Japanese writers were appropriating another, foreign mode of visualizing, experiencing, and representing landscape in order to displace inherited domestic modes.

Some have attached great significance to this seemingly straightforward notion of *shasei*. Etō Jun, for one, tracks the roots of the realist tradition in Japan to the new technique, essentially providing an alternative history of realism in Japan.[33] Karatani Kōjin relates the technique to the subject-object split that occurs with the "discovery" of landscape in Meiji.[34] And yet this immediately raises a question: Why would sketching be any different from what is traditionally called realistic description—that is, the metonymic joining together of details to produce a linguistically constructed reality effect? Is it simply realistic description applied to the natural world? In English, "sketching" implies something hurried, preparatory, or provisional, yet the Japanese term implies far more. A sketch (though a detailed one) of the genealogy of the term can help illuminate its meaning in the early twentieth century and its significance in Katai's novel.

In the world of letters, it was not the naturalists, but Masaoka Shiki (1867–1902) who pioneered the use of the new technique in his efforts to revitalize traditional poetic forms, such as the haiku. Kajiki Gō stresses that for Shiki the appeal of *shasei* lay precisely in its ability to transcend boundaries between the arts, for in true literati fashion, Shiki himself dabbled in just about every form of writing during his brief career, even the visual arts toward the end of his life.[35] Tsubouchi Toshinori goes so far as to claim that *shasei* was for Shiki the master technique held in common by all the arts.[36] Shiki borrowed the idea from his painter friend, Nakamura Fusetsu (1866–1943), and discovered that transposing the practice into the world of letters allowed him to bleed residual traces of lyricism and self-dramatization from his verse and to shift poetic practice to objective, microscopic observation.[37] Although Shiki has frequently been taken to task over the decades for coldly treating living things as if they were dead objects through this technique of sketching, his pronouncements on *shasei* suggest that his intentions were the opposite.

The clearest illustration of Shiki's ideals can be found in his short critical piece, "Jojibun" (Descriptive Prose), published in the then new literary journal *Hototogisu* (The Cuckoo) in three short installments in 1900. The essay may just as well have been entitled "Shasei," since Shiki uses it as a synonym for the titular concept. Admitting to borrowing the idea from the visual arts, Shiki defines *shasei* as "copying something just as it is in reality" (*jissai no ari no mama o utsusu*).[38] Our present-day skepticism of the possibility of unmediated contact with the real would lead us to critique the naiveté of this pronouncement, but this would be unfair, as Shiki's primary interest lies elsewhere. He conceives *shasei* as a vehicle for conveying emotion: "When one sees a landscape or an event that is captivating, one wants to convey this interest to a reader through words. Without embellishment or exaggeration, one must copy this phenomenon just as it is [*ari no mama*] and just as one sees it [*mitaru mama*]."[39] As Shiki makes clear, sketching is the technique par excellence for conveying to a reader the same emotion felt by the artist on viewing the object—not in spite of but because it opts for a precise, detailed description free of both embellishment and the subjective imprint of the writer. Yet *shasei*, in Shiki's hands, is a vehicle of sentiment that creates a bond between reader and writer through the mutual appreciation of a beautiful object. The object observed by the artist must be re-presented in words for the reader who did not see it firsthand, thus making language a "supplement" of vision, in the deconstructive sense of that term.[40]

Furthermore, as Tsubouchi notes, the object of Shiki's sketching was, with a few exceptions, the natural world, not the world of human society.[41] With sketching's emphasis on microscopic observation rather than on the totality of a landscape, these imperatives imply the necessity of selecting details from nature: "Selection implies choosing what is interesting and leaving out what is not. It does not necessarily imply choosing the large and throwing out the small or favoring the long over the short."[42] Shiki does not elaborate on his criteria for selection, but Mark Morris has argued quite persuasively that the poet's subjective idea of beauty is what validates his selection of details.[43] The poet's personal experience of beauty would be captured by detailed, unembellished representation, illustrating how subjectivity infiltrates the technique despite Shiki's claims of objectivity. In his advocacy for giving preference to the trees over the forest, so to speak, Shiki ultimately advocates for a narrowing and focusing of the artist's gaze in order to see the fine grain of nature so as to best convey a subjectively experienced beauty to the absent reader.

Shiki's ideas found currency among his poetic disciples, most notably Takahama Kyoshi (1874–1959), whose work we will examine in a later chapter. But the technique arguably had its greatest impact in the genre of prose. Influenced by the French painter Jean-François Millet (1814–1875), the Japanese watercolorist Miyake Katsumi (1874–1954), and John Ruskin's (1819–1900) influential book, *Modern Painters* (1843–1860), Shimazaki Tōson appropriated the technique and recast it for fiction. Still, Tōson objected to aspects of Shiki's practice, which he saw as excessively analytical, and instead advocated incorporating the human element and historical forces into the landscape being depicted.[44] In his *Chikuma-gawa no suketchi* (Chikuma River Sketches), which consists of impressionistic essays about Komoro written at the turn of the century but not published until 1912, Tōson is careful to depict a landscape that is inhabited and shaped by the people, but with the important exception that Tōson's brand of sketching, like that of Shiki, was more often directed at objects in the natural world.

In an essay entitled "Shasei" (1907), Tōson discusses how he borrowed the technique of sketching from the world of painting (he does not acknowledge Shiki) as a means to "practice looking at things." He elaborates: "Like a painter looking at an object, one begins by observing a part of it (trying to take in the object in its entirety is futile) and then proceeds to capture the 'truth' of that object."[45] Tōson's stance is similar to Shiki's point that sketching involves making a choice about what to include and what to leave out, with detail privileged over the larger landscape. Like Shiki, Tōson underscores the emotional connection created between reader and writer through the technique; drawing on the authority of Millet, he insists that the purpose of sketching is to "move the human heart" and "make another rejoice."[46] Once again, by sketching in minute detail a captivating object, the technique becomes a vehicle for the transmission of sentiment to an absent reader by, again, making language a supplement of vision.

In this short essay on *shasei*, Tōson mentions how he once created a homemade notebook and ventured outdoors to practice his art by recording his observations of the clouds at different times of the day and in different months. He is likely referring to his impressionistic essay "Kumo" (Clouds), a prose summary of the literary sketches he did while in Komoro as a country teacher, inspired as he was by the discussion of the clouds he found in Ruskin's *Modern Painters*, which he mentions by name at the outset. The essay was first printed in the journal *Tenchijin* (Heaven, Earth, Man) in 1900 and then found its way into his volume *Rakubaishū* (A Collection of Fallen Plum Blossoms) the following year. Tōson's interest in Ruskin-style categorization is very much on display in this work, which includes lists and even charts to form a kind of typology of clouds. The piece displays a sharp eye for detail in its descriptions of the shifting shape and color of clouds and in the observations of the relations between the clouds and other aspects of the landscape. Certainly nature's capacity to give us pleasure through its beauty comes across quite powerfully; and yet even more Tōson emphasizes transformation, with "change" being among the most common motifs in the essay; "Nature is always changing" (*Shizen wa tsune ni kawariyukeru nari*), he states definitively at one point.[47] The artistic capacity to record minute changes within the natural world suggests that Tōson was drawn to sketching as a technique that helped him satisfy the demands for rich, descriptive verisimilitude as he journeyed from lyric poetry to fiction, and thus, like his fellow travelers, from romanticism to naturalism. It also suggests that the emphasis on fine-grained observation was designed precisely to train the artist's eye to observe the most subtle transformations in the landscape, thus linking the naturalist appropriation of *shasei* to the movement's interest in objective, "scientific" description, with the eye conceived of as being a kind of microscope or camera lens. It is a tool for teaching people how to look anew at their world rather than through the eyes of their classical forebears.[48]

Interestingly, one can also find a brief piece called "Kumo" among Shiki's writings, published in *Hototogisu* in 1898. No doubt inspired by Ruskin's sensuous description of the sky, clouds became a privileged object for those practicing *shasei* and became embedded in a dense intertextual network through which borrowed ideas and methods were transmitted across national borders and passed along among the different artistic genres within Japan. It may be that Meiji writers were captivated as much by Ruskin's gorgeous descriptions *of* clouds as they were by the actual clouds they observed in nature.[49] True to Ruskin's method, Shiki creates a list of cloud types, discusses the relations among clouds and other objects in the sky, and uses clouds as analogies for the seasons, all of which overlaps with the interests of Tōson's much longer essay. For our purposes, the most important aspect of the piece is the way Shiki links nature as an ever-changing entity to sketching as a vehicle for conveying sentiment:

> Consider the clouds that appear overhead in the solitary valleys or underfoot in the distant mountains; these are dramatic vistas, so who would not be moved? But there may be few who would notice the clouds over the plains or in the clear, blue sky. The clouds in a pristine sky also change, but it is un-dramatic and thus moves us when our hearts are at peace.[50]

Dramatic vistas in nature can be appreciated by anyone, but the strength of sketching is that it disciplines the eye of the artist, allowing the writer to see the beauty of everyday elements of a landscape. By extension, if sketching is a vehicle of sentiment, as Shiki claims in his critical essays, then we can see how the artist's trained eye, sensitive to the most minute changes in the natural world and conditioned to select out of the landscape the most salient and moving details, is able to compellingly represent this unnoticed beauty to the absent reader. Relating this to the efforts to free literary discourse from the hold of the past, we might hypothesize that "un-dramatic" beauty corresponds to the beauty of objects heretofore unnoticed in literary discourse because the weight of the poetic tradition had conditioned the artist to see other things in the landscape. And yet sketching, like so much premodern poetry, is generally centered on the representation of nature, with clouds being only the most prominent example. Lying at the intersection of *ari no mama* discourse, the new literary language of *genbun itchi*, and the imperative of freeing the natural world from the hold of classical literature, *shasei* itself is a technique of separating nature from society, on the one hand, while concentrating the pen or brush on the task of capturing subtle changes within the natural world, with the larger goal of creating a like-minded community of readers.

In the nineteenth chapter of *Inaka kyōshi*, Seizō ventures out, notebook in hand, to a place called Hirano (also rendered Heigen) with the goal of sketching the clouds there. After recording the changing details of the landscape in his notebook, he proceeds to write a summary entitled, "A Study of the Clouds at Hirano" (Hirano no kumo no kenkyū). On a diegetic level, Seizō is engaged in sketching, and the word *shasei* is explicitly used to describe his activity (109). But there is also an intertextual dimension to this enterprise, which we glimpse in Seizō's motivations for his outing:

> Taking a cue from the poet who wrote *Hitohabune*, Seizō decided that he would engage in a similar study of clouds. He could not, of course, examine the complex changes of the clouds such as one might find in Takahara in Shinano, but there were still many splendid, colorful clouds encircling the mountains of Hirano here on the vast Kantō Plain. (109)

The "poet who wrote *Hitohabune* [The One-Leaf Boat]" and had roots in Shinano (present-day Nagano Prefecture) is none other than Shimazaki Tōson, whose name is invoked countless times in the novel's pages. Seizō is here mimicking Tōson's sketching activity in "Clouds."

Seizō undertakes his "Study" after a complex sequence recording a psychological seesaw between hopeful ambition and weary resignation. It begins with the narrator charting Seizō's desire to test his literary talent, like Goethe or Doppo when writing their early works (103–4). Unfortunately, Seizō's initial efforts come to nothing and he grows despondent (105). The narrator then gives us Seizō reflecting on the disparity between the high level of learning of a local priest and the man's anonymous life in the provinces (108–9). The fact that Seizō goes out to sketch the clouds immediately after this suggests a lingering desire to avoid the priest's fate. In this case, sketching is an act of mimicking literary heroes who have already achieved fame (Tōson as creator of *Hitohabune*; Doppo as the author of the widely read collection *Musashino*; Goethe as the author of the immortal *Sorrows of Young Werther*) and thus remains part of the larger treatment of literature as a metaphor for worldly success. The implied readers of the "Study," then, are the members of the *bundan*; Seizō is seeking their attention in order to gain the kind of social recognition promised to ambitious youth.

In such early passages, sketching is a fundamentally literary activity, for Seizō's descriptions of the clouds are recorded with words in his notebook (*techō*), as are Tōson's and Shiki's, which are then summarized and polished in his "Study." Later in the novel, though, Seizō will have in hand not a notebook but his sketchbook (*shaseichō*), and when he ventures out to engage in *shasei*, he will be creating visual representations rather than linguistic representations (155, 219, 223). The slight difference in terminology is important, and the transition from one medium to another is indelibly linked to Seizō's growing despair and sense of failure. For example, a friend's suggestion late in the novel that Seizō move closer to the school rather than remain in his temple lodgings in a neighboring town brings forth the following reflections on his life:

> Seizō could not help but consider how different his feelings were now from the time when he had lived at the temple. Compared to those days, his hopes, goals, and feelings had changed completely. *Gyōda Literature* had folded. The friends who had gathered around it had gone their separate ways. Nowadays he spent more time making sketches for paintings and adapting for the organ the melodies he gathered from music sheets. (147)

The crucial phrase here is making "sketches for paintings" (*kaiga no shasei*). It is likely that the specific medium is watercolor, since that is where his interest in the visual arts began (144), but whatever it may be, Seizō's sketching has shifted from prose to the visual arts, and there is something symbolic in the incompleteness of these works, for we never see him produce a finished piece. Recall that *shasei* transcends the boundaries between the arts and that its principles can be transposed into different media; this facilitates the subtle rotation of sketching from literary to visual representation.

It also means that the purpose of sketching has changed. Literature is the master metaphor of *risshin shusse* in Katai's novel. But *Gyōda bungaku* fails, and the literary-minded youth who had earlier gathered around it with such enthusiasm pursue instead more practical routes to worldly success. As the protagonist becomes aware of his inability to escape the liminal state of social inertia, he turns away from literature and takes up the visual arts, with sketching providing the fulcrum for this shift. As if to emphasize this, not a single literary work is mentioned in the final quarter of the novel. The protagonist's early literary activity may be geared toward connecting to an audience and garnering recognition and fame, but his later artistic activity has become a solitary pursuit that yields pleasure and consolation not for an off-stage reader or viewer, but for himself alone. This parallels the separation of nature from the countryside, which is also founded on the protagonist's growing despondency. As we saw, unmasking or revelation is the rhetorical maneuver utilized in the novel to separate a homogeneous countryside into nature and provincial community. Sketching is the technique that then turns nature into a privileged compensatory object among those available to the protagonist.

It would be reckless to claim that the naturalist text always performs this work of rescuing nature from the countryside. However, I would like to briefly illustrate how the analysis of the phenomenon we have uncovered in Katai's oeuvre can be extended to other works in the naturalist canon. Tōson's *Hakai* offers a similarly ambivalent portrait of the provinces, if not a drama of unmasking. In it we are given a story of the lingering discrimination in the new era against a segment of the Japanese population who had been dispossessed for centuries. Since the story of discrimination is set in the provinces, provincial society itself is inevitably represented negatively as a space of hostility, hypocrisy, and irrational prejudice, all of which conspire to prevent the dispossessed from participating in modern self-fashioning and social mobility (*Hakai*, too, is a novel of *risshin shusse*, after all). As he debates whether or not to reveal his identity as a *burakumin*, the only consolations for the protagonist, Segawa Ushimatsu, are the love of a local woman and the beauty of the natural world. Perhaps in any portrait of a sympathetic protagonist in a harsh provincial society, nature will be separated off as distinct so as to function as a compensatory object.

❖

To read Japanese naturalism as a literature of compensation, as I have done here, is to move beyond thematic analysis. Whether we take the movement's central obsession to be sexuality, degeneracy, science, or even the city-country dichotomy, it is difficult to exhaust the movement's concerns or to subsume them under a single thematic heading. Our reading here suggests that it may be fruitful to conceive of the naturalist novel (and the prose narrative is the favored mode of naturalist writing) as a site for an exploration of modernity's shortcomings. In Katai's oeuvre, and perhaps in that of others, this exploration is regularly augmented by some kind of textual mechanism dedicated to the production of compensatory objects for modernity's failure to deliver on its promises.

To illustrate the point as a way to conclude this chapter, I return to a question raised earlier: Why the strange evocation of war and nation-building within a novel ostensibly concerned with the story of the individual's experience of social inertia? The opening of hostilities between Japan and Russia in 1904 (210) and the victory of Japan over its gigantic rival the following year (260) are clearly marked in the novel, and, in a way that can only be intentionally planned by Katai, Seizō's illness and death are exactly synchronized with the Russo-Japanese War. Indeed, Seizō's death and Japan's victory occur on the very same day, described by the narrator in a bravura montage-like chapter that moves back and forth between the dying Seizō indoors and the increasingly raucous celebrations of wartime victory outdoors (259–61). We are given an implicit contrast between interior and exterior, the home and the streets, which mark a boundary between the isolated individual and the victorious communal body.

Nonetheless, as Seizō loses hope and becomes resigned to life as a failure, he becomes an increasingly fervent supporter of the war, a notable transformation considering his indifference to such matters at the outbreak of hostilities. At one point, he is even on the verge of tears because his illness prevents him from joining the military to fight for his country. Seizō despairs to the doctor in charge of his care: "Many are shedding their brave blood for the sake of the nation . . . and here I shamefully lie, bedridden by illness" (255). The closer he comes to death's door, the more Seizō dwells on the war and on his inability to be at the side of comrades at the front, as we see in the novel's final inside view of its protagonist:

> There was the suffering of those who fell in the fields. For one on the verge of death, fame meant nothing. Such men surely missed their parents. Surely they longed for the fatherland and for their natal homes, too. But, they are still more fortunate than me. Here I am fallen on my sickbed devoid of all hope. Such were Seizō's thoughts as his mind turned to his compatriots fallen on the lonely, barren fields in Manchuria. (259)

Although our hero's self-flagellation stands out here, just as notable is his longing to be a member of the battered, bloodied troops on the front line. This is the embrace of a very different community from the first part of the novel, during which Seizō's focus lay with the small homosocial group of ambitious provincial youth. We would certainly be justified in adding nationalism to the plethora of compensatory objects in the novel. Seizō's inability to climb the social ladder and join the ranks of the successful leads to still another psychological displacement: his replacing of ambition with nationalism and an embrace of the fighting forces in wartime.

Still, we might be tempted to interpret this puzzling intrusion as a sleight of hand on Katai's part, an endeavor to ameliorate the tragedy of an ambitious youth who dies a failure in the provinces with a hurried display of feel-good patriotic fervor. Or one could read this development as the symbolic integration of the disaffected individual into the larger collective enterprise—that is, as a disavowing of individual striving and an advocacy of national community. Or we could perhaps treat the protagonist's unnoticed death in the midst of nationalist revelry as irony, as some critics have.[51]

The last is the most compelling, for it allows us to connect war and another puzzling intrusion: the railroad. Not only has Katai synchronized his protagonist's illness and death with the war and daringly connected the psychology of failure with nationalism, in the same chapter in which the narrator notes the outbreak of hostilities between Japan and Russia, we read the narrator's retrospective comment that the Tōbu railway had not yet been built (211). In the chapter in which our hero witnesses the funeral for a fallen solider (225), we read that construction had begun on this railway (227). A station for this line is built in the area (240) in the chapter that gives the reader news of the stunning Japanese naval victory at Port Arthur (245). The development of the railway is meant to facilitate the movement of men and material for future wars. The novelistic coordination of war and railway construction therefore signals the link between imperialism and industrial development. Punctuating this novel of the provinces is the growth and centralization of national power (the terminus of the rail line is Ueno Station in Tokyo). Its centrifugal force entails the remaking of the novel's provincial setting into a periphery—what we might call the "provincialization" of the countryside—thereby homogenizing a diverse rural society and subordinating it to the nation's capital. It is a narrative treatment of what Kären Wigen has called a "regional inversion," whereby "the making of regional peripheries *was* the making of a national core."[52] Along the way, individual desires have been subordinated to national imperatives in Katai.

The dénouement of the novel is centered on a visit by Hideko to the unkempt grave of her former teacher, but the final sentence of the novel is completely owned by the now completed railway: "The train that ran on the Tōbu line along the forest on the way to Ashikaga raised its piercing whistle day and night" (264). Even as our protagonist lies in his grave, dead from tuberculosis rather than combat wounds, the countryside has been symbolically integrated into the national polity, and this effect is reinforced with the frequent mention of newspapers carrying accounts of the war to the far corners of the nation. The nation-state has come into its own, but time has left our hero behind. Despite Seizō's embrace of nationalist sentiment on his deathbed, I can only read this final, short chapter as ironic, as if Katai were trying to contrast Seizō's inertia and struggle to reach Tokyo with those who will now be streaming into the capital with the opening of the rail line. Indeed, the train's whistle almost seems to mock the remains of the protagonist, who has died in obscurity, his dreams of success unrealized. Dreams of love are also extinguished as Katai brings in Hideko for a final appearance, this time to further highlight what was foreclosed for Seizō.

This tone of irony is entirely in keeping with the naturalist enterprise, which reveled in pitting the individual against an inhospitable society in stories that often ended in tragedy. Naturalism in Japan, much like its counterparts in other national literatures, was invested in depicting the individual hounded by uncontrollable forces, whether an irrepressible sexuality, the brutal anonymity of the industrializing city, or, as I have emphasized here, hegemonic ideologies such as that of upward mobility. It is easy to see why this last theme would be attractive to the Japanese naturalists, in particular, for it allowed the writer to focus on those who were seized by the desire to rise in the world, but whose ambitions were ultimately thwarted.

This recounting is typically performed by a narrator (and author) who has already accepted the fact that the human condition involves being buffeted by forces outside of one's control, all while maintaining the ideal (or perhaps facade) of objective, detached narration throughout. The rhetoric of unmasking is ultimately what brings these two perspectives into alignment, thereby compelling the reader to see the world from the perspective of the naturalist writer and facilitating the reader's adoption of naturalism's position on modernity. That is, the maneuver we uncovered in Katai spuriously produces the "revelation" of the truth (natural law?) that naturalism has supposedly known all along: that the dream of modernity and the reality of modernity do not coincide; that, despite the promise of self-fashioning, the individual is not in control of his own destiny. At the same time, and as a complementary impulse for social insights that are painful to acknowledge, Katai is also committed to the production of a host of compensatory objects for an incomplete modernization. Naturalism is thus not without a didactic dimension, though it takes some effort to bring to the surface. In the next chapter, we will take up a very different representation of the provinces in a popular genre that wears its ideology on its sleeve.

CHAPTER 2

A Utopia of Self-Help: Imagining Rural Japan in the Novels of Ambition

The type of person needed in today's society . . . is the man who will create his own destiny with his own hands.

—Murakami Shunzō, inaugural issue of *Seikō* (1902)

In September 1906, the ethnologist Yanagita Kunio (1875–1962), a lifelong friend of Tayama Katai, published an expanded version of a speech he had addressed earlier to the Greater Japan Agricultural Association (Dai Nihon Nō Kai) concerning the vexed relationship between the city and the country. His essay, broadly entitled "Inaka tai tokai no mondai" (The Problem of the Country versus the City), had as its goal to sound the alarm over Japan's rapid urbanization and suggest some proposals for reversing the flight of the rural population to the growing metropolitan areas. Apprehension of the prospect of abandoned towns and villages may well have been the primary impetus for Yanagita's sizable intellectual output and, most famously, his career-long project to recover and preserve oral tales from all corners of provincial society.[1] In his essay, Yanagita encouraged economic investment in villages, towns, and provincial capitals so as to strike a better balance in the geographical distribution of resources, knowledge, and wages in Japan's expanding capitalist economy. He aimed not so much to indict capitalism per se: this would have run counter to his mission, in his position in the policy section of the Agriculture Ministry, of advocating for the modernization of the countryside through capitalistic rationalization.[2] Rather, his goal was to raise awareness about the fate of the countryside within the broad historical dynamic of the concentration of capital and opportunity in a handful of major urban centers. Yanagita clearly recognized that economic motivations underlie the choice to move to the city, and this realistic perspective informed his analysis of what he, following the conservative rural advocate Yokoi Tokiyoshi, would call "city fever" (*tokai-netsu*).

Yanagita shows himself an idealist, however, when he meditates on the cultural implications of what he fears may be the imminent emptying of the countryside. Gone would be the organic community rooted in village and soil, and, along with it, the traditions and sense of cultural identity that it nurtured. Furthermore, as Irokawa Daikichi has observed, Yanagita strategically links the nation, the rural family, and cultural identity. Using the increasingly powerful family-state model of nationhood (*kazoku kokka*), which defines the nation as the family lineage (*ie*) writ large, Yanagita argues that the destruction of the rural *ie* through urbanization would not only undermine authentic cultural values but would also weaken the basis of loyalty and patriotism (*chūkun aikoku*), thereby threatening the survival of the new emperor-centered polity.[3] Going even further, Yanagita frames the entire problem of urbanization in terms of the relationship between the individual and the collective. Modernization, he writes, gives birth to a nation where the individual's will and desires take priority over those of the family lineage. Coining a neologism, Yanagita calls the reckless flight to the city an act of "domicide" (*ie-goroshi*) against the ancestral home, leaving no doubt that he considers urbanization to be a moral crisis, a cultural threat, and an economic problem all at once.[4] By implicitly associating the city with individualism—with the perilous insistence on the here and now of the individual at the expense of past and future generations of the family—and the countryside with the collective, Yanagita idealizes rural society as the sanctuary of the organic community and authentic cultural values.

Even as Yanagita concedes that the destruction of the countryside is forcing many rural poor to flee to the cities in search of a livelihood, he notes that "city fever" is being stoked in individuals in part by "the quite understandable desire to rise in the world."[5] Yanagita's analysis of the troubled relationship between city and country within capitalist modernity is thus linked to the larger discourses on social mobility and success. *Risshin shusse* is not the focus of Yanagita's essay, but if we were to continue to follow Irokawa's suggestive lead in viewing Yanagita's real concern as the retention of the old landed elites in their ancestral homes in order to preserve traditional values and the organic community, we would find many hidden connections linking urbanization, social class, and the new cult of social advancement. In other words, Yanagita has glimpsed within the ideology of success something I have already argued: *risshin shusse* is a mechanism created by industrial capitalism to move a mostly rural population to the cities. Yanagita wants to halt this process by reasserting the priority of the collective over the individual. This reprioritization is also a return to tradition in his eyes.

Yanagita's short essay highlights a nexus in which the dichotomy between the city and the country, the relationship between the individual and the collective, and the ideas of social advancement and the traditional organic community are joined together within a moral framework. He was not alone in his worries. The aggressive industrialization and urbanization that followed in the wake of Japan's first two modern wars made the rejuvenation of a threatened countryside into a pressing concern for intellectuals, ideologues, and even the bureaucrats in Tokyo.

Our concerns here will be with how the literary imagination grapples with the inevitable problems confronting an industrializing nation. The impact of economic development on the countryside is registered with precision in a large number of literary works; among them, Shimazaki Tōson's *Ie* (The Family, 1910), with its closely observed portrait of the gradual disintegration of an established family enterprise in the provinces due to industrialization, is a canonical work that comes immediately to mind.[6] However, I wish to focus on a group of related noncanonical texts that collectively develop a stringent pro-countryside and anti-city position. Investigating this almost unexplored terrain will allow us to map one more imaginative response out of many within the domain of fiction to the discourse on ambition as the long, event-filled Meiji era was drawing to a close.

The authors of these works labeled them *risshi shōsetsu*, a term that means literally "novel of purpose," but that we could better render as "novel of ambition" or "ambition novel," provided we remember that the Japanese *shōsetsu* can refer to a prose narrative of any length, from a short story to a Victorian triple-decker. *Risshi shōsetsu* have in common a protagonist with a burning desire to climb the social ladder, usually from a starting point very near the bottom, thence to achieve material success and social respectability. The closest equivalent to this genre in the

English-speaking world would be the rags-to-riches stories of Horatio Alger (1832–1899), with their surefire combination of luck and pluck.[7] But the homegrown *risshi shōsetsu* are less familiar to contemporary Japanese than Alger's world-famous fiction, and, despite the high sales and wide circulation these novels of ambition enjoyed in their own time, not one example of the genre can be found in the voluminous compendiums of Japanese literature published today. These novels are forgotten works.

This chapter partakes of the growing effort to retrieve from the archive the overlooked narrative fiction of the past—including potboilers like these ambition novels—and, after blowing the dust off their covers, to use them to facilitate the collective process of defining the contours of the modern novel across as large a spectrum of examples as is feasible.[8] Once we expand the category of "literature" to include more than what has traditionally been called "literary," how do works that were either ejected from the canon or never entered the canon in the first place help us to think about the novel, the dominant literary form of modern Japan? How do such works contribute to our understanding of the way the literary imagination engages the socioeconomic processes of modernization? Answering these questions will require yoking together several different theoretical perspectives—on narrative, on the representation of space and time, and on media culture—within the general framework of discourse analysis.

Risshi shōsetsu may be viewed as socially symbolic acts. In *The Political Unconscious*, Fredric Jameson defines this mode of reading as one in which the literary text is seen as performing ideological work by offering an imaginative or formal solution to real social tensions and contradictions.[9] A social problem that is so vexed and convoluted as to be insoluble in reality can be disentangled by the literary imagination, and—through narrative construction, formal closure, the character system, and strategies of representation—achieve resolution. Indeed, precisely because the problem is insoluble in reality, the literary text becomes a site for testing alternative social configurations. This methodology allows us to understand that escapist entertainment is as much a participant in the contentious dialogue on Japanese modernity as are Yanagita Kunio's essays or the fiction of Tayama Katai. As a reading of an archetypal novel of ambition will show, the authors of *risshi shōsetsu* are confronting a social problem: the relationship between the individual and the collective when the conjoined forces of urbanization and industrialization are poised to destroy provincial society. Their solution is a rural utopia that has reinstated the organic community within a new national framework and relocated the path to success in the countryside, thus instantiating a formal reversal of "city fever."

Reading these works as socially symbolic acts preoccupied with the countryside suggests that within the representational system of these texts, *risshin shusse* is closely linked to a particular conceptualization and construction of social and national space, as well as to the ideology of progress. We will therefore be drawing once again on the idea of the chronotope of success developed in the introduction. To reiterate, ambition is a form of desire that is forward-looking and resolutely social in its orientation, propelling the individual from poverty to the attainment of success. In the normative view of *risshin shusse*, this life unfolds in the space of the nation: Tokyo is at its center, and the ideal route to success leads from the provinces to the capital. The *risshi shōsetsu*, however, offer an alternative idea of success, one rooted in the countryside; they construct a chronotope whose temporal dimension is identical to the normative trajectory of success, but whose spatial dimension is anchored in the organic community of the village rather than in the metropolis. Whereas Katai had inverted the entire chronotope of success in order to thematize social inertia, the ambition novels overturn the spatial axis of the chronotope of success. The ideological effect of this literary strategy is to counter the "provincialization" of the countryside and the new centrality of Tokyo.

These ambition novels are inseparable from their media context, for they appeared either as serialized fiction or as complete books published by a magazine devoted exclusively to the new ideas of ambition, success, and self-help. In order to uncover the transactions between text and context, I develop a historicist approach to media analysis and view the media context as an intertextual field defined by advertising and hence by desire. Within a media framework that will allow us to shuttle between form and content, and between text and context, I combine a general discussion of the *risshi shōsetsu* as one species of the modern novel with a close reading of an iconic example, drawing on other specimens of the genre to support the discussion.

Novels of Ambition and Their Readers

One prolific author of *risshi shōsetsu* was Horiuchi Shinsen. Little is known about his life. Born Horiuchi Fumimaro in 1873 in Kyoto, he attended the prestigious First Higher School in Tokyo but left before completing the curriculum. He decided on a writing career, and, after a short stint at Tokutomi Sohō's *Kokumin shinbun* (The Nation's Newspaper), he took the pen name Shinsen and became a literary disciple of Kōda Rohan. In addition to being a novelist and critic, Rohan was also a regular contributor of inspirational self-help articles to several periodicals, and, though Shinsen could never match the preternatural gifts of his accomplished mentor, he had a certain flair for manipulating natural imagery for symbolic effect.[10] Shinsen's first works were in the genre of the "home novels" (*katei shōsetsu*)—mostly domestic melodramas—that were in vogue at the turn of the century, but, finding little success with this genre, he turned to novels of ambition. Although he did not invent the *risshi shōsetsu*, Shinsen soon came to dominate this genre, which was still in its infancy at the start of his career. He was extraordinarily prolific in this arena, turning out at least one, and often two or more ambition novels every year between 1902 and the early 1920s, in addition to short stories, poetry, and essays. The titles of his novels—such as *Kikyōki* (A Record of a Journey Home, 1907), *Hito ichinin* (A Man Alone, 1910), *Ase no kachi* (The Value of Sweat, 1910–1911), and *Kono chichi kono ko* (This Father, This Child, 1912)—indicate a consistent thematic preoccupation with the ancestral home, family ties, self-reliance, and hard work. He knew English well enough to translate from it, rendering such works as Walter Moody's bestselling *Men Who Sell Things* into Japanese as *Shin hanbai jutsu* (New Sales Techniques, 1909). The date of Shinsen's death is not known for certain, but 1925 is probably a good guess, since the literary output of this man who lived by his pen seems to have stopped abruptly in this year.

Even if some of the preoccupations of Shinsen's novels of ambition can be traced to his biography, certain aspects of the genre transcend the circumstances of a single life. In fact, in the approach I am advocating here, the lack of biographical information about the author is an advantage. Consideration of a group of texts within its media context presumes that it is best to approach a genre from outside a traditional author-centered paradigm. The thematic preoccupations of the *risshi shōsetsu* are embedded in a matrix that includes editorial decisions, readers' expectations, the publishers' ideological agenda, and advertising needs; accordingly such genre staples as the novels of ambition are best studied by shifting attention to their media context so as to uncover the interaction between the individual work and the media framework in which it participates.

Many *risshi shōsetsu*, by Shinsen and others, appeared in the pages of the magazine *Seikō* (Success), a seminal publication of the early twentieth century and one that has been the focus of a good deal of scholarship on modern Japanese media culture.[11] Published for thirteen years, between 1902 and 1915, the magazine was comparatively long-lived in an era known for the ephemerality of its "three-issue serials." *Seikō* was begun by the enterprising Murakami Shunzō, who got the idea from the popular American magazine, *Success*, which was in circulation around the turn of the century.[12] Murakami lifted his magazine's title from its American precursor, but gave it an auspicious subtitle: *Risshi dokuritsu shinpo no tomo* (Friend of Ambition, Independence, and Advancement). The magazine eventually reached a circulation of fifteen thousand among paying subscribers, a respectable number compared to the average periodical in circulation in that era. *Kokumin no tomo* (The Nation's Friend), a prominent magazine for the educated class, had a circulation of about twenty thousand at its height. Large as these figures are for their era, they are still far lower than that of *Taiyō* (The Sun), undoubtedly the paramount general-interest magazine of the period, with subscriptions that peaked just shy of one hundred thousand.[13]

Numbers, however, do not tell the entire story. As is well documented, after the ideology of personal advancement attained hegemonic status in the wake of the Sino-Japanese War, the early years of the twentieth century witnessed a phenomenon appropriately called the "*seikō* boom," and, as might be expected, the magazine that best represented the spirit of the age played a decisive role in spurring men from all walks of life to climb the social ladder and achieve material prosperity and social distinction.[14] The turn of the century was the moment that saw *risshin shusse* spread from the elite and the old samurai classes to society at large, and the appearance of *Seikō* is one sign of this turn. The magazine was also the hub of a large publishing network, the Seikō Zasshi Sha (Seikō Magazine Company), which, in addition to its flagship magazine, produced a number of journals as well as shelf after shelf of books devoted to self-help, schooling, business, and commerce. Murakami drew on a group of prominent contributors and other supporters, including literary, political, and intellectual heavyweights such as Kōda Rohan, Ōkuma Shigenobu, and Tokutomi Sohō. *Seikō* was a magazine with respectable sales that kept pace with attention-grabbing monthlies of its era; more importantly, it penetrated deep into society and had high cultural visibility. *Seikō*'s impact, though impossible to measure precisely, certainly extended well beyond its already sizable circle of paying subscribers.

The stereotypical reader of *Seikō* was the poor, struggling student (*hinshosei*), at least according to the witty picture-essay "Shinbun zasshi no aidokusha" (The Devoted Readers of Newspapers and Magazines) from *Kokkei shinbun* (The Humor News).[15] This piece acquires its humor through trafficking in stereotypes of the day, some examples of which are the prurient male student reading *Jogaku sekai* (World of Women's Learning) and disgruntled laborers reading the socialist *Heimin shinbun* (The People's News). A stereotype also underlies the caricature of the iconic journal of self-help in *Kokkei shinbun*. The illustration of the poor student, lying on his back on a dirty *tatami* floor in his cramped rooming house, left hand supporting his head and left leg propped on the right knee, as he reads a magazine entitled *Seikō,* pokes fun at those who harbor grand visions of their future when finding themselves in a drab and grubby present.

A more nuanced view of *Seikō*'s readership has been made possible by the painstaking research of Ameda Ei'ichi. Although students were an important segment of the magazine's regular readers, *Seikō* also circulated widely among low-ranking teachers, bureaucrats, and military men, both in the countryside and in the cities.[16] Initially the magazine was also sympathetic to the Labor and Socialist movements, and advertising in workers' magazines suggests that *Seikō* was soliciting readers from the working class.[17] However, most subscribers came from among those who were on the lower rungs of the emerging professions and from those who hoped to join their ranks—that is, the lower middle class. Stated in psychological terms, the magazine attracted most of its readers from among young men without much to their name apart from the dream of social advancement in their chosen profession.

Thus, it should come as no surprise that the dominant message of *Seikō* was that of self-help or that the magazine's most enduring contribution to intellectual history was the construction of the "self-help type"[18]—the man who operates in the spirit of self-reliance. Clearly *Seikō* had fully absorbed the message of Samuel Smiles's book, *Self-Help*. Rendered into Japanese in 1871 by Nakamura Masanao as *Saikoku risshi hen*, the international bestseller had, according to contemporary anecdotes, drawn hordes of disaffected samurai, who lined the streets in front of the bookstores, eager to catch a glimpse of the glories of the modern era extolled in the book's pages.[19] The message had become legitimated and even more potent in the early twentieth century.

Fueled by these ideologies, the *risshi shōsetsu* appeared in a number of forums. The genre is, however, most closely associated with *Seikō*, which published the vast majority of these works and had on its payroll the most successful of the genre's writers, Horiuchi Shinsen. Beginning in 1905 a veritable deluge of *risshi shōsetsu* were published as stand-alone novels by the magazine's book publishing division. Shorter works appeared in the "home column" (*katei-ran*) of *Seikō* from the magazine's first issue in 1902. The titles of these short pieces—such as "Kesshin" (Resolve) and "Kibō" (Hope)—are all variations on a single theme, already foreshadowing the formulas that would come to define the genre. The "home column" disappeared during the Russo-Japanese War and was replaced by more militaristic, patriotic fare. In 1907, the magazine got a facelift and the "arts column" (*bungei-ran*) made its debut. Short *risshi shōsetsu* reappeared in this column two years later. In 1910, when the magazine received another facelift and the distinct columns disappeared, these works appeared in the table of contents as independent entries along with all the other articles and features. At this time, serialized *risshi shōsetsu* became the norm; first novellas appeared in installments over three or four months and eventually full-fledged novels were serialized over a year or more. Most of these long works next appeared as books, released by the publications wing of the magazine to stand beside the many novels produced independently of serialization. These trends were in effect right up to the last issue of *Seikō* in 1915. The first works in Japan bearing the subtitle *risshi shōsetsu* appeared as early as the 1880s and were mostly less than one hundred pages. The genre lasted into the 1920s, with the peak being the decade from 1905 to 1915, during which the novels were often substantial; it was common for a *risshi shōsetsu* to appear in two thick volumes of several hundred pages each, printed on cheap paper.[20] This peak decade happens to have coincided almost perfectly with the lifespan of *Seikō*.

Novels of ambition were highly visible in their own day. Advertisements in the magazines of the era testify that third and fourth printings were commonplace, with popular works running to six and seven printings, and ten or more reprints for the biggest sellers. Shinsen's greatest success, *Hito no ani* (The Brother, 1905–1906), undoubtedly the best known and most widely read *risshi shōsetsu* of its day, was in its twelfth printing by the end of the Meiji era, in 1912, and in its fifteenth printing by 1915, a decade after its first appearance.[21] This novel was so prominent that the phrase "by the author of *Hito no ani*" became the standard way of introducing a new novel by Shinsen. Given the large number of reprints most of these novels went through, the number of readers of *risshi shōsetsu* must have far exceeded the number of subscribers to *Seikō*, where many of the works first appeared.

We should not, however, exaggerate the prominence of these novels. Large though they may be, the sales (and hence, by implication, the social penetration) of the *risshi shōsetsu* fell far short of the level achieved by such Meiji-era melodramatic blockbusters as Ozaki Kōyō's *Konjiki yasha* (The Gold Demon, 1897–1902), Tokutomi Roka's *Hototogisu* (The Cuckoo, 1898–99), and Kosugi Tengai's *Makaze koikaze* (Demonic Winds, Passionate Winds, 1903), all of which had long afterlives. We will examine Tengai's novel in chapter four. A comparison of the *Konjiki yasha* and *Hototogisu* with the successful ambition novels, which generally saw one reprint per year, is sobering: *Hototogisu* went through a hundred printings in nine years and almost two hundred additional printings by the end of the Taisho era in 1926. *Konjiki yasha* saw similarly strong sales figures in its own day, as well as another 189 reprints during the Taisho era.[22] In addition, although ambition novels were advertised in publications other than those controlled by Seikō Zasshi Sha, unlike the big melodramas, they were never reviewed in the major contemporary literary journals of the day, such as *Bungei kurabu* (Literary Club), or in general-interest magazines that published fiction, such as *Taiyō*. After 1910, in the wake of Japanese naturalism, the novel ceased to be regarded as a novelty and was already separating into two large categories, serious fiction and everything else.[23] Tayama Katai helped develop the first category; the authors of *risshi shōsetsu* unapologetically penned fiction that fell into the latter.

Using a new-historicist approach, I uncover the intertextual network that links these ambition novels to their media context. In that it can move across a range of texts without regard for culturally demarcated zones, new historicism helps to destabilize the boundaries of literature and thus lends itself particularly well to a media approach to fiction. This methodology can reveal a "poetics of culture" (to use Stephen Greenblatt's term),[24] whereby certain tropes, narrative archetypes, and utopian fantasies circulate between text and media context. Although, for some, this approach strips the literary work of its artistic power and authority, I would argue for new historicism's expansive conception of textuality in that it locates the literary in surprising places outside the narrow circle of canonical texts. In any case, ambition novels have no artistic pedigree that would require us to pause. At the same time, not wishing to erase the distinctiveness of novels of ambition, I also draw inspiration from the approaches to media taken by scholars who pay close attention to the rhetoric of individual texts.[25]

A new-historicist approach involves the juxtaposition of specific texts. But how do we justify the use of particular works over the thousands that survive in the archive? The solution, I believe, lies in a conception of intertextuality rooted in the market. Since the advertising network linking a specific body of mutually resonant works plays such a large role in drawing attention to and generating demand for those works, it sets the boundaries, however attenuated, for a particular media context. Advertisements lead the reader of one work to similar works, thus forging connections among texts from different parts of the entire media field. The print publications of Seikō Zasshi Sha, for example, can be seen as constituting an intertextual field generated by its advertising network, and, by paying careful attention to advertisements, such published fiction as the novels of ambition, and published nonfiction, we can uncover the major tropes that circulate within a given field and indeed that help delimit that field. A poetics of culture rooted in such a bounded media context avoids the quite legitimate charges of arbitrariness that critics often level against new historicism; at the same time, it allows for conceptualizing the media network as attempting to align its own ideological agenda with readerly desire. In this formulation, the commonality we will be seeking among texts has less to do with themes as with the expression of a particular wish fulfillment.

Without reducing the text to its media context, then, we should acknowledge the market as a crucial factor in the production and circulation of a given work. To this general principle, we can add two further refinements: first, to the extent that the media context conditions both the writing and the reading of texts appearing under its auspices, a given work derives much of its meaning from the medium in which it appears; second, the formal apparatus of a literary work depends greatly on the type of media in which it appears, since serialization and other modes of production play a large role in shaping narrative structure and genre conventions.

In the August 1, 1912, issue of *Seikō*, there appeared an advertisement for several *risshi shōsetsu* by Shinsen in a format that regular readers would have seen countless times in different guises in the books and periodicals of the entire publishing network of the Seikō Magazine Company. In boldface type arranged horizontally across the top, one finds the imperative declaration "Gendai risshi seinen hitsudoku sho" (Required Reading for Ambitious Youth of the Modern Age). The layout of the page—two rows of three titles each, with titles in large print and plot summaries in small print, together with notes on page length and price—conforms to the basic template for such advertisements. Each work has the same subtitle, *risshi shōsetsu*, and the page includes a range of recent and older titles. This particular advertisement lists *Tada ikki* (In a Single Breath, second printing), *Kono chichi kono ko* (This Father, This Child, third printing), *Hito no ani* (The Brother, twelfth printing), *Hito ichinin* (A Man Alone, fourth printing), *Kokyō o izuru ki* (A Record of Leaving Home, fifth printing), and *Kikyōki* (A Record of a Journey Home, eighth printing).[26]

The ways in which the rhetoric and the layout hail and construct readers remain constant, even as the titles change. Like any novel in a commercial economy, the *risshi shōsetsu* is a commodity that circulates on the fiction market in competition with other works. Yet these ambition novels are both differentiated from works in other genres and grouped together by means of the common subtitle ("a novel of ambition"); they thus occupy a distinct niche, which, to some extent, reduces competition with other novels. In this way, by demarcating certain products in the fiction market from their neighboring genres, advertising helps define a particular kind of work and reader.

The advertising for the novels subsumes the intended reader into the category of *gendai risshi seinen* (ambitious youth of the modern age). This gendered term immediately implies a male student in the upper reaches of the educational system, including both the elite college preparatory schools and the universities, but it can also encompass those of a similar age who are not in school, whether farm workers in the country or the younger members of the emerging professional classes. The advertisement suggests that these young men will want to read these works so as to learn how to succeed. The ambition novels thus have pedagogical value, as indicated by the phrase "required reading." The advertisement encourages the reader to identify with the category of "ambitious youth" and consume the texts less as fiction or entertainment than as sources of inspiration and practical knowledge.

Nonetheless, pleasure has not been banned from this corner of the literary world. In his path-breaking essay, Wada Atsuhiko argues that these novels create a mechanism of identification whereby the struggling reader sees his own pain and hardship reflected in the protagonist of the novel. The novels of ambition present a lower-middle-class protagonist and, in following his exploits, generate a unique form of readerly pleasure, in which gratification is obtained more by witnessing the struggle itself than by following a telos that ends with the hero's success—although such closure is obviously mandatory for the genre.[27] In formulating his ideas, Wada probably got a hint from Takeuchi Yō, who had observed that *Seikō*, especially after the Russo-Japanese War, began downplaying the telos of success—whether conceived in terms of social status or personal wealth or both—and instead emphasized the path to success. Struggle as a test of one's spirit gradually takes on moral overtones, and the reward itself is of secondary importance.[28] The same message thus emanates from the magazine and from its serialized fiction, and advertising constructs a genre whose appeal lies precisely in its didactic qualities.

The advertisement's constant repetition of the subtitle "novel of ambition" suggests in yet another way that this genre is associated with pleasure. Implicitly the layout of the advertisement claims that a reader who has found satisfaction in one ambition novel will find similar gratification in these six titles. In addition to sharing resemblances of format and structure, works in the same genre constitute an intertextual field yielding similar readerly pleasures and similar ideological messages, all of which are mediated by advertising. Genre also describes a communal experience. The emphasis on the number of reprints of a given work shows that many others have purchased and liked it; it is popular and continues to sell. This guarantees satisfaction to the readers of the advertisement and presages the creation of a community of like-minded readers who will gain similar pleasures from a particular print medium. Advertising simultaneously differentiates the *risshi shōsetsu* from other fictional commodities on the market and constructs them into a coherent group through the common reading experience they offer.

Advertisements for ambition novels often occupy the same page as advertisements for university guidebooks, self-study guides, the correspondence courses that were so popular at the turn of the century, as well as books promising the secret to success, thereby demonstrating that ambition novels are one of many related print commodities. The genre of the *risshi shōsetsu* helps sell success, and the society-wide preoccupation with success helps sell the novels. By the end of the Meiji period, the discourse on success itself had infiltrated the market, and, within the same discursive field, the genre of ambition novels formed a symbiotic relationship with other commodities. Repetition of a central message within an intertextual network is crucial to the reproduction of social ideologies, and fiction plays an important role in propagating a particular ideological agenda among a broad spectrum of readers.

Yet books are not ordinary consumer goods in the same way as are toothpaste and shoe polish. Consider an advertisement bearing this typical exhortation: "Those with resolve must read these works on new shortcuts to success!!!" (*Kokorozashi aru mono wa risshin seikō no shin-shōkei taru honsho o yome*!!!).[29] In the top left quarter of the advertisement is a blurb for *Risshi shōsetsu: Zenryoku no hito* (A Man Who Gives It His All: A Novel of Ambition), a "famous work by Horiuchi Shinsen," together with a brief description. Occupying the entire right half of the advertisement is a description of a new edition of the popular title *Dokugakuhō* (Methods of Self-Study). The lower left quarter of the advertisement briefly introduces other titles: *Jinkaku to unmei* (Character and Destiny), *Jikan katsuyōhō* (Methods of Using Time [Wisely]), *Nōryoku yōseihō* (Building Brainpower), and *Jinkaku no yōsei* (Cultivating Character). All of these works are touted as "shortcuts to success," and the fictional work is included in this grouping. In addition, the large number of titles with *jinkaku* (character) and the advertisement's preoccupation with the efficient use of time indicate that these books are not to be consumed as ordinary commodities. As is consistent with the apotheosis of struggle that Takeuchi has described, any product advertised in *Seikō* acquires an aura of moral sanction, because the magazine itself, and the discourse of which it is a part, tout ambition and success as moral imperatives: study for wealth and honor; carve out your own future with your own hands. This explains why fiction and nonfiction alike are included in the same advertising space: they offer similar moral and pedagogical programs.

By the same token, the novels of ambition occupy a magazine space consisting of a variety of columns and features, including short biographies of eminent people (often cast as rags-to-riches stories), advice for making the best use of time and money, tips on how to pass the university entrance exams, and a large number of practical "how-to" articles. Here again, the magazine's dominant message is self-help; hence, the dominant message of the novels of ambition, whatever routes they trace to the inevitable dénouement, must also be about self-help. In considering the novels of ambition in their media context, then, we again encounter the didactic imperative: the novels are meant to inspire the pursuit of success. The advertisements for many ambition novels indicate that they are based on real life, thus giving them the aura of truth. Whether they are purely imaginary or rooted in the lives of real people, the novels of ambition invite their readers to identify with the protagonist, just as they would with the eminent persons appearing in many a biography carried in *Seikō*. The fictionality of an ambition novel is blurred by its surrounding context, as each novel oscillates between its status as a work of fiction yielding pleasure to the empathic reader and its status as a work that approaches the authority of nonfiction and has pedagogical value for ambitious youth.

By scrutinizing the advertising of novels of ambition, we can draw a number of conclusions about the efficacy of the genre as an ideological instrument and about the intermingling of didacticism and pleasure. First, the ideology of *risshin shusse* came into circulation on the market by the late Meiji period; as social advancement through education became prescriptive, the market responded with products that help people negotiate the hurdles. Fiction, which helped sell success, was itself a commodity whose commercial viability depended greatly on the continued reproduction of this hegemonic modern ideology. Second, the common subtitle of this group of novels, *risshi shōsetsu*, demarcates the contours of a particular genre. Distinct from other products on the fiction market, this genre created a community of readers looking for a particular form of pleasure. Third, as noted by Wada Atsuhiko, identification with a novel's hero was the chief mechanism that linked the reader of an ambition novel with the larger discourse on success; from this discourse, the reader derived the gratification of witnessing a protagonist who, like himself, was struggling against the odds. Fourth, text and context sent mutually reinforcing messages: the theme of the novels is, not surprisingly, the dominant message of the magazine, thus lessening the impact of individual authorial creativity. Fiction was part of a larger moral program of self-help propagated within a particular media network. This program gave priority to pedagogical value over entertainment value, thus endowing the genre with a didactic feel. Finally, the discourse of success, which permeated the publishing network of Seikō Zasshi Sha, created a particular narrative of a socially significant human life. This was the narrative of someone who begins in poverty and, through resolve and hard work, achieves success; the emphasis was on the process itself rather than the achievement of the goal. Through engagement with this narrative, novels of ambition offered a forward-looking and future-oriented subject position for their readers.

The study of advertising provides a window onto how a genre is constructed and grants particular forms of pleasure and subjectivity in the reading experience. Yet, such an approach has limitations. Unless we read the works themselves, we cannot know how individual texts position themselves in relation to larger aesthetic and social concerns, and we risk flattening out differences between the novels. But this type of in-depth reading is rarely applied to noncanonical fiction. Literary critics too frequently assume that the popular fare appearing in magazines is complicit with the dominant ideology, the preoccupations of which are supposedly self-evident. However, many of the new theoretical methodologies of the past quarter-century have questioned the boundaries between canonical literature and popular culture and placed increasing importance on noncanonical texts. By neglecting to read across the divide between canonical and noncanonical fiction (still a new division in late Meiji), we risk falling into the trap of seeing popular fiction as nothing more than a reproduction of the dominant social ideology rather than as part of a larger, highly contested struggle over representation. A close reading of a novel of ambition will show that, rather than reinforcing the dominant conception of success in Meiji Japan, the genre, in fact, challenges it.

The Value of Sweat, the Victory of Sweat

To illustrate this point, I take up a novel that appeared in serialized form and as a book. The first half of Shinsen's pungently titled *Ase no kachi* was serialized monthly in *Seikō* from January through November 1910. With a few exceptions, each installment consisted of five short chapters, but the serialization ended with chapter 53. Appended to the end of Shinsen's short story, "Gakusei shafu" (The Student Rickshaw Man), which appeared in the December 1910 issue of *Seikō,* is a note saying that *Ase no kachi* had ceased to be serialized in the magazine because it would be published as a full-length novel. The note adds that the second half of the work would appear together with the prior installments in a single volume in January 1911, to be published, of course, by the Seikō Magazine Company.[30] Shinsen must have been hard at work in December, as the completed novel of over three hundred pages in eighty-five chapters did indeed appear in January as scheduled.

The advertisement for *Ase no kachi*, which appeared in the December 1910 issue of *Seikō* and several issues thereafter in the usual flurry of publicity, occupies two facing pages. The layout is typical for a new novel of ambition by Shinsen, and the pastoral scene that serves as a backdrop for the text of the advertisement would be repeated time and again with other works, subtly evoking the ambition novel's pro-countryside position. Spread across the top of the two pages in large type is the hyperbolic line "Look!!! Look at this great ambition novel that marks the onset of a brand new year!!" (*Miyo*!!! *Shinnen dai-ichi hekitō ni okeru kono dai risshi shōsetsu o miyo*!!). Perpendicular to this horizontal running line, following the author's name, is the title, *Risshi shōsetsu: Ase no kachi*, in gigantic typeface. A lengthy description follows:

> Poverty gives birth to struggle, struggle gives birth to ingenuity, and ingenuity, in the end, gives birth to success. If there is anyone who does not comprehend the value of sweat in wrestling with and overcoming poverty, then there is no point in talking with him about the struggle for survival. One with weak will and weak resolve, heedlessly lamenting his own bad fortune on seeing his hopes dashed, will never discover the scope of life. The hero of this novel was born into a poor family in a cold-swept village. The hero of this novel is without parents or siblings. He has not the slightest

> capital. Through laudable struggle, he comes to understand in the end both the bitterness and sweetness of poverty and the value of sweat. In him grows a great desire to save the struggling people of his home village from dire poverty, and in the end our hero constructs a great model village; he is respected to such an extent that it is impossible to tell whether he is man or god; then he advances even farther, accomplishing great deeds for the nation. In these pages are a beautiful young woman and an evil miser. There are those who come to the assistance of our hero, and there are those who try to defeat him. People from all walks of life appear in this novel for various ends. Those who peruse this volume even once will gain hope and courage if they are from a poor family, and will learn a lesson about life if they are from a wealthy family. Every reader will become motivated by explosive ambition. Every youth under heaven must read this novel!!![31]

The purple rhetoric positions the novel as a pedagogical instrument that will teach the reader what he needs to know about the struggle of existence and stoke the fires of ambition in his breast. *Ase no kachi* is represented not as entertainment but as a life lesson, in keeping with the way advertising constructs the genre in other venues. We see the presumed audience—the ubiquitous *seinen*—and the kind of pleasure this novel is meant to deliver: the gratification of witnessing the spiritual struggle that inevitably leads to moral and material victory. This promise of pleasure is compressed into the opening lines: "Poverty gives birth to struggle, struggle gives birth to ingenuity, and ingenuity, in the end, gives birth to success." This message of social Darwinism is also the most concise description available for the basic narrative template of a novel of ambition.

As suggested in the advertisement, a symmetry encompasses the enormous quotidian detail of this novel: poverty and setbacks are the main themes of the first half, whereas struggle and success occupy the second half. From a psychological perspective, the first half shows passivity whereas the second shows activity. Moreover, as the novel's advertisement hints, the hero is the recipient of the welfare of others in the first half but becomes the benefactor of others, including his fellow villagers and the nation as a whole, in the second. However one chooses to characterize the two halves, the pivot between them occurs a little more than halfway into the novel, when our hero listens to a pair of speeches, one about self-help and the other about the early-modern agrarian reformer, Ninomiya Sontoku (1787–1856). The two speeches together constitute the transformative event that spurs the protagonist from passivity into action and self-transformation; and every novel of ambition has such an event at its midway point, even if the details differ from one work to the next.

The novel's symmetry is linked to the process of serialization and production as a book. The first half, the chapters serialized in *Seikō*, shows the hero, Sakutarō (*saku*, "to create," is an auspicious name for the protagonist of an ambition novel), as he confronts trials and suffering, including the death of his father, a lack of capital with which to make his way in life, inherited debt, and even a life-threatening illness. These challenges are presented in extended scenes filled with lengthy dialogue, generally unfolding over five chapters, the allotted span for monthly installments. This structure is conditioned entirely by the presentation of the novel as a serialized work; that is, discrete scenes of dialogue are designed to fill space in the magazine and generally end with a moment of suspense. In the second half of the novel, Sakutarō's recovery from his illness in answer to his fiancée's prayers is a metaphor for his rebirth; after hearing the inspiring speeches, he is determined to pull himself up by his own bootstraps. In contrast to the deliberate pace of the first half of the novel, the narrative gathers speed at this point, passing rapidly through days, weeks, months, and years to recount in summary fashion—without lengthy scenes of dialogue—the hero's triumphs, which, as promised in the advertisement, not only turn him into the paradigmatic self-made man but also enable him to better the life of his fellow villagers and bring glory to the nation.

Form and content are inseparable, however, and the tempo and symmetry of the two halves of the novel are also mandated by ideological imperatives. The long-drawn-out scenes in the serialized portion of the text reinforce the novel's central message: challenges and setbacks ("the bitterness of poverty" in the advertisement) must ultimately be assessed as positive experiences ("the sweetness of poverty"), precisely because such adversity breeds the ingenuity and willpower needed for "the struggle for survival." Given this ideological position, it is no wonder that the novel lavishes detail on suffering in lengthy scenes and then presents struggle and success in increasingly foreshortened summaries.[32] That is, the act of valorizing the process over the telos is formally marked by a drawing out of suffering and a compression of the path to success, with every agony of the former dutifully, even ecstatically recorded, and the latter presented in a kind of rapturous frenzy. The symmetry of this novel compels us to read it as a formally encoded lesson symbolized by the duality of its title: the novel teaches the "value" (*kachi* 価値) of hard work, with "sweat" functioning as a metaphor for that effort. But the conquest of poverty through effort and willpower invests the title with another meaning: written with a different ideograph, *kachi* 勝ち can also mean "to win"; so, undoubtedly, the other intended message of the novel is "the victory of sweat." In the symmetrical design of *Ase no kachi*, our hero learns the value of sweat in the first half and tastes the victory of sweat in the second.

The beads of sweat in *Ase no kachi* are shed in a particular narrative topography, the organic community of a village far away from the metropolis. Not surprisingly, the magazine in which the novel was serialized was, at the same time, vigorously promoting rural society in its editorials and essays. As previous scholarship has traced, *Seikō* began with a naive and uncomplicated message of self-help (to which it clung tenaciously throughout its history), flirted briefly with the Labor and Socialist movements only to repudiate them, and finally turned to touting nationalism and imperial expansion in the wake of Japan's victory over Russia.[33] What has been overlooked, however, is the way the magazine began steadily pushing a pro-country, anti-city vision of success from the final years of the Meiji era into the Taisho period. Here are a few examples just from the year during which *Ase no kachi* was serialized. An essay by Yasuda Zenjirō, the founder of the Yasuda financial group and a regular contributor to *Seikō*, highlights the difficulty of getting ahead in Tokyo and then bluntly concludes: "No matter how attractive Tokyo appears to be on the surface, it is a kind of hell for those without money."[34] Though not quite so alarmist or melodramatic, Miyake Yūjirō, better known by his pen name, Setsurei, also listed the disadvantages of urbanization, as did Yanagita Kunio, focusing especially on the loss of tradition, with which he was particularly concerned.[35] Kaneda Eikichi, the president of Keiō University, pushed the pro-countryside view and, stressing the overlap of personal interests with national interests, argued, "It is crucial that the sons of the rural elite establish themselves in their home villages and work for the benefit of society."[36] Mizuno Rentarō, of the Home Ministry, urged readers to reject the old post-Restoration fantasy of rising from obscurity to become prime minister and to work instead to establish a business in one's home village and so improve one's lot in life.[37]

It is ironic that established Tokyoites would exhort those following them up the ladder to give up their dreams of success in the city and make their mark in the provinces instead. The magazine had to walk a fine line between acknowledging that educational opportunity was concentrated in the cities, especially Tokyo, and urging its readers to make their ancestral home their base for rising in the world. Both the magazine *Seikō* and the *risshi shōsetsu* so closely associated with it were busily engaged in reimagining the countryside as the primary locus of an authentic and meaningful success. The alternative they proposed to the then-current paradigm of *risshin shusse* retained the future-oriented temporal dimension of the dominant chronotope while shifting its spatial dimension to a beleaguered countryside in need of rejuvenation.

Concern about the imminent destruction of rural society at the dawn of the twentieth century was widespread both at the provincial level and among bureaucrats in Tokyo. Some scholars have marked this historical moment as the beginning of the reactionary "modern agrarian nationalism" (*nōhonshugi*) that locates genuine communalism, authentic cultural identity, and true patriotism in the organic community of village life.[38] This intellectual current was a response to capitalism, which by the turn of the century was beginning to work profound changes on the countryside, as farms and a rural handicraft industry were pulled into the growing national market economy at a dizzying pace.[39] Rapid modernization affected all social groups in the provinces. In the poorest stratum of provincial society, the dislocations were often severe enough to lead to organized unrest among tenants, while the landed elites found themselves threatened by both industrialization and the discontent of the rural poor.[40] To defend their position, wealthy families began to assert the importance of class solidarity and to champion what they declared to be the time-honored conventions of village life. However, the discourses that are of primary concern in this chapter emanated mostly from the middle tier of rural society—the small landholding class. Under the system of primogeniture, the second and third sons of these middle-level farmers, having little to inherit, often fled to the urban centers in search of a better life, but they were then drawn into the low-wage labor pool to fuel the furnace of industrialization.[41] Unable to move up the social ladder as they had expected, these youth launched furious critiques of the city and strongly advocated service to the rural society from which they had emerged.[42] Although the discourses feeding the rural bias of the ambition novels came mostly from this disaffected provincial middle class, the Meiji state was also increasingly concerned about the dislocations in rural Japan, and city bureaucrats added their voices to the call for such reforms as promoting agricultural improvement, strengthening the fiscal and administrative capabilities of the villages, and increasing state control over rural society.

Among the many strands of thought within agrarian reform, the two that had the strongest impact on the media network under discussion were the Local Improvement Movement (Chihō kairyō undō) and the Repayment of Kindness Movement (Hōtoku undō). The Repayment of Kindness Movement, founded by the early-modern agrarian philosopher Ninomiya Sontoku, mentioned earlier, began as an effort to forge communal networks of support in rural society in response to the famines of the 1830s and early 1840s. As Tetsuo Najita has observed, the movement increased its purview and modernized itself so as to confront new problems facing rural society in the age of industrial capitalism.[43] Drawing on Sontoku's ideals about the value of ethical conduct and mutual welfare, the modern movement emphasized local self-rule, cooperation between classes, savings, and the spirit of self-reliance.[44] The scholarly consensus on the Local Improvement Movement, which aimed to modernize the countryside and establish state institutions there, is that the government, primarily through the Home Ministry, was promoting its agenda less from charitable motivations than as part of a strategy of breaking what was left of the old rural power structure, thus bringing the whole of provincial society under the national banner once and for all.[45] The impetus for this came with the government's realization that its efforts to instill national consciousness in the provinces during the Russo-Japanese War had run up against resistance.[46] The Local Improvement Movement was one facet of the larger process of nation-building in the wake of the Meiji Restoration, but with the specific goal of turning rural residents with regional loyalties into national citizens by systematically dismantling the remnants of those local institutions to which they traditionally owed allegiance.[47] The Local Improvement Movement was a government-sponsored initiative, whereas the Repayment of Kindness Movement was a grassroots reform effort, but the two were imbricated in complex ways at the end of the Meiji era, as the latter was forced to revise itself within the new legal structure. The magazine *Seikō* represents the complex intersection of these two movements and a syncretic blend of Ninomiya

Sontoku and Samuel Smiles, with the ideals of diligence and economy in the former fusing with the emphasis on self-reliance and concern with the welfare of the nation in the latter.

Discourses such as these, growing out of the tropes and motifs recurring across a given media network, can be better grasped by juxtaposing salient texts from different genres and identifying the fundamental concerns that straddle culturally demarcated zones. One text that stands out because of its ubiquity across the entire advertising network of the Seikō Magazine Company is a little book called *Ninomiya Sontoku: Kinken chochikuhō* (Ninomiya Sontoku: The Method of Thrift and Savings), written in 1909 by the journalist and aviation pioneer Midoro Masuichi (1886–1973). Its subject, as its title indicates, is the ideals of the early-modern agrarian reformer and modern cultural hero. When the first half of *Ase no kachi* was serialized in 1910, a standard one-page advertisement for *Kinken chochikuhō* appeared in no less than five issues of the magazine,[48] and another advertisement appeared among the group of ads collected at the end of the book version of *Ase no kachi*.[49] Judging by advertisements in *Seikō* alone and by the fact that the book went through three printings in as many years, Midoro's work was popular. Though not a runaway bestseller, this adaptation of Sontoku's philosophy for an industrializing Japan was one of the most heavily promoted books in the entire list of *Seikō*'s publication wing.

The implied reader of *Kinken chochikuhō* comes from a family fallen on hard times, and the chief emphasis of the book is on the gradual accumulation of capital in order to overcome adversity. The author acknowledges the existence of setbacks, bad luck, the death of loved ones, and other misfortunes, but insists that such things account for only "1 percent" of the impact on an individual's life, the other "99 percent" stemming from one's own resolve and effort.[50] Wealth and poverty, he admits, are realities, but these are largely the outcome of one's own choices in life: "The poor man works because of the need to settle accounts from yesterday, while the wealthy man works for the future."[51] The resolve not to sink into poverty and the persistence to stick to a plan of gradual accumulation of capital for future ventures, however modest those ventures may initially be, are inseparable components of this future-oriented vision of self-reliance. Midoro goes so far as to attach a numerical value to this idea: the solution to poverty lies in Sontoku's strategy of "budgeting" (*bundo*) or, alternatively, "savings" (*chochiku*), in which 70 percent of one's earnings are plowed back into one's current ventures and maintenance, while the remaining 30 percent is put away, either for future investment or to guard against unexpected misfortune.[52]

The ideas of gradual accumulation and fiscal responsibility are perfectly captured in the book's chief mantra: "Accumulate the small so as to accomplish the great" (*Shō o tsunde dai o nasu*). In its linking of forward-looking optimism, individual striving, the gradual accumulation of small amounts of capital, and eventual success, Midoro's mantra is also a succinct statement of *Seikō*'s central message of self-help—one that is, in fact, more finely attuned to the overarching ideology of the magazine than the British aphorism made immortal by Samuel Smiles: "Heaven helps those who help themselves." For present purposes, the chief interest of Midoro's slogan lies in its inscription within a poetics of culture as the centerpiece of a system of potent rhetorical figures rooted in a rural topography.

The dominant spatial metaphor in *Kinken chochikuhō* is that of a wilderness or wasteland (*arechi*).[53] This uncultivated land can, through the continual impress of labor, yield a peculiarly rural form of bounty. The spatial dimension of the metaphor is here envisioned as empty of significance until made to yield wealth through human effort, and these riches, accumulated bit by bit over the years, eventually lead to the accomplishment of great things, thus imprinting a temporal dimension onto the *arechi* to form a rural chronotope of success. The two dimensions together take on national, even mythic, significance because Midoro links the individual's efforts to gain wealth from his land to the project of nation-building in his metaphor of the "opening of the realm" (*tenchi kaibyaku*). This old-fashioned phrase implies that the aggregate of subjects striving to achieve success by cultivating their own "plots of land" (either literally or metaphorically, depending on whether the reader is in the country or the city) is the same mechanism by which the nation itself is founded.

A specific set of historical circumstances has allowed Midoro to link the individual and the nation through his favorite metaphor: the conceptualization of the nation as a work in progress requiring the collective efforts of its subjects so that it can be completed. Such a conceptualization also requires the replacement of a traditional cyclical conception of time with a progressive sense of time, in which any moment is the equivalent of any other but these moments cumulatively build to a whole greater than the sum of its parts. Stefan Tanaka dates these new spatio-temporal ideas to December 7, 1872, when the Meiji government elected to abandon the lunar calendar and adopt the Western Gregorian calendar. A seemingly simple decision had profound ontological implications, for it inserted Japan into the world system of capitalist nation-states and new systems of knowledge. The implementation of linear, homogeneous time, Tanaka has shown, is connected to the emerging awareness of the nation through "the loosening of local, place-based ideas in favor of a national space oriented toward economic growth and military power."[54] This new temporality is synonymous with the concept of evolutionary progress, which envisions the development and perfection of the nation-state at some undetermined point in the future. These ideas underlie Midoro's treatment of the wilderness as a metaphor that subtends the individual and the nation. The transformation of the *arechi* into arable land represents success for the individual and for the project of nation building.

The image of the wasteland so captivates the imagination of Midoro that he extends it to encompass human subjectivity in his metaphor of "the wilderness of the heart" (*kokoro no kōbu*). This carries distinct connotations of a deserted and desolate internal landscape, which harbors an unfocused desire for social advancement. It also includes a temporal component: the internal landscape acquires shape and social significance only after one sets one's mind on self-transformation. Furthermore, Midoro's chief slogan, "Accumulate the small so as to accomplish the great," carries a didactic message about the social value of perseverance and hard work within a narrative of success achieved through gradual fruition. The individual's nonstop forward movement toward a promised land of wealth and social respectability also empowers the larger collective of the nation. Through the potent metaphor of the wasteland transformed by cultivation, the temporal and spatial dimensions of this particular chronotope are fused within this media network into a vision of a hopeful future-oriented national subject who tills the soil for the betterment of himself and his country.

Making allowances for the heterogeneous voices that find expression through the publications of the Seikō Magazine Company, one can still justifiably claim that the chronotope just described is the prevailing mode of representation of the spatial and temporal dimensions of success in this particular publishing network in the era after the Russo-Japanese War.

The chronotope also extends to other media networks. Consider, as one example, the following speech given by one Suzuki Fujisaburō and published in the pages of *Shimin* (The People), the official mouthpiece of the Central Repayment of Kindness Society (Chūō hōtoku sha). Suzuki casts his speech as an autobiographical account of how he achieved success as the result of a fortuitous encounter with the writings of Sontoku, whom he here elevates to sainthood. Much like Midoro, Suzuki seeks the "spirit of *hōtoku*" in the "taming of the wilderness" (*arechi kaikon*). For Suzuki, this central metaphor, which draws together the values of perseverance, diligence, hard work, thrift, and optimism, can inspire people of all professions.[55] Thus, the taming of the wilderness becomes a kind of master trope for those advocating the rejuvenation of rural society along with strengthening the nation as a whole.

The *arechi* is also a prime rhetorical figure in the fiction of Shinsen, whose *Ase no kachi* began serialization the year after *Kinken chochikuhō* appeared in print. Once the fictional Sakutarō, the hero of *Ase no kachi*, recovers from illness, he is overcome with a desire to strike out and make a success of his life, though he simply does not know how to begin. As if on cue, he receives word from a friend in nearby Mishima that "two or three gentlemen from Tokyo" would be giving speeches and that he should come to hear them. Of the first speech we learn only the title: "Sontoku's Strategies for Forging One's Own Destiny." However, mere mention of the agrarian reformer is undoubtedly meant to evoke the tenets of the Repayment of Kindness Movement, and Sakutarō's reactions to the speech are clearly delineated: "Upon listening to this discourse, his whole body was suffused with courage, and the road before him was lit up instantly with hope. It was as if tissue had grown on the bones of a deceased man and blood had begun to circulate in his body" (240). The other speech is entitled "The Path Youth Must Now Take." Of this speech, which could easily have been the title of an article from *Seikō*, the following snippet is recorded:

> Over the next ten or twenty years, the state of society will steadily change. It will thereafter become impossible to conduct one's life according to the old ideals of learning, in other words, through spiritual ability. So, youth of the land, I say to you, rather than try to become independent through education, you should, starting this very day, cultivate physical ability and discover a way to live according to the power of your arm. Those who can accomplish this will achieve victory in life. (240–41)

This speech affects Sakutarō as profoundly as the first. Having realized that study in Tokyo would be useless, he resolves to achieve his success and reestablish his family lineage by following these dictates—in the countryside.

Sakutarō begins his inevitable rise most humbly, using the power of his arm to cut down and sell the bamboo in the tiny patch of soil that remains to his name; for his efforts he earns a hundred yen, a substantial sum in that era. How he uses his newly won money, and all the money he would later earn, underscores that Shinsen's novel shares a discursive space with *hōtoku* ideals: he follows the prescription of *bundo*—investing and saving the funds in a ratio of about seven to three. More crucial, however, is the novel's message of perseverance, gradual accumulation, financial responsibility, and relentless forward movement. With the land cleared, Sakutarō decides to invest some of the money for planting, which means he must till the land. He plans to till three *tsubo* per day (one *tsubo* is approximately thirty-six square feet), but the work is so grueling and the soil so unyielding that he is able to prepare only a single *tsubo* on the first day; thereafter things improve, albeit slowly. As the narrator alerts us, "He was so tired that his body felt like cotton. He could not imagine having the strength to continue the next day" (271).

But continue he does, and at this point the text begins to lavish attention on Sakutarō's laboring body with the objective of constructing an ideal masculine body for the "ambitious youth of the modern age." The seventieth chapter, entitled "Rei to niku" (Spirit and Flesh), contains a remarkable passage of transformation, couched as literal masculine self-fashioning in keeping with the gendered nature of the term *seinen*:

> Over the course of a month, he endured and bore up to the harsh labor. As a result, his muscles were forged and tempered. His body became hardened to the point that he felt if he were to strike his own arm with a hammer, the tool would spring back as if it had hit iron. . . . In the course of a month, through this kind of rigorous labor, the fuel of his courage was created. All that was left was to simply allow that fuel to burn. This pure courage rose up like flames from the depths of his being. He had become a man who could accomplish any great task and could get back on his feet after any setback. (276)

Sakutarō's body is at first unaccustomed to hard labor, but, as he becomes gradually acclimated to it, his exertions also affect his mental state. Shinsen underscores the continuity between the body and the mind so as to show that labor tempers the flesh, which in turn tempers the spirit. The courage that Sakutarō had prior to this experience—which the narrator oddly characterizes as a "cramped courage" (*keiren teki yūki*,, 275) so as to suggest its untapped potential—has now become "true courage" (*shin no yūki*, 275). The narrator makes an observation that unambiguously links the representation of labor to the discourse on *risshin shusse*: "As his body became acclimated to the labor, he developed true courage. But that was not all. He also gained unyielding ambition [*tawamanu nesshin*] through the rhythm of his exertions" (281). Here once again, as in the advertisements for these novels, the narrator stresses that the process is more important than the end result.

The potent combination of a masculine body toughened by labor with true courage and boundless ambition constitutes the prerequisites for Sakutarō's success. The narrator contrasts this complex of attributes with the idea of success through education: "It did not matter if he had little schooling. Lacking education was nothing to lament. A man with only schooling and formal education was not a man who could attain success [*risshin shusse*]" (280). By representing Sakutarō as having only a middle school education and as being able to overcome one setback after another in the first half of the novel to accomplish great things in the second, *Ase no kachi* radically devalues the idea of attaining success through schooling, which at the time was regarded as the primary route to social advancement. Instead, the novel valorizes success achieved through equal application of wisdom and labor, free of the corrupting influence of the classroom. This vision of *risshin shusse* is perfectly consistent with the traditional de-emphasis on formal education within *hōtoku* thought and the celebration of the Smilesian power of self-help in article after article appearing in *Seikō*.

Sakutarō learns these valuable lessons as he impresses his labor on the soil, clearing fields and preparing them for planting, thereby transforming the wilderness into a socially significant landscape. In their emphasis on the direct continuity of land and labor with body and mind, Shinsen's novel and Midoro's treatise share an identical ideological framework. "A healthy spirit can be housed only in a healthy body" (275), the narrator of *Ase no kachi* proclaims, and then depicts the taming of the land as an act of training body and spirit. *Ase no kachi* insists that the protagonist must proceed through a specific temporal sequence entirely in the space of the provinces: he must experience hardship, gain resolve through a transformative moment, develop body and mind through labor, acquire true courage and ambition, and achieve success.

Shinsen's iconic novel of ambition highlights how one individual learns a hard lesson about sweat, but Sakutarō's transformation also has ramifications for the larger collective. In this connection, the categories supplied by Yanagita Kunio, in his essay on the vexed relationship between city and country can shed light on the novel, even though Yanagita was a spirited opponent of the Repayment of Kindness Movement.[56] Yanagita implicitly linked the city with individualism and the country with the preservation of the collective. Applying these correspondences to the study of *Ase no kachi*, we might pose the question: What is the relationship between the individual and the collective in this novel of the provinces? The text's dominant message of self-help seems to suggest a total focus on the individual. When examined closely, however, Shinsen's novel reveals an abiding relationship between Sakutarō and the village in which he is born and raised and achieves his fame.

What Sakutarō accomplishes through his agricultural endeavors is shown to be the direct result of the operation of his entrepreneurial spirit, but it is also inseparable from his life as a member of the collective, for Sakutarō shares the fruits of his labor with the entire village and even persuades the villagers to specialize in the mandarin orange (*mikan*) trees that he has cultivated with such stunning results. Success is thus represented not as the outcome of competition for wealth or scarce resources, but as a reciprocal relationship that plays out in the fundamental symmetry of the narrative: many of the villagers had come to Sakutarō's aid when he was encountering a seemingly interminable series of setbacks in the first half of the novel, and so, in the second half, he repays their kindness in the spirit of Sontoku's *hōtoku* ideals—by becoming the benefactor of the entire collective. The village is thus a community that unites individuals in a common purpose and an affective bond.

Going even beyond these ideals, Sakutarō's efforts also benefit the greatest collective of all. When the nation comes under threat during the Sino-Japanese War, he volunteers to go off to fight in a foreign land, where he is wounded. Sakutarō's bravery and initiative are instrumental in Japan's victory over the Chinese in a crucial battle (332–37). The depiction of the war is not necessary to the plot of *Ase no kachi* and occupies only a single, relatively short chapter near the end; but it is ideologically important in that it provides an opportunity for the author to emphasize that the ultimate beneficiary of the hero's personal struggle is the nation, which is strengthened through the collective efforts of all its citizens. Throughout the novel, the nation is kept constantly before the reader's mind in less than subtle ways. Sakutarō's village is located in the Sunshu region, which lies in the shadow of Mount Fuji, a national icon that is repeatedly mentioned with each changing season. Moreover, to make an impression upon the reader's mind at the outset, the book version displays a drawing of Mount Fuji on the first page of the first chapter.

To underscore the importance of undertaking individual efforts not just for oneself but for society at large, the author has all those characters in *Ase no kachi* who pursue self-interest at the expense of the collective meet unpleasant fates. This is especially true of Sakutarō's chief antagonists, the miserly Kantarō and his son, Kanji (an *akushōnen*, or juvenile delinquent), both of whom end up financially ruined after they try to fleece the villagers. Although not given lengthy treatment, the details of this plot strand impart an unmistakable message: in the figure of Sakutarō the novel celebrates individual initiative put in the service of society yet opposes an individualism, like Kantarō's, that fails to rise above self-interest. In opposition to radical individualism, the novel represents success as being the product of collective enterprise. At the same time, the individual is portrayed as the foundation on which the health of the collective rests.

The novel ends by offering a brief but distinctive picture of rural society. Sakutarō's village has acquired advanced social services, symbolized by a library and a hospital. The village is also an exemplar of local autonomy and self-rule. Crime has ceased to exist because everyone is productive and no one pursues self-interest at the expense of his fellow villagers. The water is clean; all land in and around the village is put to productive use; and *mikan* trees—the most important symbol of entrepreneurial ingenuity and economic prosperity in this novel—stretch out as far as the eye can see. All the villagers live by a common creed, the equal application of wisdom and sweat; without feeling alienated, they thus enjoy their labor, as well as the fruits of that labor (342–43). This is what the advertisements for the novel call the "model village" (*mohan mura*, a propaganda term during the war with Russia) enabled by the hero's efforts.

Sakutarō's village is a rural utopia, with a didactic dimension as well as implications for the nation. The novel closes with a brief remark stating that, if every village in the land operated by these principles, Japan would "undoubtedly be the strongest country in the world" (343). Self-help seems to have the power to reshape individual, family, village, and nation—in that order. We have at the end of the novel the prospect of a country that is made up of rural utopias supporting a rich state and a strong army; that is held up by the two pillars of economic individualism and reciprocal assistance; and whose every part is joined together by a free market and an entrepreneurial spirit that spread good ideas and specialized products from one rural community to another.

Through tracing the narrative movement from poverty to success, Shinsen's novel proposes a major alternative to the dominant form of *risshin shusse*, and especially in relation to the spatial imagination of this discourse. In the hegemonic version of the chronotope of success, recounted in numerous novels, autobiographical works, and eventually films, the protagonist leaves the countryside, goes to school in Tokyo, acquires as much education and cultural capital as possible, and then joins the ranks of bureaucrats serving in the nation's capital or the emerging class of white-collar workers struggling in the big cities. This is the rat race for success, worked out according to the ideology of individualistic competition. *Ase no kachi* offers a critique of the radically individualistic, city-centered vision of *risshin shusse*; more significantly, it wrests *risshin shusse* from the city and, while retaining the future oriented element of this discourse, relocates authentic success in the village, where agricultural rhythms and distinctive patterns of collective support and reciprocal help hold sway.

Incorporating the ideology of *Seikō* and the discourses of agrarian reform found in both the Local Improvement and Repayment of Kindness Movements, *Ase no kachi* instantiates a formal inversion of "city fever" and articulates a vision of individual and collective triumph. Imagining success in this way constitutes a socially symbolic act that is firmly rooted in rural society. Yet, even as *Ase no kachi* banishes smokestacks, factories, and all vestiges of the industrial city from its pages, it retains traces of the struggle over representation, making us feel the presence of the city through its conspicuous absence. Confronting the ravages of industrial capitalism and the "provincialization" of the countryside, the text offers a utopia of self-help that has, within the literary imagination, rejuvenated the old organic community. However, since this community never really existed in the first place, it is more accurate to say that Shinsen's novel has produced an idealized organic community as an act of wish fulfillment.

❖

My close reading of this one specimen of the genre of *risshi shōsetsu* shows how one particular text provides a formal or imaginative solution to a concatenation of seemingly intractable real-life problems within capitalist modernity. But a genre featuring a common narrative blueprint would be truly formulaic if every text within its domain offered the same formal solution. To return to the discussion of the genre as a whole, it is useful to draw upon Fredric Jameson's distinction between a utopian impulse and a utopian program. The former implies longing for a solution to problems, the latter the actual elaboration of a vision that resolves them and also offers the satisfaction of formal closure.[57] The genre of the ambition novel spans the whole gamut from expressions of a vague longing for the countryside to fully developed visions of a rejuvenated rural society.

Our reading of *Ase no kachi* has revealed one pole of this spectrum: the utopian program. To illustrate the utopian impulse at work, let us turn to Horiuchi Shinsen's bestseller in two volumes, *Kannondō* (The Hall of Kannon, 1908).[58] This novel features Imamura Kōkichi (his name contains the ideographs for "village" and "filiality"), who faces the challenges of his father's death and a lack of capital with which to rise in the world, two of the common burdens borne by the genre's protagonists. Like many of his ambitious fellow heroes, however, Kōkichi has advantages: he is honest (*shōjiki*) and filial (*oya kōkō*), and he is highly motivated to succeed. The head of his village, trying to comfort the grieving Kōkichi after his father's death, stresses the importance of these advantages: "As long as you don't lose those qualities [honesty, filiality, and ambition], there will be people who will lend you a hand wherever you go, and the path of success will open before you" (1:91). In a grand gesture, he also gives Kōkichi a copy of *Saikoku risshi hen*, Nakamura Masanao's translation of Smiles's *Self-Help* (1:92–93). When taking a ship from his village to Kobe, Kōkichi reads this book and is transformed:

"With each page he read, his spirits soared and hope welled up within his breast. A vision of the single path he must travel appeared before him" (1:133). Kōkichi's path takes him to Yokohama and then to Tokyo, there to rise spectacularly.

Throughout *Kannondō* are fortuitous events and encounters that lead the hero to his success, but all these events seem to stem from the occult power of Kōkichi's personal transformation; also, it does not hurt that he possesses something of a magical talisman in the form of the Japanese translation of Smiles. In addition, before leaving his village, Kōkichi visits the dilapidated Kannon Hall, the symbolic center of his ancestral home, where he makes a vow to dedicate himself to the pursuit of success. This religious site is connected in the spiritual geography of the novel to the Kannon Temple in Tokyo's Asakusa district, which Kōkichi visits as soon as he arrives in the capital. Thus, Kōkichi's success, like Sakutarō's, is represented not as chance, but as a product of his character and resolve, with the eyes of the gods looking favorably on him.

Kōkichi achieves success by becoming the right-hand man of an important entrepreneur. After seven years in this position, he returns to his village in order to visit old friends, sweep his parents' grave, and marry Osono, an orphan raised by his family. Eventually Kōkichi takes Osono back to Tokyo to make a home there, just as the discourse on success demands, but before he departs he endows the local school (2:166) and provides a substantial amount of money to rebuild his own home and the Kannon Hall of the village (2:163). The title of the novel draws our attention to the Kannon Hall, and it is significant that the novel begins with this structure in a state of dilapidation and ends with the building's renewal. Read metaphorically, the Kannon Hall itself connotes the ruin of rural society or its rejuvenation, depending on the structure's physical state. Furthermore, this narrative of rural transformation is overlaid upon the story of individual transformation and success in a tale of the idealization of the provinces. The values of the ancestral home supply the seed for the eventual success of the hero, whose nostalgia for and gratitude toward the countryside lead to his symbolic rebuilding of a rural community that had fallen into disrepair.

At the other end of the spectrum, where the problems menacing rural society do not much occupy the narrative, lies Shinsen's most commercially successful novel of ambition, *Hito no ani* (The Brother), published in two volumes in 1905–1906. The brother in the title is one Kakuichi (*kaku* can encompass both status and character; *ichi* indicates that he is the eldest son). In the first of the two hefty volumes, Kakuichi's father, Ikehata Kakunoshin, dies a long-drawn-out death, leaving the hero to care for his younger sister, Hatsune, and brother, Kakuji, and to rise in the world with little to his name but ambition and character. In the second volume, a series of events that are both improbable and inevitable lead to the hero's success. Despite these thematic similarities with other novels of ambition, *Hito no ani* takes place in Tokyo and displays the author's command of the capital's geography. The chronotope of this novel is consistent with that of the standard, city-centered version of *risshin shusse*, but the novel's urban setting is as unusual as is the vision of a utopian rural society in *Ase no kachi*.

Both *Hito no ani*, dating from the Russo-Japanese War, and *Kannondō*, from 1908, feature a success that occurs in Tokyo, but the latter work also presents an idealized countryside and the symbolic rebuilding of rural society that is figured in the reconstruction of the Kannon Hall. Moving from *Kannondō* to *Ase no kachi*, serialized in 1910 and published as a book in 1911, we see that this nostalgic longing for the countryside has grown into a full-fledged utopian plan, in which *risshin shusse* has been wrested from the city and planted firmly in the soil of provincial society. Farther down the road, Shinsen's *Tada ikki*, published in 1912, continues this development and further expands the geographic contours of the genre. In the first of two volumes, the protagonist leaves the countryside and sets sail for the United States, where he labors in an ironworks, all the while learning everything there is to know about the trade. The second volume sees our hero return to his home village, where he puts his accumulated knowledge to use by establishing a factory that brings prosperity to the hero and the local community. Thus, as we approach the end of the Meiji era, Shinsen's novels grow more resolutely rural in their orientation and more focused on the rejuvenation of provincial society; this, in turn, helps to develop what was initially a utopian impulse into a utopian program. As already noted, the magazine *Seikō* was moving in exactly the same direction in the wake of the Russo-Japanese War, with an increasing number of essays condemning the ills attendant on urbanization and urging the nation's youth to make their ancestral home their base for rising in the world.

The genre of *risshi shōsetsu* presents the utopian organic community as wish fulfillment. The genre exhibits what Ernst Bloch, in a discussion of the utopian function in the arts, memorably referred to as a "militant optimism."[59] From the perspective of the canonical novel (for example, those of Tayama Katai), this optimism must appear naive in its uncritical acceptance of the promise of self-fashioning and its wholehearted celebration of the organic community. Moreover, even though the ambition novel, like many canonical works, explores the relationship between the individual and the collective, it comes down decisively on the side of the latter, in contrast to the canonical novel, which tends to focus on the embattled individual.[60] Such differences aside, the collective project of the *risshi shōsetsu* constitutes not simple escapism but the same intense engagement with a modernizing society that we usually ascribe to canonical works of fiction. The genre participates in the larger debate on Japanese modernity, alongside important novels, essays such as those of Yanagita Kunio, magazine articles, and other works. If we are to understand the full range of demands society placed and still places on the novel, as well as the full range of responses to modernity offered by the novel, we must remove these literary works from isolation and put them in dialogue with nonliterary texts; additionally, we must continue to bring new paradigms to bear on the venerated texts and we must also explore the forgotten works in the archive. In chapter four, we will examine another such novel that was popular in its day but that has been largely forgotten over time, Kosugi Tengai's *Makaze koikaze*, but before that, we will turn to the figure at the very center of the modern canon and examine some of his most sophisticated novels.

CHAPTER 3

Topographies of Value: City, Gift, and Money in Natsume Sōseki

"I don't like to borrow money."
"You don't have to borrow it." "I don't want to receive it as a gift either."

—Natsume Sōseki, *Nowaki* (1907)

This chapter takes us from the provinces to the metropolis. I want to begin by examining several moments from Natsume Sōseki's *Mon* (The Gate, 1910), which centers on the married life and past indiscretions of Nonaka Sōsuke, a middle-aged government bureaucrat who hangs by his fingertips to the bottom rung of the middle class. An enigmatic novel, *Mon* relentlessly probes the effect of the failure to meet familial and societal expectations on individual psychology. In the fifth chapter, Sōsuke engages in one of his many mundane activities: a trip to the dentist. Experiencing the usual boredom in the waiting room, his eye alights on the periodicals on the table:

> He picked up a magazine called *Success* [Seikō]. At the front were many short articles under the heading "The Secret of Success." One claimed "one must push ahead no matter what," whereas another discouraged rushing madly forward, urging instead, "one must put one's march forward on a firm foundation." After reading these two pieces, Sōsuke put the magazine back. There was a tremendous gap between himself and *Success*. Until now, Sōsuke hadn't even known there was a magazine with this title.[1]

The two uses of the word *Success* (*Seikō*) in italics above are enclosed with brackets (「成効」) in Japanese, which is also true of the original serialization. The first is clearly a magazine title, but the second usage is ambiguous: it could be the magazine *Success* or, possibly, the idea of success (I have rendered it as the former because the final sentence mentions the magazine). The ideographs used in the passage are not the standard pair for either the word or the magazine title; both are normally written with the following characters: 成功. This is possibly a printing error, but it is more likely that Sōseki is attempting to fictionalize a well-known magazine in order to put distance between the world of *Mon* and real life.

Still, the implied reader of the novel is clearly expected to be familiar with the iconic periodical, for we are given no information apart from brief mention of two characteristic articles. To recall the previous chapter, by the time of *Mon*'s publication in 1910, *Seikō* had embraced the ideas of nationalism and imperial expansion and begun advocating a pro-countryside, anti-city vision of success, but it was also still peddling the ideas of self-reliance and the inevitability of success with the application of effort.

It is surely no accident that before Sōsuke finds the exemplary journal of *risshin shusse*, he first flips through some unnamed women's periodicals, leafing through "the many pictures of women gathered at the front of each" (414). At exactly the moment Sōseki became a writer, just after the turn of the century, magazines directed exclusively at the growing stratum of women readers were appearing in quick succession.[2] Sōseki's juxtaposition of such publications with *Seikō* only serves to underscore the gendered message of the latter all the more: it was a masculine imperative to be ambitious and rise up the social ladder. One's personal worth and family security were at stake. When Sōsuke feels a gap between his own life and success, it is surely such gendered ideas from which he feels the most estranged.

The scandal instigated by Sōsuke's marriage and betrayal of a friend, Yasui, in a triangular relationship common in Sōseki, compelled Sōsuke to drop out of his course of study at the imperial university in Kyoto. He has been forced off the path to a promising future and thus, more abstractly, derailed from the standard course of *risshin shusse.* This manifests spatially through Sōsuke's journey after the scandal, from Kyoto to Hiroshima and finally to distant Fukuoka. Sōsuke moves in a quest for stable employment, but on a more symbolic level, he embarks on a route of failure, not unlike the hero of Katai's *Inaka kyōshi.* Because *Mon* so strenuously thematizes the guilt felt by Sōsuke and his wife, Oyone, over their betrayal of Yasui, this route of failure can also be viewed as a journey of penance, as if the couple cannot be allowed to return from the periphery to the center until they have experienced hardship and suffering in recompense for their flaunting of social mores. All this is recounted in the novel's three increasingly lengthy analepses. The couple eventually returns to Tokyo, where the narrative present is set. By that time, Sōsuke has secured a low-level government job through the assistance of an old university friend, and Oyone has become expert at stretching his modest salary so that they lead a respectable life in the eyes of others.

The nature of his suffering imparts on Sōsuke a sense of both freneticism and futility in his daily life. Like his fellow petty bureaucrats, Sōsuke works six days a week and has only Sunday to relax, even if he is often too tired from the workweek to do so. This yields an alienated relationship to the city:

> He was a man who breathed the air of Tokyo all year long. He took the streetcar to the office each day, passing through the bustling city streets every morning and evening. But he was always so tired in mind and body that he passed through it in a daze, and recently it never occurred to him that he lived in the midst of so much activity. He was so busy he never noticed it. But when Sunday came around each week, and he had the opportunity to relax, he would suddenly become aware of his high-strung nerves in his daily life. Each time he realized that he didn't really know Tokyo even though he lived here, a strange melancholy always took hold of him. (356)

His Sunday walks seem to pass in a haze, and Sōsuke experiences the city passively as a space of advertisements and shop windows: on the train, the framed advertisements for a removals firm, a new model of gas burner, and a new translation of a Tolstoy novel; on the streets, a display window for a bookshop; a jeweler with gold watches and chains; an umbrella shop and a Western-style haberdashery; a display window of a Tokyo branch of a Kyoto shop; a newsstand (357–58). Sōsuke wants to make a purchase, almost as if he believes that consumption will cure his alienation, but his wallet never seems to have enough bills to acquire any of the wares vying for his attention.

As Sunday seems to draw to a close faster than any other day, Sōsuke imagines the office on Monday: "the large room with too few windows and little sunlight" (362). Sōsuke's psychological state is externalized in descriptions of the city that insistently stress light and darkness, but actual sunlight seems rarely to penetrate Sōsuke's world. A modicum of relief from the dark, claustrophobic office that saps Sōsuke's energy six days a week can be found only in the city's shop windows, illuminated by a sun that always appears to be on the verge of setting.

After a day of work or a walk on Sunday, Sōsuke returns to his home, which is similarly described using light and darkness. Sōsuke and Oyone rent a house in an unspecified part of the capital at the bottom of a cliff, at the top of which lives their landlord, Sakai. The house and neighborhood are described in the second chapter:

> Passing the fish vendor Uokatsu and continuing beyond that for five or six buildings, one turned at a place that was neither an alley nor a side street. There was a tall cliff at the far end of the street with four or five rental houses, all in the same style, lined up on either side. . . . Sōsuke's house was on this street, at the far end on the left hand side. As it was at the very foot of the cliff, the house got little sunlight, but it was also the farthest from the main road. After consulting with his wife, Sōsuke, thinking the place would be fairly quiet, decided to take the house. (362)

In this and other descriptions, we can see that the world of *Mon* is constructed around resonant dichotomies: Sōsuke's dwelling at the base of the outcropping and Sakai's at the top; Sōsuke's cramped house is enshrouded in darkness, whereas Sakai's spacious abode is bathed in sunlight; Sōsuke and Oyone are poor and childless, whereas Sakai is wealthy, his house filled with a lively brood of children; whenever Sōsuke is at home, he seems exhausted by work, whereas Sakai leads a jovial life of leisure; adjectives such as "cramped" and "secluded" are used abundantly in reference to Sōsuke's house and his life, whereas Sakai's home and social connections are broad.

The dichotomies drawn here comment on class divisions, to be sure, but, more importantly, they highlight one possible future now lost to Sōsuke and Oyone and show how withdrawn the couple has become as a result. As the narrator frequently reminds us, they have no close friends and almost never have callers. Even visits from relatives are few and far between due to familial tension over the fact that Sōsuke was cheated out of his inheritance by a swindling uncle, Saeki. This claustrophobia is reinforced by the novel's topography: with the exception of the few isolated pages depicting Sōsuke's Sunday outing, space in the narrative present occupies a single house in an undisclosed, isolated, and shadow-enshrouded corner of Tokyo.[3]

Sōseki is preoccupied in *Mon* with the psychological effects of alienation and guilt, but he also stages three crises in order to move the story forward and explore other themes: the Saekis claim to be unable to support Sōsuke's brother, Koroku, as he tries to get into university; Oyone gets critically ill about halfway through the novel; hearing a rumor that Yasui has returned to Japan from the colonies, Sōsuke flees to a Zen temple for several chapters, its gate providing the novel with its title. The friendship with Sakai, which develops through a series of exchanges of assistance during these crises in the novel, turns out to be instrumental in resolving the novel's central dilemma about Koroku's education. Sakai is deeply sympathetic to Koroku's situation and ends up offering the young man lodging and material support in exchange for his service in the Sakai house. Koroku's duties are intentionally modest, allowing him to continue his studies in university without undue burden. This is essentially a gift from Sakai to Sōsuke, even if it takes the form of artfully disguised employment. Sōseki is working through some of the novel's chief symmetries here. Sōsuke is a failure in the eyes of others, but there is every reason to expect that Koroku will be a success with Sakai as his benefactor. In contrast to Sōsuke, Sakai is wealthy and respected. His younger brother is the failure and even becomes friends with Yasui, the very man whom Sōsuke and Oyone betrayed. With Koroku settled, the novel's major crisis has been solved. Moreover, the burgeoning friendship with Sakai coaxes Sōsuke out of his self-imposed isolation, however tentatively. To be sure, the novel ends with Sōsuke's skepticism about his prospects in his current job, yet the resolution of the novel's central crisis leads to Sōsuke's highly symbolic, if partial and contingent, reintegration into society.

Drawing on this discussion of worldly success, the experience of the city, and relations forged through reciprocity providing a frame, we will explore more fully the novel *Sorekara* (And Then), which was serialized in the *Asahi shinbun* (Asahi News) from June 27, 1909, until October 14 that same year in 110 installments, then published as a book. Usually, *Sorekara* is seen as part of an informal trilogy together with its predecessor and successor novels, *Sanshirō* and *Mon*, respectively, although none of these features the same characters.[4] The first treats youth, the second adulthood, and the third middle age. *Sorekara* addresses many of the same themes as its companions, though it ultimately shares more terrain with *Mon*. *Sorekara*, too, uses the topography of the capital as a canvas with which to explore the failure to meet social and familial expectations. The estrangement experienced by its protagonist is an individual psychological experience, but it is also a reaction to a city inhabited by other human beings and collectively fashioned into a space of false fronts and naked ambition that repels our protagonist.

In addition, *Sorekara*'s engagement with social Darwinism makes it a crucial context for this book, linking the novels discussed in this chapter with the writings of Horiuchi Shinsen, discussed in the previous chapter, and those of Takahama Kyoshi, discussed in the fifth chapter. Julia Adeney Thomas has studied the influence of the theory of social evolution on early Meiji political thought and concludes that its energy was largely spent by the turn of the century. In her words, "it sanctioned neither Japan's claims to international equality nor the tight domestic authority sought by the Meiji oligarchy."[5] Although this is true of official state ideology, it is worth recalling that in Japan the writings of Herbert Spencer were the most widely translated of all European thinkers.[6] The influence of Spencer and other proponents of social evolution on a variety of fields beyond politics was enormous, and social evolution theory was tightly imbricated with the ideology of *risshin shusse* well into the twentieth century. This is aptly described by the historical sociologist Takeuchi Yō: in their quest to advance up the social ladder according to the imperatives of ambition, individuals became engaged in fierce competition with others in such a way that success became coded as the survival of the fittest.[7] In *Sorekara*, Sōseki shows us a Darwinian world that threatens to instrumentalize social relations, especially among urban dwellers, which, in turn, motivates a novelistic grappling with what has genuine worth in such a society. Drawing on theoretical work in anthropology, I will show that Sōseki juggles his varied themes under the trope of value, both monetary and emotional. Engaging *Sorekara* in this way will allow this chapter to add the urban space of Japan's capital to our growing novelistic map of worldly success in Meiji Japan. Additionally, a close reading of *Sorekara* will enable a new view of Sōseki the author: we will reposition this most canonical of writers on the map of modern Japanese literature as perhaps the most incisive and trenchant critic of the discourse on *risshin shusse*, a view that can shed light on his entire oeuvre.

The Alienated Hero and the Experience of the City

Mon announces its engagement with social mobility through Sōsuke's perusal of the iconic magazine of self-help. *Sanshirō* declares itself a *risshin shusse* novel by opening with the protagonist on a Tokyo-bound train about to enter university.[8] The image of the youth brimming with energy and drive, with his eyes fixed on dreams of future success, seated on a train bringing him to the seat of Japanese modernity embodies the trope of success better than any other representation in Meiji Japan. It is less apparent that *Sorekara* is similarly engaged with the theme of worldly success. The middle novel of the trilogy centers on the deepening relations between the protagonist, Nagai Daisuke, and Michiyo, now married to Daisuke's friend Hiraoka. Daisuke and Michiyo eventually declare their love for each other. As a result, Daisuke is disinherited, and the novel ends elliptically with its protagonist in the midst of deciding how to proceed. None of this seems to have much to do with *risshin shusse*.

This feeling is strengthened when we observe that, with his constant recoiling from the frantic, noisy metropolis and his prioritization of the contemplative life, Daisuke seems far removed from the typical characterization of either the ambitious man or the social failure. Within the critical work on *Sorekara*, it is common to view him as a member of a highly educated leisure class or as a cultured aesthete who has withdrawn from the public world into a purely aesthetic realm of private experience. Some have tried to expand on these basic paradigms. Takahashi Kazumi calls Daisuke an "intellectual" (*chijikijin*), as others have before him, but one who exhibits both "a critical spirit" (*hihyōseishin*) and "apathetic *nil admirari*" (*mukandō niru adomirari*).[9] Drawing on the evidence of what Sōseki was reading when he began writing *Sorekara*, Kenmochi Takehiko sees Daisuke less a member of the "educated leisure class" (*kōtō yūmin*), as so many have, and, instead, views him as a "child of pleasure" (*ikko no kairaku shugi sha*) of the kind that populated so much fin-de-siècle European literature of the "decadent" school, such as the Italian Gaetano Gabriele D'Annunzio (1863–1938).[10] Yoshida Hirō argues that Daisuke is not just "a rational person" (*ronri no hito*), but also "a person of emotion [*jo-o*] and nervous tension [*shinkei*], that is, a person of sensibility [*kansei*]."[11] Yoshida ultimately diagnoses Daisuke as narcissistic. The critical tradition illuminates the psychology of the novel's protagonist, but does not provide much support for characterizing *Sorekara* as a *risshin shusse* novel.

A reading of the novel in the context of the concerns of this book is thus immediately confronted with the challenge of convincingly situating *Sorekara* within a framework of worldly success. An opening here can be made by first turning to the supporting cast in this story of forbidden love.[12] Nagai Toku, Daisuke's father, is the quintessential self-made man. He represents an older generation, those who successfully made the transition from samurai to entrepreneur in the wake of the Meiji Restoration and subsequent dissolution of the hereditary warrior class. Toku, in fact, thrived in the new political and economic environment and even resolved in his own mind the obvious tension between older samurai values, which sees money and merchants as despicable, and his newfound enthusiasm for commercial ventures. His eldest son, Seigō, is the quintessential success story of the post-Restoration generation, but his is a success guaranteed by his father's wealth and position and solidified by a university education. Daisuke's friend Hiraoka has converted educational capital into upward mobility, thereby using the newly established Meiji school system to achieve success, but ends up bungling his first career in banking. He begins anew at a newspaper, and every indication is that he is about to make his name for himself as a journalist by preparing a muckraking story on the business operations of Daisuke's family, which the novel suggests are of questionable legality. Though he makes few appearances in the novel, Daisuke's friend Terao is a struggling writer always seeking loans from acquaintances to meet his daily expenses; leading a hand-to-mouth existence, he is a bottom feeder within the world of letters. With the exception of Toku, these characters are elite, university-educated men, and Sōseki carefully positions his cast on a spectrum of success, from a point near the bottom to its upper reaches, allowing the author to explore the experience of *risshin shusse* for men across two generations spanning the Restoration.

This discovery of a character system linked to worldly success should spur us into trying to position Daisuke himself within this spectrum. Daisuke has received a first-rate education, like his brother, but his father has allowed him a few years of leisure before he makes his way in a profession of his choice. The first thing to note in pursuing this line of thinking is that Daisuke's leisure is made possible by a monthly allowance from his father. Daisuke's reliance on his family's largesse for his material comfort is explicitly discussed, even criticized, by several characters, and Daisuke himself seems painfully aware at times of his lack of true independence and the hypocrisy of criticizing his father's obsession with wealth while relying on that very wealth to maintain his life of the mind. Daisuke does not have to struggle like a Terao nor does he have to experience the anxiety of a Hiraoka precisely because of his generous allowance. Daisuke's position is one of privilege made possible by the good fortune of having been born in a particular stratum within a class society dominated by money, status, and worldly success. It may be possible, then, to interpret Daisuke's barely concealed contempt for the struggle faced by Terao and Hiraoka as itself being a position within the spectrum of *risshin shusse*, but that of an outsider who considers himself unaffected by the rules of the game. We might hypothesize that Daisuke has adopted an oppositional position to a worldview shaped by the imperative of upward mobility and a philosophy of opportunism and reacts by retreating into an aestheticized life of the mind.

Daisuke engages in a wide-ranging critique of a modern Japan shaped by capitalism and *risshin shusse*—everything from its citizens' infatuation with surface appearances to its obsession with money, its lack of culture, and the scramble to get ahead in life—but, as Karatani Kōjin has astutely observed, his critique of society is oddly cerebral, divorced from his inner life. With the assistance of the narrator, we as readers observe an interiority that consists of Daisuke's fluctuating moods, anxieties, and high-strung nerves, rather than a rational mind at work; Karatani goes so far as to argue—quite convincingly—that Daisuke does not understand himself.[13] Extending Karatani's thesis in a narratological direction, we can observe a gap between words and reality in the novel. The usually unobtrusive narrator sometimes distances the reader from the protagonist by revealing that he knows more about Daisuke than Daisuke knows about himself, at times even commenting on Daisuke's lack of self-understanding.

Although such moments can be found throughout the narrative, they come to the fore in the thirteenth chapter, when Daisuke tries to reconcile his burgeoning love for Michiyo with concern for a friend's failing marriage. When emotional confusion threatens to overwhelm him, the narrator steps forward to call the reader's attention to it: "This was something new to Daisuke, something of which he himself was unaware" (178, SZ 237).[14] Even more striking is the following: "He was saying illogical things on impulse, unlike his usual self. But he never doubted for a moment that he was doing this for the sake of the man seated before him" (182, SZ 243). The way free indirect discourse blurs the boundary between narrator and character can make the subject and tone of the voice in such passages ambiguous, but the narrator intervenes unambiguously a few sentences later, once again to call our attention to his protagonist's limitations: "He never thought of it as a deceptive maneuver to blind Hiraoka to his relationship with Michiyo" (182, SZ 243). What can we conclude from this gap between the narrator's discourse and that of Daisuke? Simply put, in the matter of his relationship with a university friend and his wife, Daisuke does not understand his own mind or emotions, and the narrator (and author) wants the reader to know it.

Moreover, such moments cannot be confined to narratorial intervention on the theme of love. Consider Daisuke's conversation with Hiraoka about work in the sixth chapter. Trying to explain his unwillingness to seek respectable employment to his unsympathetic friend, Daisuke remarks, "I mean that it's hard to work sincerely at a job that you're doing just to eat." Hiroaka retorts, "I think it's just the opposite. It's because you're working to eat that you feel like working furiously." Daisuke elaborates in an effort to persuade his friend: "Maybe you can work furiously, but it's hard to work sincerely. If you're working in order to eat, which do you think is the main object—work or food?" (75, SZ 105). Hiraoka can in no way be considered the moral center of the novel, but his role in such exchanges is similar to that of the narrator in other chapters: to cast Daisuke's remarks in a critical light, to provide a counterpoint, even when, as in this moment, they are not quite speaking the same language when it comes to the goal of work. Hiraoka draws on the Darwinian strain of *risshin shusse*, whereas Daisuke references sincerity as an ideal for work. Because of Hiraoka's skeptical comments in such scenes, when Daisuke connects his own unwillingness to work to the larger international context—as when he says "it's because the relationship between Japan and the West is no good that I won't work" (72, SZ 101)—we cannot help but view this as an act of rationalization, pure and simple. Daisuke even expands on his theory: "A people so oppressed by the West have no mental leisure, they can't do anything worthwhile. They get an education that's stripped to the bare bone, and they're driven with their noses to the grindstone until they're dizzy—that's why they all end up with nervous breakdowns" (72, SZ 102). The protagonist's effort to link the scramble for success to a national nervous breakdown and to justify his own leisure by appealing to global politics is thoroughly unconvincing; as readers, we bear witness to his self-delusion.

We can conclude from this that our protagonist has withdrawn from society less for philosophical problems with modernity, though this is what he says, than as part of a more visceral reaction to the world around him, and this is what the narrator shows. The modern Japan of *Sorekara* is shaped by competitive struggle and brute social climbing, though Daisuke's allowance shields him from this unforgiving world through most of the novel. Because his family's wealth keeps him away from the proverbial grindstone, Daisuke is able to construct his sense of self-worth in opposition to the other characters in the novel, each of whom measures himself and others according to the imperatives of worldly success. When we recall the poststructuralist lesson that an oppositional position to a hegemonic discourse always rests on some kind of appropriation of the terms of that discourse, we are able to read Daisuke's life in relation to worldly success. Daisuke's opposition is typically cast as an aesthete's distaste for this world, but one that he does not himself understand as such, leading the narrator to delve into his mind to show the reader the forces shaping the protagonist's worldview.

There is something oddly seductive about Daisuke's complex, even paradoxical, personality: he is at once disagreeable to twenty-first-century readers yet representative of a whole lineage of protagonists in twentieth-century Japanese literature; some even see Daisuke as the precursor to this lineage.[15] This puzzle has tended to lead critics to an analysis of the individual psyche in essays centered entirely on the novel's protagonist, but we can also view Daisuke as a man immersed in a larger environment that includes both city and nation. In a bravura historicist reading of *Sorekara*, Ichiyanagi Hirotaka shows the way a discourse on nervous tension arose in response to the Darwinian strain of *risshin shusse* in Meiji, which we see in our novel in such phrases as the one quoted above: "with their nose pressed to the grindstone . . . they all end up with nervous breakdowns." The individual body was conceived as a site that registered the negative effects of society's imperative to compete with others, move up the social ladder, and thereby achieve success. With this evidence in hand, Ichiyanagi argues that Daisuke's extreme sensitivity and high-strung nerves are reactions to the "struggle for survival" that resulted from the yoking together of upward mobility and the theory of social evolution.[16] In other words, the world of competition and social climbing that surrounds him impacts Daisuke on a physiological level—all the way to his nerve endings.

Just six years before the publication of *Sorekara*, George Simmel (1858–1918) argued in "The Metropolis and Mental Life" (1903) that the characteristic experience of modern metropolitan life is "the intensification of nervous stimulation which results from the swift and uninterrupted change of outer and inner stimuli."[17] There is no evidence that Sōseki was familiar with the German sociologist's work, but there is an uncanny resemblance between Simmel's metropolitan type and the protagonist of *Sorekara*. Simmel observes that the metropolitan inhabitant "develops an organ protecting him against the threatening currents and discrepancies of his external environment which would uproot him."[18] Simmel dwells the most on the "protective organ" he calls the blasé attitude, which shields the modern individual from the buffeting winds of modern urban life, but he is equally interested in how larger historical forces converge to shape the metropolitan personality, including the rule of the clock, the money economy, and capitalist rationality.[19] Connecting this to Ichiyanagi's reading of the novel, we can say that, in addition to an aesthetic withdrawal from society, Daisuke develops an apathetic or blasé attitude as an outer shell or "protective organ" for living in a cutthroat world of *risshin shusse*, yet his inner world is one of turmoil and high-strung nerves.

The complex psychological state can perhaps be best summarized as ennui, a term that is used with some frequency in *Sorekara*.[20] This is evident in Daisuke's reaction to Hiraoka's home. Upon his return to Tokyo with Michiyo in tow, Hiraoka takes up residence in the Koishikawa district of the capital, and this is where Daisuke visits him. The area is filled with homes that were hastily erected in a mad rush to keep up with the population flooding into the metropolis after the turn of the century. We view the couple's new abode through Daisuke's critical eyes, and the narrative discourse reflects his displeasure: "It was an exceedingly crude, unsightly construction. And Daisuke was especially sensitive to its shortcomings. There were only about two yards between the gate and the kitchen door [*genkan*, or entryway, in the original]. Next to this house, in every direction stood similarly cramped houses" (65, SZ 91). To Daisuke's judgmental eyes, this new housing is a "memento to the struggle for survival" (65, SZ 92)—an observation linking Darwinism and reckless urbanization. Moreover, given that these new constructions are erected for those like Hiraoka who are streaming into the capital looking to get ahead in life, this is a critical reaction to both social evolution and *risshin shusse.* Yet Daisuke's contempt for these new homes is characteristically cast in an aesthetic register.

This new housing takes on a national hue when Daisuke calls it "the most accurate symbol of modern Japan" and characterizes the viral spread of the shoddy housing as "the advance of defeat" (65, SZ 92). Here is exactly the kind of image—so prevalent in *Sorekara*—that has quite rightly led some critics to invoke terms such as degeneration, the opposite of Darwinian evolution.[21] The national image takes on additional connotations with Daisuke's second visit to Hiraoka:

> He followed the banks of the Edogawa River from Gokenchō, and by the time he crossed the river, the spiritual fatigue that had beset him during his afternoon walk had lifted. Climbing the hill and coming out at the side of the Denzūin, he came upon a tall, narrow chimney, spewing dirty smoke from between the temples into the cloudy sky. (96, SZ 131)

What is important to note here is the close relationship between the city and the hero's psychology, for his mindset is frequently impacted by the topography of the capital, and the representation of Tokyo, in turn, is colored by Daisuke's mental state.[22] In this particular scene, he sees a creeping industrialization that plunges him once more into melancholy, and he cannot help but see the small smokestack as the "labored breathing of a puny industrial force struggling to survive" (96, SZ 131). The frameworks of social Darwinism and *risshin shusse* are thus placed within an international context, and now it is Japan that is engaged in a furious struggle for survival in an industrial competition with other, stronger nation-states. The fact that Hiraoka lives here links the individual struggle to ascend the social ladder within Japan to the national struggle to advance within a competitive international arena, a connection Daisuke himself makes explicit: "He could not help half-consciously associating this chimney with Hiraoka, who lived nearby" (96, SZ 131–32). The struggle of the individual in a national topography is analogous to the struggle of the nation in an international context, and, conversely, the nation's international struggle can be glimpsed in microcosm in the individual's personal struggle up the domestic social hierarchy.

Daisuke's hostility to the modern metropolis and the fact that the novel rarely leaves his point of view help explain the circumscribed urban space in which the novel's plot unfolds. It is useful to juxtapose the space of the middle novel of the trilogy to its companions. We have already seen the contraction of novelistic space in *Mon* to a shadow-enshrouded home at the base of a cliff. Though firmly rooted in the university milieu of the Hongō district of the capital, the first novel of the trilogy, *Sanshirō*, takes its protagonist wandering throughout Tokyo and even references the provinces through the protagonist's exchange of letters with his mother back home. Daisuke is frequently on the move, as was Sanshirō, and there is even a scene of him visiting the Ginza to purchase a gift, but the protagonist of *Sorekara* does little more than shuttle within the vast sprawl of Tokyo between the three locations of Ushigome, Aoyama, and Koishikawa. His own home is in the first area, that of his family the second, and Hiraoka and Michiyo are in the third. Furthermore, Daisuke spends much of the novel shut up in his own home, even within one room of his home—his study—where he laments the state of modern Japan and seeks refuge from its troubles in his many books, mostly Western volumes.

A Chronotope of the Threshold

For nearly the entirety of *Sorekara*, Tokyo has been represented as the city of ennui. The capital receives a different treatment in the novel's concluding pages. In the final chapter, Daisuke's brother visits in one last effort to convince Daisuke to cement a socially advantageous marriage; when Daisuke refuses, Seigō vows never to see him again, as the father had done in an earlier scene. After his brother storms out, Daisuke half-heartedly informs Kadono, his houseboy, that he is going out to look for a job. As Daisuke rides the streetcar with no real plan and no sure destination, the combination of the summer heat, a personal crisis, and family censure causes Daisuke's head to spin, and the city transforms frighteningly before his eyes:

> Suddenly a red mailbox caught his eye. The red color immediately leaped into Daisuke's head and began to spin around and around. An umbrella shop sign had four red umbrellas hanging one on top of the other. The color of these umbrellas also leaped into Daisuke's head and whirled around. At an intersection someone was selling bright red balloons. As the streetcar sharply turned the corner, the balloons followed and leaped into Daisuke's head. A red car carrying parcel post passed close by the streetcar in the opposite direction, and its color was also sucked into Daisuke's head. The tobacco shop curtain was red. A banner announcing a sale was also red. The telephone pole was red. One after another, their signs painted in red. Finally, the whole world turned red. And with Daisuke's head at the center, it began to spin around and around, breathing tongues of fire. Daisuke decided to go on riding until his head was completely burnt away. (257, SZ 343)

One cannot help but recall George Simmel's characterization of the experience of the modern metropolis as one of heightened nervous stimulation, a partial inventory of which includes, in Simmel's phrasing, "the rapid crowding of changing images, the sharp discontinuity in the grasp of a single glance, and the unexpectedness of onrushing images."[23] In *Sorekara*, the red objects in the landscape—mailboxes, umbrellas, balloons, cars, curtains, banners, telephone poles—leap into Daisuke's head one after another and accelerate the spinning sensation. In this troubled hallucination, everything in his vision is cast in a reddish hue, on the verge of fiery destruction. Once again, Tokyo is the site of an expressionistic projection of the hero's mental state and nervous tension onto the city's topography, now figured as an apocalyptic space.

Sōseki has prepared the reader for the onrush of red imagery and for the theme of death from the novel's opening pages, when a red camellia falls to the floor, waking Daisuke from a deep sleep (1, SZ 3).[24] Like many things that startle him throughout the novel, the camellia's fall on the opening page makes Daisuke feel the blood pulsing in his veins. The narrator offers an explanation of the significance of color to the protagonist in the fifth chapter. Daisuke is reading some of the writings of D'Annunzio in which the Italian writer discusses décor: red should be used for rooms that called for excitement, an example being the music room, whereas blue should dominate in rooms that called for repose, such as the bedroom

(48, SZ 68). Red thus takes on the meaning of the excitation or stimulation of the senses, and Daisuke admits that it is a color that causes him physical pain. The onrush of red imagery in the closing pages of the novel indicates the hyperstimulation of the senses, the awareness of the circulation of blood, and the overloading of the protagonist's mental faculties. For Daisuke, who seeks D'Annunzio's blue and instinctively shies away from anything that causes his blood to rush through his body, the overwhelming of his senses by red imagery indicates an excruciating physiological experience and a changed relationship to the city.

The reason for this transformation is that Daisuke has transgressed social mores in declaring his love to Michiyo and is subsequently disinherited. With his allowance gone, Daisuke now has no choice but to join in the struggle for survival inherent in the economy of *risshin shusse.* Worse still, he will need to put his connections to good use to secure a position, in exactly the kind of instrumentalization of social relations he has decried throughout the novel. He will be working to eat rather than working according to ideals. The change in the protagonist's material and moral circumstances is reflected in the shifting representation of the metropolis: the estrangement, deadened senses, and blasé attitude that characterize ennui shift to the experience of painfully heightened senses and apocalyptic imagery that accompany society's opprobrium.

But the novel ends without telling us more, just as Sōseki warned in the advertisement to *Sorekara* that appeared before serialization commenced.[25] As we saw, Sōseki will explore the outcome of such censure in *Mon,* in which a transgression very like the one committed by Daisuke and Michiyo becomes a past that haunts the present. In *Sorekara,* on the other hand, the theme has been traced in a more straightforward, linear way, though one that incorporates a complex past before the novel opens and projects a bleak future. Given its elliptical ending, it also compels a reader to speculate further about what has happened and what may happen—"and then?"

Uchida Michio has done more than speculate. Making use of the sparse references to historical events in *Sorekara,* he calculates that the novel opens at the beginning of April and concludes in mid-July 1909, with references about the lives of Daisuke, Michiyo, and Hiraoka extending as far back as 1902.[26] The span of time within the narrative present is three and a half months and encompasses one season—spring—in its entirety. Seasonal references regularly punctuate the novel, alerting readers to the fact that even as its narrative unfolds in a distinct season, it is bookended by the end and beginning of the preceding and subsequent seasons, respectively, a structure that, when we consider that individual seasons have distinct connotations, imparts multiplicity and richness to *Sorekara*, loading those months with meaning.

In this sense, the use of seasons here is not unlike the use of light and darkness. As Jay Rubin has observed about Sōseki's oeuvre, wherever there is light, there is darkness, too, and the light will always find a way into the darkest shadows.[27] The same can be said of the seasons. Each novel in Sōseki's first trilogy is able to draw on a range of positive and negative connotations. Sanshirō's world, to take the novel to which Rubin devotes the most attention, is filled with the sunshine of summer, which even fills the autumnal present of its story. Yet it ends on a surprisingly wintry note, from both a thematic and a seasonal perspective, and there are a number of harrowing incidents in the novel that interrupt its youthful brightness. The crises facing Sōsuke in the third novel increase with the onset of autumn and the deepening winter, yet the novel ends on a positive note, for the crises are averted, and spring arrives. Nevertheless, Sōseki will not allow the reader to close the book in a happy frame of mind, for in response to Oyone's relief at the first signs of spring, Sōsuke sourly reminds her that winter will soon return. The dominant spring setting of *Sorekara* reinforces the growing love between Daisuke and Michiyo, which dispels the lingering cold that opens the novel, but the tale concludes with the intense heat of early summer, which works in conjunction with the novel's apocalyptic imagery to foreshadow a bleak future for the new couple, if they even have one; Michiyo, after all, is on her sickbed when we last see her, and the situation appears dire. These three novels are as intricately structured in reference to the symbolism of the seasons as any work in premodern Japanese literature; each tempers optimism with pessimism and undermines hopeful moments with harrowing incidents and premonitions of impending disaster.

Putting together these observations on time in *Sorekara* with the earlier discussion of the novel's representation of space, we can enumerate the features of its chronotope. *Sorekara* offers a cross-section of a human life at a specific point in time, a cross-section that features a dramatic moment centered on a fateful choice in that life, making the novel different from a typical *bildungsroman*.[28] *Sorekara* condenses time to a season to make use of its rich symbolism to add weight to the enormous gravity of the protagonist's situation. It encompasses the broader context of that situation through recourse to narratorial comments filling in gaps in the reader's knowledge. The novel joins this moment with the protagonist's subjective experience of the city as a space of ennui and alienation. Like its treatment of time, it condenses space to a few privileged locations crucial to the novel's tale of the protagonist's relations with a handful of individuals. At the end, the novel opens up to a larger cityscape once the fateful choice is made.

Bakhtin would call this a "chronotope of the threshold," where "threshold" can be taken literally—a door, a gate—or metaphorically, such as, in Bakhtin's words, "the breaking point of a life, the moment of crisis, the decision that changes a life forever."[29] In *Mon*, the protagonist crosses the gate of the Zen temple, where he is forced to confront his betrayal of Yasui. In the final chapter of *Sorekara*, Daisuke crosses a threshold by leaving the house and ventures out into the city to look for a job; the threshold thus extends out into the larger city, which, in its fiery red glow, has an expressive function that gives it symbolic and metaphorical dimensions. This chronotope—featuring the condensation of time with an elliptical ending and the constriction and final opening of space—allows for a drama of interior struggle and moral choice that is tightly imbricated with the discourse on worldly success.

It is, however, not reducible to *risshin shusse*, for love is also central to the drama. In the broadest terms, *Sorekara* pits love against familial and social expectations, as well as friendship. Such drama is a frequently utilized literary strategy for exploring what is truly important. I will argue in the next section that Sōseki is primarily interested in an exploration of value in society, and the plot positions monetary and affective value against each other in complex and ambiguous ways. Like *Mon*, the second novel privileges the city as the site in which this drama unfolds, and we need to grasp that Sōseki's city of alienation and apocalyptic imagery is a rejoinder of sorts to an antagonist that is only implied in the novel, but not explicitly addressed. We have glimpsed its shadow in the thematization of social Darwinism, but a close reading of a text embodying to the full this Darwinian city of *risshin shusse* will clarify the stakes of Sōseki's drama.

A Novelistic Scale of Value in a Darwinian City of Competition

In 1909, Watanabe Kōfū published a curious book entitled *Risshi no Tokyo* (Ambition in Tokyo), which also presents the capital as a city of competition, but one that engenders a different representation than it does in *Sorekara*. The volume includes a preface by Ozaki Yukio (1858–1954), then Tokyo's mayor, who, in response to the seemingly endless growth of population in his city, predicts that the text will be indispensable to those navigating the "swamp" of the capital.[30] Watanabe's own introduction paints a similarly pessimistic portrait of Tokyo, but he shifts the terms of the discussion even more resolutely toward social Darwinism: "Bread is the fundamental necessity of life," he exclaims (1). Its acquisition stems not from cooperation, in his view, but from fierce competition, a view shared by Hiraoka, as we saw. Watanabe's metropolis is thus the theatrical backdrop for the fight over spoils: in his melodramatic phrasing, "Tokyo is the grand stage of the struggle for survival" (4). This is as succinct a statement of the Darwinian strain of *risshin shusse* in the capital as one is likely to find in Meiji-era writings.

We must look to what at first appears to be a peripheral section of *Risshi no Tokyo* in order to fully understand Watanabe's adherence to this worldview. What emerges in the appendix is a vision of a society in crisis, and the cause is what Watanabe, following the standard term of the age, calls *shūshokunan* (employment difficulty): the inability of recent graduates from university to find jobs befitting their education and intellectual training. Watanabe is referencing the contemporary historical context: the period following the Russo-Japanese War was a time of intractable economic malaise. The immediate cause was the financial panic of 1907, which plunged the country into a lengthy recession and created the dire job situation to which Watanabe alludes.[31] Watanabe himself draws a firm line between early Meiji and the contemporary crisis and then goes on to survey a diverse set of career paths—bureaucrat, academic, even writer—in order to show that success in these fields is no longer possible because wages have become inadequate to meet life's needs in "the struggle for survival."

Yet there is something more than nostalgia in his critique. Watanabe is hostile to the new professions, which he sees as turning people into wage slaves, and, in contrast to the matter-of-fact tone in the body of his text, the appendix features him at his most strident on this topic. As he asserts in that section, his goal in the book is to spur people out of the salaried professions (what he calls *gekkyū seikatsu*, or a life that depends on a monthly wage) and into entrepreneurial paths and self-employment (what he polemically calls *dokuritsu seikatsu*, that is, "an independent life") by severing the connection between social mobility and education. Indeed, for all of his parsimonious attention to wages and prices, Watanabe espouses a surprisingly liberal view of education; for him the purpose of schooling is to develop one's innate abilities and character, and he decries an instrumental conceptualization of learning, which treats schooling as one mandatory step on the path of upward mobility. But education is ultimately peripheral to his main concern, which is to show that success, a good living, and high social status can be better attained through entrepreneurialism rather than through the emerging professions and the enticement of a regular, stable wage, which Watanabe views as illusory.

Watanabe provides an encyclopedic array of information so as to "detail the many occupations in Tokyo and to introduce the means to live independently," as Ozaki Yukio phrases it in his preface. Watanabe envisions his audience not as members of the leisure class, but as "those living in the middle tier and below" (*chūtō ika no seikatsusha*, 5). At a practical level, this means those earning a monthly income of fifty yen or less, and Watanabe's book is filled with lists of the necessities of life—everything from rent to rice, sugar to soy sauce—and the prices one can expect to pay for these commodities. Much of the book is dominated by a series of household budgets, neatly divided by occupation and income. He is nothing less than earnest in his effort to supply readers with the means to rise in the world through work and savings rather than through education—although, in a nod to reality, he does provide a budget for students, too.

Watanabe devotes a chapter to "Shūshoku no chūi" (Pointers for Those Seeking Jobs) and another to "Rōdō no chūi" (Pointers for Laborers). Each is subdivided by profession: in the former, bank tellers, reporters, postal employees, and bus drivers, among others, jostle for limited space. Ironically, these are exactly the wage-earning professions that

Watanabe decries in the appendix, but they are decidedly middle-class professions, most from the lower end of that spectrum: the bank teller rather than the bank manager, the newspaper reporter rather than the daily's editor. The latter chapter is also subdivided by profession—rickshaw driver, printer, milk deliveryman, and such—and the tightened budgets clearly indicate that this category is the working class. Still another chapter is devoted to "Eigyō no chūi" (Pointers for Those Running a Business) and geared toward his favored small shopkeepers, including those running a boarding house, operating a milk delivery business, or selling inexpensive commodities from small shops.

A Meiji reader from this stratum would no doubt have looked up his or her profession in the table of contents and turned to the appropriate pages for specific occupational advice. Such readers may have even modeled their spending on the budgets provided in the second chapter. It is unlikely anyone would have read the work in its entirety, yet *Risshi no Tokyo* is fascinating when examined as a whole and against the grain of Watanabe's stated intent. Especially intriguing are the links between pages, implying an economic connection. The government bureaucrat, for example, is encouraged to budget one yen, twenty sen for daily milk delivery (7), and Watanabe also offers practical advice to those who operate a milk delivery business (106–15) and their deliverymen (140–43). Salaried workers (7), students (16), and laborers (19) are encouraged to set aside fifteen sen each month for a daily newspaper so that they can keep up with current events. Sure enough, Watanabe also has a section for newspaper delivery boys (143–47) and wisdom to share with the newspaper reporter (50). Watanabe has practical advice for students trying to decide on a boarding house (15–16) and for those running such establishments (103–6). He has a line for savings in almost every household budget and much advice for the bank tellers processing those transactions (49). There are uncanny connections of this kind throughout the volume.

In *Risshi no Tokyo* everyone is, thus, at the same time a producer and a consumer. The capital is implicitly represented as the site of a minute division of labor, with each person occupying a discrete niche in this network, while at the same time the framework of social Darwinism imparts dynamism to this model and casts it as an upwardly mobile, entrepreneurial society. Everyone supplies something others need and buys the goods and services that others provide in the competition to get ahead. What emerges obliquely in the book is the exchange of commodities within a highly interconnected metropolitan economy. The manifest content of Watanabe's treatise is a Tokyo that has become the dramatic stage for the struggle for survival, but its latent content is a vast network of goods flowing like blood through the city's circulatory system, bringing sustenance to everyone within its reach, all the while creating networks of dependent relationships out of them in the process. We are given a portrait of a society in which individuals compete to advance, but are also dependent on others for that very success. It is thus a world where human relationships are seen as having instrumental value.

At the center of this system is, of course, money, which makes the exchanges possible in the first place. Watanabe's carefully crafted budgets reveal a world in which everything can be given as a value in yen or sen, the currencies of the realm. Of course, money had existed for centuries in Japan and was already the main mediator of trade during most of the Tokugawa period, even if rice was the ostensible foundation of the economy. Nor is the image of the metropolis as a vast circulatory system particularly novel in Watanabe's day; similar characterizations go back at least as far as Ihara Saikaku's (1642–1693) celebratory descriptions of Japan's vast, interconnected cities in the late seventeenth century.

What is new in Meiji is industrial capitalism and the class structure it engenders, the most distinctive stratum being the emerging professions and the monthly salaries they receive. David Ambaras has usefully elucidated the difference between these two as an "old middle class" of small shopkeepers and a "new middle class" of salaried professionals.[32] Using these terms, we might argue that what Watanabe desires, though he is never explicit, is to turn back the clock in an era of deep recession and return a city increasingly filled by the salaried professionals of modernity (Ambaras's new middle class) to an era of small shopkeepers and apprentices of the type that dominated the early-modern metropolis (the old middle class). At the same time, he retains the hegemonic ideological orientation of Meiji modernity, that of social Darwinism and the idea of *risshin shusse* that it, in part, supports. But such tensions abound in the book. Watanabe decries the salaried class as a dependent group, yet shows us a city of dependent economic relations. The real object of his scorn is unstated (and possibly unconscious), but we can conjecture that what Watanabe does not like about the professions is that they do not produce any visible object or product at the end of the workday. Unlike the romanticized shopkeepers of yesteryear, salaried workers receive compensation but do not contribute a tangible good to a market in which buyers and sellers meet.

It is illuminating to juxtapose Watanabe's *Risshi no Tokyo* with the fiction of Natsume Sōseki. The former is hostile to the salaried professions, whereas Sōseki's characters are almost always representatives of this new social stratum (Sōsuke in *Mon*, for example) or students aspiring to join its ranks (Sanshirō, for one), with a few exceptions (such as Daisuke of *Sorekara*). Watanabe accepts social Darwinism as gospel; Sōseki, who understood very well the disturbing racial implications of the doctrine and the way it utilized nature and science in order to justify Western imperialism, treats it with great skepticism.[33] These are stark differences, but there is shared terrain as well. For one, Daisuke may like to think of himself as independent of society and its Darwinian value system, but, from a material perspective, he is thoroughly dependent on others in a way that is not dissimilar to the world of dependent relations in Watanabe. More importantly, the two writers grapple with the question of value in a world in which money abstracts specific goods and blurs the distinctions among them. In such a world, we see the leveling of which George Simmel memorably wrote: things "all float with the same specific gravity in the constantly moving current of money, and all, since they are on the same level, are distinguished only by the size of the pieces that they cover."[34] This leveling is the replacement of qualitative distinctions by quantitative ones. There is a moral dimension to this picture: as we will see, Sōseki is deeply interested in the problem of how to invest select commodities with emotional, even moral value and with signs of human connection.

Our agenda in this section is to map out the exchange of objects and money in *Sorekara*, with some glances at its companion novels in the trilogy, as well, in order to extend the argument here beyond a single work. In these novels, as well as in several others in Sōseki's oeuvre, as the epigraph from *Nowaki* at the head of this chapter suggests, the author organizes significant parts of the narrative around the borrowing and lending of money, the exchange of gifts, or, more abstractly, around the motifs of reciprocity and circulation, a feature it shares with Watanabe's book. Previous criticism has highlighted the role of money in Sōseki, and I will extend this work in a narratological direction. I will argue that circulation is a technique for propelling the plot of *Sorekara* forward, and is thus inextricably connected with narrative development. It also helps organize characters into relationships that are simultaneously instrumental and affective. Combining narratology with anthropological work on the gift allows for the construction of a theoretical framework capable of showing how narrative produces value in a capitalist world of equivalence, thus rescuing the qualitative from the siege of the quantitative and the sensuous from the abstract. Though one would surely never find a copy of *Risshi no Tokyo* on Nagai Daisuke's shelf of learned books, Watanabe's city of competition will offer an illuminating comparison to the city of ennui in Sōseki.

There is precedent for the complex tale of borrowing and lending in *Sorekara* in the novel's predecessor. *Sanshirō* relies on exchange in its second half, in which we see the farcical circulation of twenty yen. Hirota is forced to borrow twenty yen from Nonomiya to help cover the expenses of moving to new lodgings. We are not given his remuneration, but as a teacher in the First Higher School, it must be less than that of Nonomiya, a university professor. Nonomiya is overworked and underpaid, and, with his monthly salary of fifty-five yen, twenty yen is a substantial sum for him. Given that Nonomiya, too, is saddled with his own moving expenses, he can only comply with Hirota's request by drawing on the money intended by his family for his sister Yoshiko's violin lessons. When Hirota finally earns some extra money, he asks Yojirō to take it to Nonomiya, but the ne'er-do-well ends up losing it at the racetrack. At a loss for how to get such a sum in a short time, Yojirō turns to Sanshirō. But the only way Sanshirō can secure such funds is by requesting it from his mother, who entrusts the money to Nonomiya and encloses an admonishing note for her son. The amount in circulation among friends is not insubstantial, though it is no fortune either. When Sanshirō sheepishly pays a visit to Nonomiya, the plot has carried us full circle, making creditors and debtors out of all the major characters in the process, as Komori Yōichi has shown.[35]

Connecting Komori's observations to narrative construction, we note that *Sanshirō* is structured episodically, and without the complicated, comical circulation of money, very little would happen in the second half of the novel. Whereas Sōseki can rely on the standard scenes of the provincial's arrival by train in the capital, his confusing encounter with the metropolis, and his gradual acculturation to the university in the first half of the novel, the repeated borrowing and lending of twenty yen provides the main contours of the story in the second half. It is a major structuring device driving the novel's action.

Sorekara, in contrast, utilizes such tropes from the opening chapter; it is the principal structuring device of the entire novel, from beginning to end. Demonstrating this will require detailed knowledge of the novel's plot. Hiraoka visits Daisuke in the opening chapter, and from the conversation between the two we as readers learn that Hiraoka, having been derailed from the course of success, has returned to Tokyo to make a fresh start. Shortly after that, Michiyo visits Daisuke, reveals that the couple has accumulated five hundred yen of debt, and asks Daisuke for two hundred yen, a large sum in 1909. For example, given that Watanabe estimates that the midlevel bureaucrat or the average company employee would earn about thirty yen each month, two hundred yen is the equivalent of over half a year's wages for such a person (6–7). Whether Michiyo is sent by her husband, who may be too embarrassed to approach his old friend directly, or comes of her own accord is unclear. Daisuke characterizes the amount as a "trifle" (47, SZ 67), but he notably does not have that amount of cash on him. (In fact, we never learn the exact amount of his allowance, but it is likely substantial.) Daisuke asks his brother, Seigō, but is rebuffed, so he instead turns to his sister-in-law, Umeko. Importantly, Daisuke is not close to his older brother and has a tense relationship with his father, so the money must come from his sister-in-law; this female control over finances echoes other novels in Sōseki's oeuvre, such as *Sanshirō*.[36] The loan from Umeko also underscores Daisuke's absolute dependency on others. Daisuke gives this money to Michiyo, not Hiraoka, and so the exchange of money maps out connections of affect, for Daisuke's efforts to help Michiyo here and in subsequent chapters stem from his sympathy for her situation.

Toward the end of the work, Michiyo and Hiraoka are still in a bind, and Daisuke hands an unspecified amount of money to Michiyo—essentially everything in his wallet at the time. Here, however, the situation has become more emotionally complicated, for Daisuke's feelings have shifted from affection and sympathy for a friend in dire straits to love for Michiyo; or perhaps it is more accurate to say that Michiyo's predicament makes Daisuke realize that he never stopped loving her. Furthermore, Michiyo's need for money to pay her family's debts and buy them a little more time while her husband reestablishes himself in Tokyo is Sōseki's primary technique for brining Daisuke and Michiyo together.

The plot of *Sorekara* advances because of the movements of the characters among the three primary locations of novelistic action for the purpose of borrowing, lending, or repaying money. Characters and money circulate together. Michiyo travels to Daisuke's home to request a loan, but this is simply the impetus for a long scene between them, one that occupies an entire chapter. Daisuke travels to Michiyo's house to deliver that money, and this becomes the fulcrum for another lengthy, emotionally charged scene between the two. Daisuke journeys again to Michiyo's home toward the end, and the act of lending money leads to a scene in which he almost declares his love for her. He summons her to his home in the lengthy and moving penultimate chapter in which he finally does make his long suppressed declaration. Interspersed among these are chapters in which much of the action centers on Daisuke's efforts to get money from his family in order to assist Michiyo.[37] The circulation of money becomes the fulcrum around which the plot turns and is indispensable to the formation of novelistic relations and novelistic action. Circulation and reciprocity bind characters together and structure the narrative. Although the primary motivation for the lending of money is sympathy and affect, there is always the danger that such relations will be merely instrumental when money is exchanged. Stated differently, the boundary between affective and instrumental motivations is deliberately obscured in *Sorekara*. The question, of course, is why?

To answer this, we should observe that the novel adds an element that complicates this picture; the story of the pearl ring provides a separate yet related moral and emotional economy for the novel. Daisuke had bought Michiyo a pearl ring as a wedding present, and when Sōseki introduces Michiyo, she is wearing it on one hand and her wedding ring from Hiraoka on the other.[38] As many have noted, when she asks Daisuke for money, she covers her hand on which is affixed her wedding ring with her hand displaying the pearl ring, thus seeming to consciously hide her wedding band and display Daisuke's present when asking for money (46, SZ 63). During one of Daisuke's visits, we notice that she is not wearing either ring, and the implication is that she consigned both to a pawnshop in order to pay the family's growing debts, which come from previous entanglements as well as new ones incurred from setting up a household in Tokyo (154, SZ 206). During Daisuke's last visit to Michiyo, she pulls out a box and reveals that she has redeemed the pearl ring at the pawnshop and has it back in her possession (173, SZ 230). Furthermore, she makes sure that Daisuke knows that her husband is unaware of what she has done. Affect and monetary need thus intersect in complex, ambiguous ways, and it is possible to detect the mercenary use of emotion, even as emotion underlies all efforts to give assistance and electrifies all exchanged objects in the novel.

It is easy to see the redemption of the pearl ring as Michiyo's preference for Daisuke over her husband, but I would like to point to something more abstract operating in *Sorekara*: an exploration of value. When Michiyo must decide among paying familial debt, redeeming her wedding band, or retrieving Daisuke's ring from the pawnshop, she must choose based on the value of those things to her. Daisuke's ring has sentimental value, which puts it higher in a hierarchy of objects than the symbolic value of her wedding band or the social value of paying off familial debt. Additionally, her decision has been placed in a larger context: sentiment has been pitted against pragmatism, and the former has won out. To return to our earlier question, by creating one economy out of the ring and another out of the borrowing and lending of money, Sōseki juxtaposes a gift with monetary worth and money imbued with affect in order to explore the problem of value in a capitalist society that erases the qualitative dimensions of objects so as to make them equivalent and exchangeable. Sōseki's novels work to undo that equivalence and return sensuous, qualitative distinctions to objects and human connections.

As so often happens in this body of writing, female characters become the primary site for the figuration of the qualitative, especially the love between the female characters and the novel's male protagonist. J. Keith Vincent, summing up a long critical tradition in Japanese, has observed that female characters and bourgeois romantic love become increasingly important in Sōseki's fictional worlds.[39] Part of this can surely be attributed to his transition in 1907 from contributions made to such male coterie journals as *Hototogisu* while still a university professor to a professional writer for *Asahi shinbun*, whose readership included both men and women. The transitional novel was *Gubijinsō* (The Poppy, 1907). Minae Mizumura (in a pivotal passage that Vincent also quotes) has said of this work, "after *Gubijinsō*, the possibility of not taking women seriously—of not succumbing to the temptation of sharing the same world with them—was no longer a viable option for him."[40] Yet it is also important to note that the tropes of circulation and reciprocity provide continuity from the homosocial early works to the heterosocial later novels, to use Vincent's terminology. The aforementioned *Nowaki*, Sōseki's final novel before becoming a professional, connects three men in a homosocial network through the circulation of one hundred yen. This is similar to *Sorekara* and the second half of *Sanshirō*, except that women play no significant role in *Nowaki*, whereas women play crucial roles in the trilogy.

It is possible to connect the increasing importance of female characters after 1907 and the continuity of the themes of circulation and reciprocity across this divide. In the Darwinian world of *risshin shusse*, we observe that the theme of worldly success implicates male homosocial bonds, as friendships forged in school become instrumental in an individual's efforts to rise in the world, as we saw in Tayama Katai. In creating such worlds, Sōseki goes beyond Katai's two-dimensional women and makes increasing use of complex female characters to signify love and, more abstractly, a qualitative realm characterized by noninstrumental relationships, divorced from the world of brute social climbing. The female characters may be more complex, but this oeuvre still relies on entrenched and hierarchical gender roles in society in its thematic explorations.

Given these transactions in *Sorekara*, let us work toward some theoretical observations, with a focus on the literary treatment of objects. Though objects in novels are really nothing other than words, they nonetheless take on an aura of reality. Certain recurring objects stand out from the flow of words and seem to do more than simply provide background detail in the realist novel. When certain objects receive this repeated close attention, they acquire layers of significance and symbolic value. They become pregnant with meaning. When such objects are given by one character to another, they create a complex moral and emotional economy that links characters in webs of novelistic relations. When that object is money, the situation becomes even more fraught, for the boundary between affect and instrumentality, gift and commodity becomes blurred.

Anthropological work on the gift provides the most productive framework for analyzing such literary situations, not least because modern novels are intent on modeling actually existing social relations at the same time that they attempt to capture the subjective experience of those relations. Being works by and for the middle class, those novels are preoccupied with the purchasing, circulation, and exchange of goods, while the novelistic interest in production tends to be confined to proletarian literature in Japan. It is helpful to return to the foundation for all scholarship on the gift, Marcel Mauss's classic work of 1925, *Essay on the Gift*. Mauss is primarily interested in uncovering an economy of the gift in archaic societies, but his book was path-breaking in the social sciences, for it opened the eyes of anthropologists and sociologists to the symbolic role of gifts and the instrumental social strategies that underlie their exchange. Two points from his essay are especially suggestive for literary study. The first is the way the gift possesses talismanic power. As Mauss puts it, in characteristically terse fashion, "originally—so much is sure—things themselves had a personality and an inherent power."[41] The best way to understand this is to view the given object as a substitute or stand-in for the giver. It is also the key to Mauss's idea of reciprocity, that is, the obligation to provide a counter-gift. The obligation to give, to receive, and to reciprocate thus creates networks of relations: "Contracts, alliances, the passing on of goods, the bonds created by these goods passing between those giving and receiving—this form of economic morality takes account of all of this."[42] *The Gift* has additional complexities, as well as the rough outline of a historical framework, but for the purposes of this discussion we need only highlight these two aspects of his theory.

As a side note, it is worth mentioning an interesting overlap between Mauss and semiotics on these two points.[43] This can be suggested fairly quickly by turning to a canonical reference point, Roman Jakobson's essay on "Two Aspects of Language." In it, Jakobson asserts, "the linguistic sign involves two modes of arrangement," selection and combination.[44] The figural faces of these two modes are, respectively, metaphor and metonymy. The first is paradigmatic, and Jakobson associates it strongly with poetry; the second is syntagmatic, and Jakobson sees it exemplified in prose narrative. These modes have been utilized by a number of scholars to examine a whole range of human phenomena as texts, most famously, within Japanese studies at least, the experience of the city in the work of Maeda Ai.[45] Mauss's idea that the gift has talismanic power because it is a substitute for the giver suggests that this facet of gift exchange is paradigmatic, like metaphor. With the moral obligation to reciprocate comes the building of networks of human relations, making the gift syntagmatic, like metonymy.

However we choose to understand them, Mauss's two central ideas can be fruitfully adapted to literary study, especially in relation to narratology. If the occult power of the gift can be seen as the substitution of the object for the person, it helps explain why some objects in a literary work take on substantive rhetorical and symbolic power. Second is the creation of bonds: the exchange of gifts (or money or commodities) functions to create connections among characters and, with its circulation, to map out a network of novelistic relations. If enough symbolic weight is attached to objects or if they circulate widely, they can even become principal devices for structuring narrative, as they often are in Sōseki.

Arjun Appadurai has cautioned against drawing too strict a distinction between the gift and the commodity, a point already anticipated in Sōseki, as we have seen. Drawing on George Simmel's classic work on money from the early twentieth century, Appadurai steers discussion of commodities away from the Marxist emphasis on production and toward a problematic of exchange. One could argue that in making this move, Appadurai overlooks the fact that Marx himself had much to say about the way the social character of commodities depends on their exchangeability, especially in his discussion of commodity fetishism in the first volume of *Capital*.[46] Nonetheless, there is no doubt that Simmel put exchange at the very heart of social life; as he phrased it in his *Philosophy of Money* (surely with Marx in mind), "exchange is just as productive and value-creating as is production itself."[47] Appadurai's preference for Simmel over Marx here is undoubtedly productive in its own way.

Appadurai's formulation of "diversion," in particular, will allow us to deepen our reflections on the literary treatment of the gift and the commodity.[48] By placing exchangeability at the center of his analysis, Appadurai is able to argue that objects have a social life and that being a commodity may be only part of an object's biography. Equally important are the ways that objects are diverted away from their status as commodities. The commodity phase emphasizes money and reduces sociality, whereas the gift reverses this, privileging social relations, as Mauss argued. (Barter, a third option, deemphasizes both axes.) Appadurai preserves the most important insights from Mauss and creates a flexible model for understanding how an object can shift between a commodity context and a gift context.

Understood this way, diversion can be seen as a major literary device in Sōseki's novels, in which the status of an object switches from being a commodity on the market to a gift. The opposite movement, from gift to commodity, is also possible. Such diversions are elaborate in *Sorekara*. When Daisuke bought the pearl ring for Michiyo, that ring changed its status from commodity to gift, the value of which is affective rather than monetary. Yet the ring does not lose its monetary value just because it is given as a token of esteem. Indeed, when Michiyo sells it to a pawnshop in order to pay expenses, the ring is diverted once more, from a gift back to a commodity. When Michiyo redeems the ring, she diverts it a third time, from a commodity with monetary value to an object with sentimental value. Sōseki essentially gives us a biography of the pearl ring, which passes back and forth between a commodity context and a gift context. Thus, following the social life of an object can serve as a method for structuring narrative and mapping novelistic relations. What is more, because the biography of the ring is linked to the circulation of money, it also allows Sōseki to explore the meaning of value and human connection in a capitalist world in which everything is, at some fundamental level, a commodity, even, potentially, the relations between people when such a relationship becomes, in a world of competitive social climbing, a means to an end rather than an end in itself.

The use of the gift for such purposes can be found throughout Sōseki's oeuvre. Returning for a moment to the novel with which we began this chapter, we saw that the crucial figure in solving the central crisis in *Mon*—what to do with Koroku—is the landlord, Sakai. His role shows that reciprocity and exchange are not limited to material objects. One night at about the midpoint of the novel, a thief steals into the Sakai home, but has an accident during his exit and ends up dropping a box with valuables down the hill, where Sōsuke discovers it the next morning. He returns it to Sakai, which leads to the establishment of cordial relations between the two due to Sakai's need to "repay" Sōsuke's kindness. This is the moral economy of reciprocity, described by Mauss and other theorists of the gift. By making novelistic use of the social imperative to reciprocate, Sōseki moves the story forward through more and more scenes that depict a deepening friendship between the two men, a friendship that contrasts markedly with familial relations in the novel, which are decidedly mercenary.

This friendship is also built on the social life of objects, in particular an ornamental screen once owned by Sōsuke's father, the last remaining possession from the estate. By bartering with an antique dealer, Sōsuke and Oyone are able to get an offer of first six then seven yen, later fifteen yen, and finally thirty-five yen for this family heirloom (430–32). The couple accepts the last amount. Later, Sōsuke learns that Sakai, having no knowledge of the screen's history, acquired it from the same dealer for eighty yen, which he considers a bargain (469). Its real value, though unstated, must be even higher. Similar to the situation with the pearl ring in *Sorekara*, we are given the biography of the ornamental screen, which is diverted through a variety of contexts: family heirloom, commodity, and part of a wealthy man's art collection. Moreover, when Sōsuke reveals the truth about the screen, Sakai feels guilty that his tenant and friend was duped by the antique dealer, and this sense of moral responsibility provides an additional impetus for Sakai to lend assistance to Sōsuke and leads, in turn, to the offer to support Koroku. This developing friendship thus has instrumental value in solving the problem of what to do with Koroku, but such value is precisely what the moral economy of the gift is supposed to obscure. Sōseki uses the inherent ambiguity in reciprocity here in much the same way that he does in *Sorekara*.

We can draw one final lesson from the literary potential of the gift when we recognize that the creation and deepening of ties between characters through exchange, diversion, and other devices is a process that unfolds in time. Pierre Bourdieu has highlighted the weaknesses of structuralist models of the gift, which do not take account of the temporal process, and points to a fundamental feature of gift exchange often forgotten: "the counter-gift must be deferred and different, because the immediate return of an exactly identical object clearly amounts to a refusal."[49] By injecting time and difference back into gift exchange, Bourdieu transforms a structural and static model of reciprocity into a dynamic temporal process that is part of a moral economy, but one whose conclusion cannot be given with certainty. This is anticipated in *Sorekara*, which shows us the exchanges of the gift and counter-gift as events that unfold in time. Indeed, it is crucial for a counter-gift to be deferred for an appropriate amount of time in order for it to be effective at deepening ties, and this process draws out narrative action to novelistic length. In sum, Sōseki provides an entire theory of the gift in *Sorekara*. He shows in this novel perhaps more than in any other how gifts acquire rhetorical power, how they build relations between characters, how diversion works to extract a gift from a commodity context or return it to such a context, how time functions within the moral economy of gift exchange, and how this exchange can be utilized to structure narrative.

❖

I would like to bring this chapter to a close by connecting these conclusions about the gift in Sōseki's fiction to the earlier discussion of the representation of the alienated protagonist in the metropolis. In the dominant portrait, *risshin shusse* creates the drive of ambition, and, in order to close the gap between circumstances and desire, characters stream into the city, especially Tokyo. Furthermore, with ambition yoked to the Darwinian idea of the survival of the fittest, human relations have value only as far as such ties help a person advance in a fiercely competitive society. Other human beings become nothing more than a means to an end. I have read *Sorekara* as an exposition and indictment of such a Darwinian city through the portrait of its protagonist. Nagai Daisuke lives in exactly the kind of competitive city described, even promoted by Watanabe Kōfū in his *Risshi no Tokyo*. The protagonist's nervous tension, ennui, blasé attitude, and posture of aestheticism can be interpreted as emotional and bodily responses to social Darwinism and its instrumentalization of human relations. The author critiques his protagonist, to be sure, showing the limitations of his perspective and of the Meiji elite male, more generally, but he also uses his protagonist to critique the larger society of Meiji Japan.

Furthermore, Sōseki explores the issue of value in this society by juxtaposing a ring with sentimental meaning and the borrowing and lending of money, thereby blurring the distinction between affective and instrumental value. Always engrossed with moral questions, Sōseki often schematized his novels in such ways, pitting two ideas against each other in a complex Manichean framework.[50] In *Sorekara*. money circulates in the novel's world of struggle and ambition. From the perspective of gender, this is the world of male homosocial relations, dominated by the imperative of upward mobility. One develops a network of male relations during school then makes use of these relations over time to secure a good position and advance in society. The ring circulates, too, but in the world of the gift, sentiment, and love. While a social biography of the ring shows how it can be diverted into a world of money, its simultaneous status as a gift demonstrates its power to transcend the fallen world of naked ambition and pure pragmatism. It is the female character—the love interest of the alienated protagonist—who points the way to a world of redemption. This may very well be the primary reason why "women and money always appear together in Sōseki," to return to the observation of Komori Yōichi.

George Simmel observed that in a fully developed capitalist economy, "objects circulate according to norms and measures that are fixed at any one moment, through which they confront the individual as an objective realm."[51] Not only is the qualitative replaced by the quantitative in this world, but the subjective experience of objects is replaced by a price, which, for Simmel, always appears to the individual as objectively determined. By valuing the ring over money, the novel makes a choice between these larger worlds, championing a subjective, qualitative realm that transcends the fallen world of *risshin shusse,* in which everything has a price. Yet Sōseki can hardly be accused of idealism, for the threshold choice of the qualitative also brings on the "red" city as summer begins, that is, the city of heightened, even painful sensory experience. This is coded as an apocalyptic city, a city in which love and death become almost synonyms. The clear-eyed and nuanced exploration of a moral universe tends to result in an acknowledgment of ambiguity and uncertainty, even pain.

Sōseki's alienated bourgeois male protagonist plumbs the novel's diegesis, seeking out objects of noninstrumental value in order to remove himself from a competitive city and the Darwinian values it embodies. In doing so, he seeks a cure for ennui and alienation. However, in the expanding world of commodity capitalism depicted in this extraordinary novel, a world in which all objects are made equivalent through money and exchange, we cannot say that anything has a priori value. Sōseki's texts must actively produce value by placing added weight and meaning on objects (and words) that are otherwise equivalent.

CHAPTER 4

Winds of Scandal: Female Self-Fashioning in the Metropolis

Tokyo is a demon pit that corrupts the female student.
—Ōtsuki Hisako (1905)

As the warmth of late spring gave way to the heat of early summer in 1906, a staff member of *Waseda bungaku* (Waseda Literature), then the bustling hub of the naturalist movement in Japan, visited Kosugi Tengai (1865–1952) at his home in Odawara, an old castle town beyond the southwestern suburbs of Tokyo. The resulting unsigned article, "Kosugi Tengai shi shinsaku dan" (A Talk with Kosugi Tengai about His Latest Work), was an update on the man who had acquired the reputation of being the first naturalist writer in Japan, with his novellas inaugurating the Zola boom at the turn of the century. Tengai had then taken a very different turn by accepting the position of staff writer at the *Yomiuri shinbun* (Yomiuri News), which then serialized his first melodrama, *Makaze koikaze* (Demonic Winds, Passionate Winds, 1903), one of the blockbusters of the Meiji era, with serialization followed by print volumes and even an afterlife on the stage.[1] When the reporter visited Tengai, naturalism was beginning to exert tremendous influence on serious literary circles in Japan, but Tengai had already abandoned its tenets and was fully engrossed in the newspaper novel trade.

The reporter tries to engage his interviewee in a discussion of Shimazaki Tōson's groundbreaking *Hakai* (Broken Commandment, 1906), which had just been published to much acclaim, especially by those promoting naturalism, but discovers that Tengai, the naturalist progenitor, has not yet finished reading it: "'Ah, yes,' he said, turning around to reach a book on the shelf behind him. 'I haven't had any time, so I've only read this far,' he lamented, showing me page 100."[2] Time is clearly in short supply: when the reporter reaches Tengai's home, the novelist greets him somewhat brusquely, explaining, "Actually, as you can see, I'm trying to write tomorrow's installment right now," and sends the bewildered visitor out to tour the castle town on his own, telling him, essentially, not to hurry back (52). After taking his time to appreciate the local scenery, the bemused reporter returns to Tengai's home to find him finishing up his work for the day: "When I got back, Mr. Tengai was addressing a thick envelope. 'Sorry, sorry about that. I just finished. That's done,' he said, tossing the package into the corner" (53–54).

Although the resulting essay seems intent on portraying an author who is out of touch with the latest work in serious literary circles by recording Tengai's babble about a major book he has not yet finished, the dominant portrait that emerges is that of a man rushing to put words on a page in order to meet deadlines. In fact, the two images are closely related: Tengai confesses to being so pressed for time that he has given up reading almost everything except the *Yomiuri* itself (57). It is surely to the advantage of the serial novelist to maintain some knowledge of his own newspaper, but the demands of the profession allow nothing apart from this. Tengai admits that his responsibilities keep him up until evening each day, occasionally even well into the night. Commenting on the prickles of conscience that haunt him when he tries to take a day off, he adds, "There's my duty to the newspaper, of course, so I normally don't take any time off and work each day according to a schedule. I generally don't stop writing. I can't stop" (52). With their weary resignation, these words reveal that Tengai has become a writing machine, laboring incessantly to get words down on the page to meet his daily quota and to create a compelling read that moves his audience to reach for the paper again the next day.

Tengai was more sanguine a few years earlier, in 1901, when he had achieved some notice as a vanguard naturalist, but before he gained fame as a newspaper novelist. A reporter for *Shinshōsetsu* (New Fiction) took down Tanga's musings about literature in shorthand and published them in the literary review as "Risō no dokusha" (The Ideal Reader). Tengai reprimanded writers who claim to produce art for art's sake with not a thought for the general reader and blasted those who write merely for the amusement of a tiny coterie of like-minded compatriots. Although Tengai expressed dismay at the vulgar tastes of many readers, he was on balance enthusiastic about the prospect of writing for a large audience: "I want to accommodate everyone's demands; I want to write fiction that can be read by everyone in society."[3] Since Tengai had written something of a manifesto the previous year very much in the spirit of art for art's sake,[4] he had apparently enlarged his ambitions by 1901 to include the entire nation. The summons from *Yomiuri* gave him the chance to reach tens of thousands of readers each day.[5] What had changed between 1901, when the *Shinshōsetsu* reporter took down his optimistic words, and 1906, when the *Waseda bungaku* reporter visited the harried writer, was that Tengai was finding the task of satisfying those tens of thousands of readers to be utterly exhausting.

Tengai would have surely agreed with the portrait of the profession offered by Ihara Toshirō (writing under his usual pen name, Seiseien) in his essay "Shinbun shōsetsu" (Newspaper Novels), also published in *Waseda bungaku* in 1906. The simultaneously morose and farcical portrait of the serial novelist begins with words of angst, comparing the newspaper to a tree that flowers in the morning and withers by evening. "Surely there is nothing more pitiable than the newspaper novelist, who agonizes over works this short-lived," he remarks.[6] More striking than this clichéd natural imagery of ephemerality is the mechanistic analogy used a few paragraphs later: "The gears of the machine turn hundreds of times each second, printing the day's news on the countless sheets of paper spinning dizzyingly through the press. In response to this, the newspaper novelist churns out his creative work each day." It is as if the machine itself were the ruler, and the writer merely a slave trying to keep up with its inhuman speed, obediently creating fictions that, like the morning news, are always in danger of being stale by evening.

This combination of transience and mechanical servitude informs the litany of complaints about the tragic fate of the serial novelist in the new era of capitalist print. While meeting the publisher's tight deadlines, he must cater to the demands of the paper's clientele. This means he must put aside any artistic ambitions he may have, for his audience desires a gratifying plot and has little interest in psychological nuance. This readership is notoriously fickle, wanting stories of scandal one day and plots filled with intrigue the next. The audience is also vast and anonymous, meaning that the novelist must supply fictions that can pique the interest of a massive and diverse body of unknown readers, both men and women. All of this condemns the serial novel to ephemerality, as Ihara observes, for, being a commodity produced solely to satisfy the tastes of the moment, it has little chance of winning a place among the canonical works of an era. As can be seen in these examples, Ihara returns again and again to two major concerns: the serial novel will always be excluded from the emerging canon; the serial novelist must draw on the fleeting interests of the day to produce appealing fiction.

With roots in the broadsheets (*kawaraban*) of the Edo period, the newspaper emerged in the wake of the Meiji Restoration in order to report on the happenings in a rapidly changing society. By the turn of the century, newspapers matured into a phenomenon of national significance, with some reaching a daily readership of nearly 100,000. The serial novel, which evolved in the 1880s and 1890s from earlier, multipart, fictionalized accounts of "poison women" (*dokufu*), had reached maturity by the turn of the century.[7] Founded in 1874, *Yomiuri shinbun* was a decidedly mass-oriented daily, whose readers were ordinary urbanites rather than intellectuals, yet it also concentrated on literature and the arts.[8] It achieved spectacular success when Ozaki Kōyō, a staff writer and arguably the most influential novelist of the 1890s, began his *Konjiki yasha* (The Demon Gold, 1897–1902). During the novel's run, Kōyō was inundated with letters from readers demanding that the plot move forward in this way or that.[9] Kōyō was pressed in so many directions that he seemed unable to bring his novel to a conclusion; it remained unfinished at the time of his death. Kōyō, too, had turned into a writing machine, but his absence was quickly filled when the *Yomiuri* decided to hire Kosugi Tengai as its new face; and the gap left by the incomplete *Konjiki yasha* was filled by the almost equally popular *Makaze koikaze*, which began serialization on February 25, 1903, even before Kōyō's death in October. Like his predecessor, Tengai was inundated with postcards and letters with suggestions for his novel in progress.[10]

Confirming Ihara's worries about canonicity, *Makaze koikaze* is now barely remembered, but it is easy to see why it was once so popular, for Tengai seemed to intuitively understand that nothing generated as much momentum for a plot in his day as a story of female virtue compromised. Our heroine is the beautiful Hagiwara Hatsuno, who is preparing for her final battery of exams at the fictional Teikoku Joshi Gakuin (Imperial Women's College) in Tokyo. Waiting for her after graduation, she believes, are "success [*risshin*], fame [*meiyo*], and fortune [*kōfuku*]."[11] It is rare in Meiji fiction to encounter a female character so closely associated with the discourse on *risshin shusse*; hence the importance of this novel as an object of study.[12] Hatsuno's hopes are ultimately thwarted, for she is faced with the unexpected challenges of becoming a surrogate mother for her younger sister, Nami, who has fled the family in rural Chiba for the capital; of securing a livelihood for the two of them while trying to finish school; of fending off predatory males, among whom is the wily artist, Tonoi Kyōichi; and of unwittingly falling in love with the fickle Natsumoto Tōgō, heir to a wealthy family and promised in marriage to Hatsuno's own friend, Yoshie. Hatsuno is ultimately ensnared by forces beyond her control, leading first to her moral degradation and finally to her death.

As if to confirm Ihara's second point about the serial novel, in his later reminiscences about his career, Tengai claimed that he had been inspired to write *Makaze koikaze* after reading the true account of a disgraced female student in the newspaper. Scholars have painstakingly sifted through the many articles on the moral shortcomings of Meiji youth in order to discover the report that seems to best fit the plot of Tengai's novel, thus wrapping up analysis in a standard author-centered paradigm.[13] It is possible, however, to approach Tengai's reminiscences from within a different framework. What if there was a closer relationship between text and context than simply inspiration? If there were elements shared by the serial novel and scandal journalism, the distinction between text and context would become blurry. We could then claim to be tracking a "poetics of culture" (again, in Greenblatt's phrase) centered on a potent trope in the Meiji era: the morally corrupted female student.

This chapter will uncover the common structure of the sensationalist press and the serial novel. It may at first sound absurd to compare a sprawling serial melodrama with brief newspaper articles, but the shared terrain is extensive. Part of our investigation will hinge on the kind of anxiety expressed so well by Ihara: the author of a novel serialized in a newspaper has to be acutely aware of the interests of the vast, anonymous readership of the era and has to be willing to cater to the changing preoccupations of the moment. Although one can find reports about decadent schoolgirls as far back as the founding of women's educational institutions in Japan in early Meiji, the establishment in 1901 of the first women's college in the country—Nihon Joshi Daigakkō (Japan Women's College)—and the sudden increase of female students to fill its ranks, as well as those of the other women's higher schools established thereafter in rapid succession, seemed to bring on a veritable deluge of articles about morally disgraced women students. This reached a crescendo in the second half of 1902, mere months before serialization of *Makaze koikaze* commenced. In his portrait of Hagiwara Hatsuno, Tengai was certainly catering to the concerns of his age.

But the desire to draw upon topics of urgent interest to readers of the day cannot fully exhaust the connections between the serial novel and contemporary journalism. I will also argue that fiction and nonfiction manifest similar anxiety over the way that increasing opportunities for higher education allow women to fashion identities for themselves free of traditional conceptions of gender and to be potentially as independent and as mobile as men in the new era. Narrative can then be viewed as a form that generates anxiety in order to master it.[14] These issues are inextricably connected to urbanization, for Tokyo, being the center of modern Japanese education, takes on contradictory meanings in this regard: from one perspective, it is a positive space of self-fashioning and social mobility for women as much as for men; yet, on the other hand, the city is more often represented negatively as a space of moral decay, figured primarily by loose sexuality. Thus we find a gendered chronotope for women, in which the danger of the metropolis occupies a particularly prominent place. Fusing historicist, formalist, and psychoanalytic approaches, we will uncover the deep structure shared by both journalism and the novel for turning social anxiety into sales.

The Meiji Schoolgirl under Scrutiny

On June 13, 1902, the newspaper *Yorozu chōhō* (The Morning Report) printed for its readers the following sensational story about an ambitious young woman:

> Around 3 a.m. yesterday morning in Etchūjima-chō, Fukagawa-ku, a young woman in her mid-teens threw herself into the river from the Chōren Bridge. One Ono Sajirō, a resident of the area, noticed her, leaped into the river, and carried her to safety. He took her to the nearest patrolman, who then escorted her to the Fukagawa Police Station, where they took down the details of her story. The young woman is one Hagiwara Kie (16), the second daughter of Hagiwara Kanekichi of Shimotsuma village, Makabeko

> district, Ibaraki Prefecture. The family is the wealthy proprietor of the Kuriyama Dairy Farm. Okie had long desired to go to school and had so pressed her father, who nonetheless refused to grant his consent, explaining that, as formal education was unnecessary to her future, there was no need for her to go to Tokyo. Okie, imagining that if she were to make her way to the capital and become a maid she could acquire the means to go to school, fled to Tokyo on the twelfth of last month. She was so occupied with household duties, however, that she had no time to study. She moved about, never staying long in any household, finally arriving in desperation at the home of her uncle, Wakayama Mokichi, a milk distributor at 1–4 Habakuri-chō, Fukagawa-ku. Deciding that, as she could not achieve her dream of an education, she would rather die, Okie went to the Kannon Temple in Asakusa two days ago to lament her fate, afterward spending the night in the neighboring park. On her way home yesterday, she attempted to kill herself by leaping into the river. The police summoned her uncle, who came to take her home.[15]

Encapsulated in this tragedy is the paradox of a *risshin shusse* in Meiji Japan. This discourse ostensibly authorized social mobility and self-fashioning to all who acquired an education, yet the presence of women trying to seize this promise highlighted the unspoken gendered nature of the new discourse and presented special dilemmas for the ideologues of the era. On the one hand, there was a widely felt social imperative for women, too, to be modern and educated; only resolute traditionalists, such as Kie's father, felt that women needed no formal education at all. Yet, an educated, independent woman also generated anxiety, for she sharply challenged both older and emerging conceptions of a segregated realm of female activity. By the 1890s, public opinion had reached an uneasy consensus: education for women was mandatory for society because women raised the country's children and were thus the first teachers of the next generation of national citizens. The call for women's education was thus put in the service of a newly constituted nationalist and patriarchal ideology in which the socially acceptable roles for women were reduced to those of wife and mother.[16] *Risshin shusse* for women became nothing more than marriage to a successful man. Yet once the discourse on social mobility was put in circulation, it could not be so easily contained or circumscribed. We do not know the fate of Hagiwara Kie, since the woman's voice never appears in such reportage, but her obvious resolve suggests that her desire for an education encompassed more than being a good wife and a wise mother in the future.

This desire is even more pertinent for the small number of women who attended the nation's few female institutions of higher education at that time. These are the so-called *ebicha shikibu*, a portmanteau word constructed from the terms *ebicha hakama*, the traditional maroon-colored formal divided skirt that became a veritable uniform of the female college student after 1900, and Murasaki Shikibu (fl. 996–1010), the brilliant author of the eleventh-century *Tale of Genji*. *Ebicha shikibu* was the colloquial equivalent of *jogakusei*, which referred to any female student between her mid-teens and mid-twenties, who had already completed compulsory education and was continuing her studies at a higher level.[17] She could be recognized at the turn of the century not only by her maroon *hakama*, but also by her frequent refusal of traditional hair styles in favor of tresses tied with a brightly colored ribbon and by her ubiquitous use of the bicycle.

It is precisely on this novel mode of transport that the fictional Hagiwara Hatsuno, the heroine of *Makaze koikaze* and another young woman very much intent on acquiring an education and achieving success and independence, speeds into the reader's consciousness in the novel's opening sentences:

> With the dinging of a bell, the Dayton bicycle burst into view, its occupant a beautiful, elegant girl of perhaps eighteen or nineteen years of age graced with slim shoulders. She wore a divided skirt and bound her hair with a pure white ribbon. Her tresses and the long maiden sleeves of her kimono billowed in the wind behind her. (150)

The description is so memorable that it is even possible for present-day readers to grasp the revolutionary newness connoted by Hatsuno's entrance in a novel written over a century ago. The heroine is marked in the novel's opening neither by a name—which we learn only in a subsequent chapter—nor by any sense of an interior life, but by specific material objects that threaten to dismantle her individuality and turn her into an icon of her times. Hatsuno wears the *ebicha hakama*, the maroon divided skirt, and, like other female students, eschews the elaborate coiffures and hair ornaments still worn by the majority of Meiji women, preferring instead a ribbon, in this case a white one denoting the heroine's purity. The long sleeves (*nagasode*) worn by unmarried women also contribute to this virginal image, while the way that these sleeves and her long tresses are billowing behind her in the wind reinforce the sense of independence and freedom (and eroticism) that was so often associated with the female student in the Meiji era.[18]

Equally important to creating this aura is the bicycle. Whereas in 1899, there were somewhere between two and three thousand in all of Tokyo, at the time of the novel's publication in 1903, the number of bicycles in the metropolis had more than doubled to just over six thousand.[19] Yet it was still an unfamiliar form of self-propelled transportation, and Hatsuno's appearance on it with all the accoutrements of the Meiji schoolgirl struck a deep chord in readers of the day. Moreover, the text specifies that Hatsuno's transport is an American-made Dayton, which in Japan generally came in a rust-colored hue—"Dayton colored," in the language of the day—adding an exotic element to the picture.[20] With the bicycle, the modish attire, and the uncoiffed hair so characteristic of the still rare female student in the highest reaches of the educational system, Hatsuno's appearance in *Makaze koikaze* is the very epitome of modernity, freedom, and mobility, all mapped onto the body of the type of young woman who evoked breathless excitement among her supporters and deep suspicion among her detractors, and even, for some, both reactions at once.

It is significant that Hatsuno gets into an accident moments after she appears in the narrative, putting her in the hospital and ruining her bicycle. This has led one critic to muse that her literal fall from her bicycle in the opening chapter foreshadows her moral fall, which it will be the task of the remainder of the lengthy novel to detail.[21] This is an astute observation, but I would not reduce the crash to this one reading. The bicycle is the initial focal point for the heterogeneous, often contradictory, meanings that coalesce around the female student and can thus be read as a the starting point for an untangling of those meanings. Revealing his indebtedness to naturalism's concept of the fictional laboratory, Tengai stages an accident to ground an exotic, liminal figure before she can speed off the page, thereby making her available for closer scrutiny by spinning a scandalous, erotic tale around her. Seeing, knowing, and eroticism animate the entire narrative and will be our watchwords for this chapter.

In an early scene, the cunning Tonoi Kyōichi manages to talk Mrs. Shimai, the proprietress of Hatsuno's rooming house, into showing him Hatsuno's quarters. He is insatiably curious about this woman who, by all accounts, is "beautiful," "virtuous," and "studious" (157). With Hatsuno in the hospital, the time is ripe to learn more about her. He follows the proprietress into her room and looks about:

> A soft light shone through the sliding paper door. He could see an ink-stained wooden desk, upon which were an ink grinding pad and a metal inkpot. There were two or three primly stacked notebooks, with a dog-eared English-Japanese dictionary set atop them, as well as a pile of blank, white paper held in place by a stone paper weight. Behind the desk was a traditional wooden book box atop a Western-style bookcase with glass doors. Paper had been pasted to the glass, so that the contents of the bookcase were not visible. Beneath the desk were a wastebasket, a coal bin, and a small, chestnut brazier. (160–61)

We have the impression of an orderly space, the kind of room we would expect to be kept by someone as devoted to her studies as Hatsuno. One of the highlights of the description is the thick English-Japanese dictionary atop the desk, dog-eared with frequent use; Hatsuno is in the Department of Letters at the college, with a specialty in English. Although the paper pasted to the glass doors hides the contents of the bookcase from view, there are surely many English-language books lining its shelves. This is not the only time something about Hatsuno will be simultaneously suggested and cloaked, a fact that subtly introduces the motif of frustrated vision.

Inwardly, Tonoi is "secretly impressed" by the evidence of Hatsuno's seriousness. Outwardly, his survey of the contents of Hatsuno's room leads him to exclaim, "It's exactly like the room of a male student" and to note that there is not a single decorative flourish that he would expect to find in a woman's room (161). This likening of Hatsuno to a man occurs several times in the novel. Sexual difference and clear divisions between men and women in the social, economic, and cultural realms are ideas to which Tonoi fervently subscribes, as we witness in his deeply held skepticism, expressed almost as soon as he is introduced to the reader, about any suggestion that women can be as serious, motivated, and intellectual as men (158). For Tonoi, biological sexual difference is inseparable from culturally constructed differences between men and women, making him a clear subscriber to biological determinism. For the possessor of such firmly entrenched ideas, the evidence of a serious female student whose room contains no "feminine" touches practically invites a skeptical probing of every corner of the room for corroboration of virtue or evidence of vice.

When the proprietress admits that Hatsuno is behind in her rent, Tonoi blurts out, "She hasn't paid last month's rent, you say? That's very suspicious. She's surely joined the ranks of the fallen students [*daraku-sei*]" (161). We learn the exact nuance behind this keyword, *daraku* ("fallen," in the sense of being morally corrupted), when a few lines later Tonoi, trying to account for Hatsuno's sudden irresponsibility, speculates that "she must have become infatuated with some man a month ago" (161). A *daraku-sei*, then, is a female student engaged in erotic escapades. Unconvinced by the proprietress's explanation that Hatsuno's spoiled younger sister made it necessary for Hatsuno to choose between providing for her and paying her rent, Tonoi presses on with his investigation, casting his gaze next on a traditional round pillow. In a moment thought by many to be the inspiration for Katai's memorable closing scene in his *Futon*, Tonoi goes so far as to sniff it, becoming flabbergasted at the scent—almost as if he had detected a hint of moral corruption (162). The proprietress explains that it is simply the smell of the hair oil commonly used by women. The comedy of this whole investigation should not blind us to what is happening here: with his curiosity and skepticism piqued by the visible evidence of a studious, industrious Hatsuno, Tonoi has abandoned the quest for virtue and is on the prowl for a sign—any sign—of *daraku* hidden behind the apparent fastidiousness.

Tonoi's unquenchable curiosity leads him to still further violations of privacy as he opens the sliding door to peak inside Hatsuno's closet:

> The closet was divided into two sections by a shelf, on which he could see a thick, folded futon made of woven cloth and colored grey-blue on one side; the tattered edge of a brown blanket; a silk quilt with green stripes and edged in faded velvet; and red nightclothes, the fabric of which was somewhat soiled and beginning to unravel in places. On top of all these items were a purple cushion and the pillow that Mrs. Shimai had stuffed back in the closet. These were piled all the way up to the ceiling board, which looked as if it would give out under the pressure of all these items. Next to these were a striped Chinese bag and two round containers of the

> kind that kimono makers used when delivering finished goods that had been ordered. The Western-style mirror was framed with mulberry wood and covered with a muslin cloth stained with face powder (162).

I quote this and other passages at such length to emphasize that Hatsuno's moral status is being defined in her absence by material possessions and physical objects rather than by thoughts or intentions. Furthermore, the novel generates a plethora of objects precisely in order to spur the search for something hidden. But here is frustration, for the orderly arrangement of things in the closet only underscores Hatsuno's moral propriety.

But Tonoi is undeterred. Sniffing further, he discovers a medicine bottle, leading him to wonder aloud, "What's this? Maybe it's medication for syphilis" (162). Hatsuno's troubles, Mrs. Shimai interjects, have led her to take sleeping pills. Tonoi next finds "two stacked wicker trunks and, beside them, an old cardboard box tied with string, from which old newspapers were bursting out. There were also women's magazines, arithmetic practice books, a round sweets can with the Fūgetsudō label, and a traditional umbrella, all stuffed into an old bag" (163). Hatsuno is clearly a voracious reader and enjoys sweets, but everything is in its place. The scene culminates in Tonoi's discovery of a receipt from a pawnbroker.[22] Hatsuno is undoubtedly selling her possessions to finance her passionate affairs with men, Tonoi speculates. But the proprietress links this back to her earlier revelation that, in trying to support her younger sister, Hatsuno fell short of cash and had to sell some of her possessions to the pawnbroker.

Each discovery of a suspicious object results in an explanation that is designed to allay Tonoi's (and behind him, the reader's) suspicions. And yet, the explanations are double-edged, for, along with Tonoi, the reader's appetite for the salacious is further whetted, and genuine scandal always seems just behind one more door or just under one more lid, awaiting discovery. With each of Tonoi's discoveries of "evidence" of Hatsuno's corruption, the reader begins to identify with him and his actions, leading to our own increased curiosity. We become co-conspirators in the persistent, aggressive quest for dark secrets, especially sexual secrets.[23]

If the voyeuristic dimensions of this scene were not clear enough, the erotic connotations of all this snooping become nakedly explicit a little later in this same chapter. Hatsuno's sudden return from the hospital forces Tonoi to make a hasty escape into the garden through the sliding door. Rather than return home, he tries to gain a glimpse of the mysterious owner of all the possessions he has been so assiduously studying. The description is focalized through Tonoi; the reader is positioned with him outside the room in the garden, peering in through a sliding door, giving him a partial—and seductive because it is partial—view of Hatsuno from behind as she changes clothes for bed, with, because of her injury, the help of the proprietress (164). Through such descriptions of flesh, the quest for signs of *daraku* has become tightly intertwined with sexuality.[24]

Such moments reveal the intertwining of knowledge—real or imagined—and voyeurism in a way that engenders the erotic investment in mastering an object. The entire scene we have been discussing reenacts one of the central gestures of patriarchal society: women, reified as "Woman," tend to be the object of knowing and the gaze, whereas the subject of both vision and knowledge tends to be conceived as masculine. Woman, as the figure of an enigma to which the man seeks a solution, is veiled in mystery, the penetration of which requires unveiling and denuding. Knowledge and the desire for mastery place subject and object in a relationship structured by the gaze and subtended by eroticism. Peter Brooks has succinctly described the mechanism at work here: "The body held in the field of vision is par excellence the object of both knowing and desire, knowing as desire, desire as knowing."[25] When the body itself is unavailable for direct viewing, as is often the case since narrative thrives on the denial of immediate gratification, substitute objects in the form of possessions take its place.

The theorization of this problematic has been most fruitfully pursued within a psychoanalytic framework, such as that employed by Brooks, and goes all the way back to the beginnings of psychoanalysis's grappling with sexuality. In the second of his *Three Essays on the Theory of Sexuality* (1905), Freud asserts that sexuality emerges in early childhood and connects this to the quest for knowledge:

> The same period in which the child's sex life reaches its first blossoming, from the third to the fifth year, also sees the beginnings of the activity attributed to the drive to knowledge, or the research drive. The drive to knowledge can neither be counted among the elementary drive components nor placed exclusively under the heading of sexuality. On the one hand its action corresponds to a sublimated aspect of mastery, while on the other

> hand it works with the energy derived from the love of looking. Its relations with sexual life, however, are particularly significant, for psychoanalysis has taught us that the drive to knowledge in children is drawn with an unsuspected precocity and an unexpected intensity to sexual problems, and indeed it may be awoken by those very problems.[26]

Without reducing the drive to knowledge to the erotic, Freud irrevocably associates it with sexuality, for the research drive is sparked by the childhood need for answers to sexual questions. Freud will vacillate in different essays between two problems for which the child seeks solutions: with the arrival of a sibling, the child wants to know where babies come from (the question of origins); or, upon noticing that boys and girls are equipped with different sexual organs, the child will seek an explanation (the question of sexual difference).[27] The latter problem more strongly links the research drive to the gaze, for the question is sparked by noticing anatomical distinctions between men and women, and the answer to the problem of sexual difference will necessitate the further visual inspection of reality. In Freud's view, the drive to knowledge, regardless of the lofty nature of the object of investigation later in life, will invariably contain the kernel of childhood curiosity about sex, and the desire for mastery through knowledge will always privilege the eroticized visual field.

Toril Moi has rendered the phrase "drive for knowledge" as "epistemophilia," and, in drawing on Freudian theory as one component of a feminist hermeneutics, has emphasized that it tends to result in frustration. The reason for this is that epistemophilia is always bound to the body and to the sexual difference embodied in it, so that "the Freudian drive for knowledge is structurally incapable of achieving total insight or perfect mastery."[28] Sexual difference will always remain the great mystery, even with the increased biological knowledge that comes with maturity. Peter Brooks, in his thinking about the inseparability of epistemophilia (the erotic investment in knowing) and scopophilia (the erotic investment in viewing), has reframed this insight around the idea of fantasy. Within the classic paradigm of male subject and female object, perfect mastery is continually frustrated because the object of the gaze is, partly or wholly, the work of the imagination.[29] That is, the object may be a real body, but it is overlaid with the subjective desires of the viewing subject.

Returning to our novel armed with these insights, we can see that, if the bicycle accident is the means by which Hatsuno's motion is arrested and she is made available for scrutiny, Tonoi's snooping turns her into an object of fantasy. With every discovery of a seemingly incontrovertible sign of compromised virtue, Tonoi encounters the sensible explanation of the proprietress. Nonetheless, with every explanation pointing to Hatsuno's innocence and legitimate financial difficulty due to the actions of others, Tonoi becomes increasingly certain that she must be hiding something, and the more aggressive his efforts to uncover the "truth" become. It is easy for the reader, like the proprietress, to become a co-conspirator in the quest for evidence of sexual scandal, even though there is no scandal to discover yet. The novel's central irony is that Hatsuno is an upstanding young woman in the beginning. Her fall is due in large measure to male fantasy; male characters have a desire to see her as corrupted, which, in turn, gives rise to situations beyond her control that ultimately ensnare her.

Yet, we should not swing to the other extreme: Hatsuno as Madonna is ultimately no less an imaginary construction than Hatsuno as Whore. Tonoi's quixotic quest for one or the other is closely related to the novel's status as a melodrama, and, though it is not the focus of this chapter, it is worth taking a moment to develop this point. Ken K. Ito has shown that the melodramatic imagination was of paramount importance in Meiji Japan, for the creative destruction all around made the modernizing nation seem as though it were a fraught moral terrain. Following Peter Brooks's study of European and American literature, Ito reiterates that melodrama's most salient feature is the logic of the "excluded middle," in which all of the so-called gray area has been removed from what becomes a stark environment of right and wrong.[30] What is portrayed is a world of good and evil, purity and corruption—that is, a highly charged moral universe with nothing but extremes. Hatsuno is the heroine in a melodramatic novel that explores the mystique of the Meiji schoolgirl by drawing on the logic of the excluded middle. Will Hatsuno cling to purity or will she tumble into the pit of moral degradation? The effort to find absolute virtue or absolute vice is a paradigmatically melodramatic gesture.

In a way that is entirely suited to the charged moral landscape of melodrama, the cast of *Makaze koikaze* is forever fretting that unflattering facets of their lives will appear in the newspapers. Hatsuno's bicycle accident, for example, is reported by a daily, which is where both Tonoi, the bohemian artist, and Tōgō, heir to the wealthy Natsumoto family, learn of it. A newspaper story helps jump-start the plot of romantic entanglement. When Hatsuno's younger sister Nami flees her rural home in Chiba to Hatsuno's side, seeking refuge from her hard-hearted brother, the story appears in the Tokyo papers, much to the chagrin of both sisters. In fact, the appearance of a developing scandal here is one of the reasons behind Natsumoto Yoshie's mother's interference with the friendship between her daughter and Hatsuno, leading to misunderstandings that help complicate the plot. The Natsumoto family also hears rumors of a developing relationship between Hatsuno and Tōgō and becomes eager to push forward the marriage between him and Yoshie; their plan is to use a quick marriage to dispel rumors of impropriety on the part of their virtuous daughter before the scandal sheets get wind of the story. This plays a role in the precipitation of the crisis that leads to the novel's dénouement. Newspapers are represented as having tremendous powers to create scandal—with a particular appetite for stories involving female students—and thus help generate plot. The newspaper draws its materials from the salacious stories in the world, and the actions of people in the world are impacted by the stories in the dailies. The entire world of *Makaze koikaze* is a fictional creation, of course, but its obsessive treatment of the newspaper suggests that profit may lie in an exploration of the real headlines.

On October 5, 1902, *Yomiuri shinbun*, the very daily in which *Makaze koikaze* would begin serialization less than five months later, reported a story that we might take as paradigmatic of the journalistic treatment of the fallen schoolgirl. The article states that two days ago (October 3), a young woman reported to a patrolman the loss of two wicker trunks at Shinbashi Station in central Tokyo—that is, trunks that would have held her possessions. Finding no evidence for a theft and with his suspicion aroused by the disheveled appearance of the girl, the officer escorted her to the station to ascertain more details about her background. The young woman turned out to be Kame, the eighteen-year-old daughter of one Aoyama Seinosuke, a resident of rural Kanagawa Prefecture. Kame moved to Tokyo three years earlier to attend a trade school in the Kanda district of the capital and lived in a nearby boarding house. She began a passionate affair with one Suzuki Shōsuke, age twenty, who was living in the same rooming house, though he attended a different school. Young men and women inhabiting the same boarding house would have been scandalous enough, even if quarters were strictly segregated, but this was overshadowed by the fact that Kame became pregnant. On learning this, Shōsuke fled, leaving Kame behind to fend for herself. Having gotten wind of the developing scandal, the authorities at Kame's school expelled her, and while Kame had no choice but to return home, her father insisted that he would have nothing more to do with her and turned her away. She returned empty-handed to Tokyo, where she caused the ruckus at Shinbashi Station in an improvised plan to turn the glare of public attention on Shōsuke for the loss of the nonexistent wicker trunks. On the morning of October 4, the father came to Tokyo to fetch his daughter and take her back to the provinces. The brief article concludes, "This is an example of the recent phenomenon of the fallen female student, for which there can be no end to our laments."[31] The newspaper's editors, too, must have also thought of this story as paradigmatic, for they gave the piece the title, "Koko ni mo hitori daraku jogakusei no hyōhon" (Another Sample of a Fallen Female Student). The article's title makes it clear that the instance recorded here is far from being the first of its kind.

In fact, such articles about morally corrupted female students were a staple of scandal journalism during the early years of the twentieth century. As Inagaki Kyōko has documented, such articles began appearing in abundance after the passage of the Women's Higher Education Act of 1899, which created a system of public women's schools to parallel those long established for men; reached a crescendo in the wake of the establishment of Japan's first women's college in 1901; and then tapered off with the reform of the original law in 1910, a reform that joined with prevailing public opinion by emphasizing that the goal of women's education was to create good wives and wise mothers for the benefit of the nation.[32] Articles about compromised female virtue rarely appear on the first page with the "hard news," but rather on the page of the daily reserved for reports on political shenanigans, love suicides, homicides, arson attempts, morally corrupted male students, and so on. News about disgraced schoolgirls, then, is a subgenre of scandal journalism and appeared surrounded by other salacious pieces. During 1902 and 1903, it was rare to go more than a month between such reports.

So standardized are the framing and telling of these scandals that one is tempted to treat them in the same way Vladimir Propp treated the Russian fairy tale in his classic *Morphology of the Folk Tale* (1928). We will be content here, though, merely to sketch the narrative presentation of the fallen schoolgirl without resorting to the diagrams and charts of structuralism. Such articles begin with a brief prefatory section detailing how attention was drawn to the suspicious activities of a young woman, with the date and place clearly indicated. In some cases, the proprietor of a boarding house reports a theft,[33] whereas in other cases a police officer notices a girl hovering near a bridge or river, seemingly intent on committing suicide, as we saw with Kie. The scenarios are almost endless. In the case of Kame, we have the ruckus over two wicker trunks. The young woman is questioned at the nearest police station, whereupon she reveals her name, age, and family background. The behavior that initially aroused the suspicion of the authorities is then discovered to be the proverbial tip of the iceberg, and an elaborate tale of scandal in the metropolis then unfolds before the reader's eyes. In the most typical examples, the "protagonist" falls in love with a morally questionable man—whether a student, an actor,[34] or someone else—has a sordid affair, and then faces all the fire that society reserves for such acts. In Kame's tale, we have one more turn of the screw: She is pregnant. Kame's story is emblematic in that such reports often dwell on the economic hardship faced by the female student, which typically leads to the petty crime that initially aroused the suspicions of the authorities. These articles usually conclude with the reporter's lament about the rising number of such cases, though many stories offer some consolation in recording how the girl's father came to the capital to take his disgraced daughter back to the provinces. It is worth reiterating that the voices of the young women concerned never manifest in the accounts except in highly mediated form. The women students are always objects of discourse.

In sum, these reports are cast as cautionary tales featuring a young provincial woman who arrives in the capital to further her education, but who then has a passionate affair with a young man whose feelings for her turn out to be less ardent. Confronted with the censure of family and school, the young woman faces social ostracism, which brings her to the precipice. At this level of abstraction, we have a narrative very much like *Makaze koikaze*, though in a rudimentary and highly condensed form. Tengai's novel, too, features a heroine who has come to the big city to get an education, but becomes entangled in a relationship with a man. She is cut off economically from her family, isolated from former friends, and struggles in vain to support herself and lead a life of independence. The heroine is ultimately rejected by her one-time love and plans a desperate act of revenge. Hatsuno is the focal point for social anxieties about female learning, independence, and sexuality freed from the disciplining confines of family, just like the newspaper articles.

My point here is not to reduce Tengai's fantastically convoluted melodrama to a brief newspaper article; the differences should also be highlighted. We can do this by shifting our gaze to the supporting cast of *Makaze koikaze*. Hatsuno ends up falling in love with her benefactor, Natsumoto Tōgō, who has been infatuated with her for many years. Tōgō, however, is engaged to be married to Hatsuno's friend and classmate, Yoshie, and was adopted into her aristocratic family to do just that. Furthermore, the match has been sealed since the two were children. The love between Hatsuno and Tōgō (never consummated, a crucial difference from most newspaper stories) thus not only works on an interpersonal level by creating a rift between two friends, but also operates on a social level by threatening the lineage of an important family. In the penultimate chapter, Hatsuno, her mind clouded with jealousy, engages in deception (her real "crime") in an attempt to keep her paramour from abandoning her and reuniting with Yoshie, but she soon repents and brings the two together on her own deathbed in the final moments of the novel (the heroine's death being another major difference between novel and most newspaper stories). For all of its elaborate subplots and detours, *Makaze koikaze* is ultimately a narrative of the mastery of the liminal female and a story of a prominent family lineage alarmingly threatened and then reassuringly restored in a tale of social reconciliation, which itself is a different kind of narrative mastery over the threat that a liminal woman poses to patriarchal ideas of familial succession.

But let us return to similarities. The utilization in both journalism and fiction of a basic narrative template is only the most obvious point of contact between the two forms of writing. To illuminate a deeper connection, we can return to the conjoining of epistemophilia and scopophilia. Freud's goal in "Three Theories" was to connect the pursuit of knowledge to the primal scene of a child's first glimpse of anatomical difference and to argue that there is no clear distinction between knowing, looking, and erotic investment. It might be objected that we are in danger, when dealing with scandal journalism or a novel, of treating the gaze as a mere metaphor and thereby making spurious connections between vision and narrative. However, narrative is fundamentally the revelation of information to the inquiring gaze of the reader through the unfolding of the plot. The issue here is the regulation of narrative information. Epistemophilia and scopophilia can be linked to narrative discourse, and this is best illustrated by considering narrative suspense in scandal journalism and *Makaze koikaze*.

Tengai is a master of the strategic revelation of narrative information, and this no doubt helped to make his melodrama one of the biggest successes of the Meiji era. He began his novel with a dramatic bicycle crash, but held back both the name and the details of the young woman involved, electing instead to slowly reveal her portrait over the next several chapters, primarily through conversations between other characters, such as the nurses in the hospital, or Tonoi and Mrs. Shimai. Of course, as we saw, it is precisely because the reader knows nothing about the young *ebicha shikibu* that Tonoi's investigation is so effective at generating curiosity and fantasy on the part of the reader. Consider but one other example among many: the eighth through the eleventh chapters. Having peered into every nook and cranny of her room and convinced himself that Hatsuno is hiding something, Tonoi has become obsessed with her. In the eighth chapter, he tantalizes Hatsuno with a financial lifeline, which would allow her to finish school, in order to create a pretext to be alone with her. The eighth chapter concludes with Tonoi forcing Hatsuno into a dark room and her unsuccessful attempt to escape. We suspect a tragedy is about to occur, but the ninth chapter, far from giving us answers, instead introduces another plot complication in the form of Nami's second flight from rural Chiba to Tokyo. It is only in the tenth chapter that we gain a kernel of information about the events that concluded chapter eight—just enough information to realize that Tonoi's attempts to be alone with Hatsuno were likely frustrated, but this comes amidst further plot developments. It is only in the eleventh chapter that we finally learn that Tonoi used force to get Hatsuno alone, but did not force himself upon her.

The techniques utilized by the narrator essentially constitute narrative striptease, eroticizing knowledge of its already eroticized central character. Narrative suspense is precisely this strategic withholding and unveiling of information for the purpose of generating curiosity and pleasure. Gérard Genette, the dean of narratology, argues that the regulation of narrative information involves both distance and perspective: in the former, "the narrative can furnish the reader with more or fewer details, and in a more or less direct way," whereas in the latter, "the narrative can also choose to regulate the information it delivers, not with a sort of even screening, but according to the capacities of knowledge of one or another participant in the story."[35] Our narrator has full knowledge of what has happened, but only reveals this information to the reader in the form of a gradual unveiling, using primarily temporal ellipses, or by selectively narrowing or expanding the field of vision through which the reader views the world of the novel, usually by adopting a character's point of view.

Brief as its stories are, journalism also partakes of these strategies of storytelling. The scandal piece typically begins with introductory information that is presented as objective, but that is also a hook to arouse the reader's curiosity and whet the appetite for more information. The police interrogators act as surrogates for the reader in questioning the young woman while they enact the drama of a male subject denuding the female object. This is structurally identical to Tonoi's prying into Hatsuno's closet: the drive for knowledge is subtended by the erotic investment in knowing, self-servingly couched as moral concern for the welfare of society. All of this questioning ultimately results both in a feeling of mastery and absolute knowledge but also of having penetrated to the heart of a sexual mystery. Having revealed her secrets (usually sexual), the young woman is branded a *daraku jogakusei* (fallen female student)—the naming itself indicating mastery—and sent back to the provinces. Anxiety has been generated and controlled, and the reader is often given a didactic lament about the sorry state of female education and women's morals in the present day. If Tengai's melodrama is more explicit about vision, this is only because narrative fiction can more freely manipulate the perspective through which the reader views and experiences the diegesis.

The melodrama shares one more feature with journalistic writing. As the stories of corrupted female students (or, indeed, any major scandal) become mired in larger networks of facts and relations, the uncovering of information by the authorities takes time. Scandal journalism may be able to report only on a small number of details on one day, leaving the larger picture still shrouded in mystery. The papers are able to report more facts on subsequent days as more information becomes available. Such a developing story becomes drawn out over multiple issues of a newspaper, thus leading to a phenomenon that is similar to the serialization of a fictional work.

Consider an incident reported in *Yorozu chōhō*, the same paper that published the tragedy of Hagiwara Kie and a daily very much enamored of scandal mongering, with its salacious pieces making it among the most successful newspapers of its day.[36] The article, appearing on the third page—*sanmen kiji*, the "scandal page"—of the daily on June 12, 1902, has the eye-catching title, "Gakusei dōshi no shinjū (shitai hyōchaku)" (Student Love Suicide [Two Corpses Wash Ashore]).[37] The article reports that four days ago (June 8) fishermen in Enoshima, near Kamakura, found the corpses of a man and a woman locked in an embrace in the offing and brought them ashore. We are told that the young man appeared to be around twenty years old. The young woman, "round-faced and pale skinned" (*kao maruku iro-jiroku*; two classic emblems of beauty), appeared to be in her late teens. Given the attire and age of the two, they were probably students. The police also discover that the young lady was about five months pregnant, leading the reporter to speculate that the two committed a love suicide in order to avoid a real-life scandal. Instead we have the makings of a posthumous scandal, for the discovery that the young woman was midway to term indicates that a sexual transgression lurks in the background of the fishermen's dramatic discovery. The student attire of the two invariably situates this mystery in the intertextual network of stories of disgraced female (and male) students.

Journalism is not so free as serial fiction, and the reader would have to wait until July 29 for the details, which came in the form of a follow-up article entitled "Jogakusei wa ichidoku seyo" (Reading the Female Student), making explicit the fact that the female student will be treated as a "text" to be read and interpreted for clues to dangerous forces at work in society. There is a didactic urgency in the piece, for the reporter, after rehearsing the main points of the original article that appeared over a month before, notes that the newly discovered facts in this story will "record the details as an admonishment to female students in danger of being corrupted."[38] In this instance, the didactic statement comes near the beginning rather than at the end. This simple amendment to the classic narrative blueprint, however, functions in a similar way to all such statements, whether fictional or factual: the didactic comment draws the reader and the reporter into a shared framework of moral concern regarding the facts that are about to be revealed, but it also guarantees that those facts will be sensational.

And it is hard to characterize the story as anything else. The young woman was one Adachi Matsue, a nineteen-year-old student from Oita Prefecture. While attending classes, she had resided at the boarding house run by the highly respectable Imperial Women's Association. The young man was Kumeno Yūta, also nineteen, who hailed from distant Fukuoka Prefecture and was a graduate of the Kanda Middle School in Tokyo. Yūta, however, is merely the last of a long list of men in Matsue's life. Indeed, without using the word itself, the article portrays her as a nymphomaniac. With her sexual urges already apparent at the age of 14, Matsue's parents, hoping to curtail her excesses with a respectable match, married her off to Oda Kōsaku, a student from nearby Hiroshima. When the two arrived in Tokyo, however, Matsue quickly abandoned her husband. The news piece refers to her as a student, but it is unclear when she pursued her studies, since she seems to have moved around from one man to another and from one boarding house to another. Having got wind of the continuing scandals, her parents even married her once more, this time to Haga Yoshio, a law student. This proved as brief as her first marriage, and she reverted to her former ways almost immediately. After a few more relationships, recounted with breathless narrative drive by the reporter, Matsue eventually met and committed a love suicide with Yūta.

I conclude this section with the report on "Kurui-Koma," the alliteration of which can, through a linguistic coincidence, be captured in English with its rendition as "crazy" Koma. This is not, strictly speaking, the tale of a disgraced female student cast in the usual mold, so I will give only a skeletal account. Koma was born in rural Tochigi Prefecture where she received an excellent education, culminating in her graduation from the prefectural normal school at the age of 19. Koma pursued a number of men in various parts of the country and the capital, moving from one teaching position to another as rumors about her spread. She eventually found herself living in dire straits in Tokyo without gainful employment, "a latter-day Ono no Komachi."[39] Her tale was serialized in five consecutive installments between March 2 and 7, 1902, the only exception being that on March 5 there was the notice that "the article on Kurui-Koma will not appear today." Otherwise, the first four installments concluded with the note, *mikan* ("incomplete," glossed with *mada aru* [more coming]), and the final installment had at the end the character *kan* ("complete," glossed with *owari* [the end]) appended. This is the same mark that generally concludes a serial novel.

The Meiji Schoolgirl in the Dangerous City

One common thread within this reportage, which tends to get overshadowed by the overt attention given to sexuality, is geographical mobility. Koma, for example, moved about the country from one teaching position to another as word of her scandals dogged her at each institution. Adachi Matsue's story is extreme, for here was a young woman who was born in Oita, on the island of Kyūshū, yet whose desire for an education led her to the capital and whose later misadventures drove her to many corners of the nation. Indeed, Matsue moved freely about the country, improbably appearing in such widely disparate locales as Hiroshima and Okayama, far to the south, the Kyōto-Osaka region, Shizuoka, in the middle of the main island of Honshū, and Enoshima, near the temple town of Kamakura. She also shuttled between these provincial locations and various abodes within Tokyo, all while assuming different identities—Abe Otsuyu was a favorite. When we join the foregrounded story of sexual scandal with the less punctuated themes of geographical mobility and changeable identity, we discover a spatial element to the anxiety aroused by the female student. She has become an independent actor, free of the supervising gaze of patriarchy and able to move freely about the country, engaging in and breaking off relations with whomever she pleases under any alias she chooses. Education provides the tools for independence, freedom, mobility, and self-fashioning, but, when appropriated by women, these assets were viewed by many as dangerous, for they turned women into liminal figures.[40]

Sensational as these accounts are, the editorials and essays condemning the corrupted schoolgirl far outnumber the reports of real women. Moreover, the shrillness of the discourse about the phenomenon makes it seem as though the social order is unraveling as we read and gives the impression that there were far more scandals than was actually the case. Miriam Silverberg, in an influential essay on the modern girls of 1920s Japan, has shown that the widespread appearance of women in the labor market generated a voluminous media discourse, the central theme of which was that the sexual freedom and economic independence of the modern girl threatened to undermine society and established gender roles.[41] The appearance of the New Woman (*atarshii onna*) in the 1910s witnessed still another spate of discourse condemning the independent woman, and here, too, reports of sexual scandal were not an insignificant component of such attacks.[42] Going back to the 1870s, the fictionalized accounts of "poison women" (*dokufu*) dwell on the swollen libidos and shrunken moral compasses of their protagonists.[43] The fallen schoolgirl of late Meiji takes her place in a long line of dangerous women who are very much a media product.[44] Her appearance on the historical stage at the turn of the century led to the widespread circulation of anxiety about female mobility and liminality, which manifested in journalistic discourse as fear mongering about sexually independent women who had freed themselves from social controls and were traversing the country at will, spreading social malaise in the process.

This social anxiety creates a relay of meanings that insistently link sexuality with the city, higher education, and moral corruption. This makes *daraku* highly overdetermined and fits all too neatly into a familiar narrative pattern, which is one of the reasons that scandal journalism about disgraced schoolgirls tends to take on the trappings of a formula and why Tengai's melodrama is simply a more flamboyant version of the basic narrative template. Inagaki Kyōko has described this narrative paradigm as follows: "'Going up to the capital' [*jōkyō*] entails separation from the family and the acquisition of freedom. The female student then encounters the seductive dangers of the metropolis, among which is the new idea of 'love' [*ren'ai*]. This develops inevitably into 'sexual relations' [*seikankei*], meaning that an 'unpleasant end' [*fukō na matsuro*] awaits her."[45] *Makaze koikaze* is too prudish to take up sexual relations directly, but it partakes of Inagaki's basic narrative of corruption. Given the consistency of the narrative in fiction and nonfiction, such stories might be productively framed not just as a theme but as a chronotope of scandal, featuring a temporal axis that borrows from the chronotope of success, but, in its anxiety over corrupted female purity, savagely distorts it so as to make social mobility impossible for the female character.

What about the spatial axis of such a chronotope? Here, too, the stories borrow the trope of "going up to the capital" from *risshin shusse*, only to deny the telos of success. The narrative of inevitable doom for the female student who moves from the provinces to the capital to receive an education underlies the persistent representation of Tokyo in journalistic discourse as a space of danger that by its very nature threatens the female student. Behind the demonization of the capital lay the anxiety over social, gender, and sexual liminality. Guidebooks to Tokyo's educational institutions, which had long existed for men seeking insight into the bewildering array of schools that had opened their doors in Tokyo since the beginning of the Meiji era, are useful here. After 1901, the number of schools for women also increased dramatically, and the market responded with appropriate information. Some books had separate sections for men's and women's schools, but there were also many devoted exclusively to women's education.

Such texts were by no means merely descriptive, for, even more than the guidebooks for male students, they typically included prefaces, introductions, and other discursive sections, which collectively framed the detailed descriptions of curricula, housing, and tuition with what we can call a discourse of the dangerous city:

> To the eyes of someone from the provinces, and especially to the superficial gaze common with women, Tokyo must appear a wonderland, filled with everything good and beautiful, the capital of everything. In the provinces one hears only of the marvels of the city and never has an opportunity to see its evils. It must be said that the city is not, in fact, an appropriate place to receive an education. Indeed, it presents great risks to female students, in particular. Students from across the country congregate in Tokyo for the simple reason that the intellectual class is gathered there. There is a saying: "Hearing about it alone is not enough; one must see for oneself." The city is certainly not as wonderful as it seems when one merely hears about it from afar. To put it extremely, Tokyo is a demon pit that corrupts the female student. One must take great care to ensure that their virtue remains untarnished.[46]

A common representation of the city, this passage draws a thick line between Tokyo and the provinces. To a provincial the capital must appear a wonderland, and Tokyo seems to do a fine job hiding its secrets. In reality, the power of the metropolis to corrupt the unwary female student is seemingly infinite. This guide was published after Tengai's novel concluded its serialization, but its tone is manifest almost as strongly in earlier texts. One that appeared the same year that *Makaze koikaze* commenced its serialization is less didactic than the guidebook from 1905, but still includes a preface with a stereotypical portrait of the city, stressing the dreaded power of the metropolis to send female students to their doom.[47] The representation of Tokyo in these texts is consistent throughout the early twentieth century. If the tone became more strident after 1903, it seems likely that Tengai's bestseller contributed.

Such portraits help generate an anxiety that manifests as a strenuous insistence on curtailing the movement and independence of women students, in other words, a kind of disciplinary imperative. Examining a passage from a book called *Tokyo-gaku* (Study in Tokyo, 1909) helps illuminate its contours:

> Those who require the strictest supervision are young women. However, as I stated, there are many naïve fathers and brothers who, wishing success and profit for their daughter or sister, send the young woman to Tokyo without heed. In most cases, they have neither relatives with good sense nor friends who can supervise the girl. Moreover, in most cases the young lady, having received an incomplete education at home, is wanting in morals and judgment. As soon as such a girl arrives in Tokyo, she immediately becomes the plaything of some man and ends up falling into the swamp of corruption. Even if such a disgraced girl should be expelled from one school, she simply goes to another and to still another, moving recklessly among institutions.[48]

Every anxiety of the era comes together in this brief passage. The audience for the book is represented as a naive family in the provinces thinking of sending their daughter to further her education in Tokyo. Seduced by the slick charms of city men as soon as they set foot in the capital, the daughters of provincial families become ensnared in erotic webs that lead to their moral degradation. Once her virtue has been compromised, such a woman is portrayed as alarmingly mobile and independent, moving unsupervised from one place to another, a moral threat to society.

Such anxiety about the capital and its pernicious effects on the female student helps us see that a didactic intent informs the seemingly neutral representation of space in Tengai's *Makaze koikaze*. This may not be immediately apparent as we glimpse, with Tonoi and the proprietress, Hatsuno's small room in the beginning of the novel. This space, as we saw, is orderly and free of distractions. Every feature of the room points to a serious student trying to pass her exams and graduate from college; and every seemingly suspicious article discovered by Tonoi can be explained by pointing to Hatsuno's unanticipated need to support an immature and egotistical sister, who arrived unexpectedly in the capital with nothing. Yet the text also gives us reason to pause. Hatsuno, after all, is a native of rural Chiba and has no relatives in Tokyo. She must therefore find a place to live in the city while she goes to school; she has chosen the Shimai House, a private rooming house (*geshuku*) catering to students studying in the capital. Students lived in one of the small, Japanese-style rooms that filled such establishments, and their monthly payments typically included room and board.

The Shimai House, located in the Komagome district of Tokyo and thus an easy bicycle ride to most of the women's educational institutions in the city, has a rocky history to which the narrator is eager to call the reader's attention:

> It was only recently, in the spring of last year, that the continuing scandals involving female students elicited a strong public outcry. Until then, the Shimai House flourished, almost never having a vacancy among its ten rooms. It was an officially sponsored boarding house of the Imperial Women's College. With the School Reform Law, however, that official status had been revoked, and the Shimai House had sunk to its present lonely state. In addition to the two or three relatives who had rooms, there was a student who went to another women's college, a nurse who was looking for new employment, a midwife, a new teacher who had not yet seen her first payday, and a woman who suffered from a sickness severe enough to require her to commute daily to see a doctor. This was the pathetic group of lodgers at the Shimai House at present (155).

The fictional Shimai House was once an officially recognized rooming house that catered exclusively to female students who attended the fictional Imperial Women's College, an institution respectable enough to be able to welcome the Empress herself at the ceremonies celebrating the tenth anniversary of its founding (149). This status was revoked with the passage of reforms spurred by the public outcry over the spate of newspaper articles reporting on the disgraced female students haunting the capital.

Our suspicion is that these newspaper articles are exactly the kind we have already examined, and those suspicions are confirmed a few paragraphs later. The proprietress had always engaged in various side businesses, which gave her a wide circle of commercial and social relations in the city, and the Shimai House routinely saw the comings and goings of merchants and vendors of various stripes. But rumors also began to spread that men of questionable character appeared to have free access to the establishment (155–56). Tonoi Kyōichi, a bohemian painter long acquainted with Mrs. Shimai, is a perfect example, and we are introduced to the pair immediately after the above description of the establishment. Tonoi seems to come and go as he pleases, generally to banter with Mrs. Shimai; but precisely because of this friendship, he can easily co-opt the proprietress to his schemes, beginning with the transgressive inspection of Hatsuno's room and continuing with his efforts to get Hatsuno alone and ultimately culminating in his efforts to have her sister Nami live with him while Hatsuno finishes school. Such is the danger represented by the boarding house.

Tengai's novel shares this negative representation of the boarding house with the polemic editorials and essays in the newspapers, magazines, and books of the era, all of which were preoccupied with keeping intact the virtue of the young boarders of the *geshuku*. Public discourse recommended curtailing the movements of female students and stepping up supervision of their activities. Within the vast, menacing topography of the metropolis, the private boarding house was singled out as a place of particular danger, coming to be increasingly perceived, in the apt words of Inagaki Kyōko, as "a dangerous space into which the supervisory capability of the family could not penetrate."[49] Tengai's novel draws on the representations of the day: as the narrator suggests, scrutiny began to fall on the private boarding houses, which aroused suspicions that licentious behavior lay concealed behind their walls, and the status of many of these establishments was revoked with the passage of stricter regulation of the schools and with the schools' own interest in protecting their reputations and those of their charges, most of whom came from families of stature.

To acquire surer footing navigating this space, let us return for a moment to the claustrophobic guidebooks to women's education. The author of one acknowledges that "the greatest difficulty for the female student come to the city to study is lodging." She notes that some schools have dormitories and that this is certainly the most convenient form of lodging, but she insists that the best solution is for the student to live with relatives or some other trusted family friend who can function as a kind of policeman (or "guarantor" [*hōshōnin*] in her phrasing). The discourse of the dangerous city bursts forth once again in the final two sentences of the section: "There are also those renting rooms, but such places are the foundation for moral corruption [*daraku*], and women who move to a private boarding house [*geshukuya*] will end up being tainted by a degradation that can never be washed away. The reader should beware."[50] Similarly, an anonymous editorial that appeared on June 27, 1902, notes with approval the increase in educational opportunities for women and the visible increase in the number of female students in the capital, but warns that, although most school dormitories provide adequate supervision of their female charges, the private boarding houses (*geshuku*) are danger zones that will lead to moral disgrace.[51] In October that same year, the *Yorozu chōhō* published an unsigned editorial that made a similar claim: lax supervision of their student charges among the proprietors of boarding houses has led to widespread moral corruption among female students studying in the capital. The author recommends that all students live with relatives or in dormitories.[52]

Private boarding houses were universally reviled, and Tengai borrows the discourse in whole. Seeking relief from the machinations of her male admirers and a refuge where she can concentrate on studying for her upcoming exams, Hatsuno moves approximately halfway through the novel to a small, thatched-roof building on the property of one Sen'emon, a farmer and plant nurseryman in Komagome (270–71). Surrounded as it is by trees and a bamboo grove, Hatsuno's new abode has a semirural feeling, with almost no hint of the metropolitan din. Hatsuno's room is small and rustic, and, struggling to live on the meager funds left to her (she has been cut off from family by this point), the only furnishings are two desks—one for each sister—lined up in front of the sliding doors that open onto a pleasant view of the garden. A reader might think these spartan quarters perfect for Hatsuno as she nears the time of graduation, for our heroine valorizes not only independence, but struggle and hardship, as well—as proof of freedom from men and of the ability to materially support herself. However, even as Hatsuno's new quarters retain these positive valences for her personally, the narrator immediately raises doubts about them by giving the reader the perspectives of others. Ever the spoiled sister, Nami is unhappy with the place, saying that she feels isolated and forlorn in the sisters' new home. Additionally, from the perspective of Yoshie and the other characters who represent the respectable class and the moral center in the novel, a young, single woman living alone with her sister in rented rooms with no hint of tasteful bourgeois decoration has a distinct air of disreputableness about it.

Hatsuno is living in even more straitened circumstances by the final chapters of *Makaze koikaze*, and the reader is encouraged to see a causal relationship in this state of affairs: an economic and moral fall that reveals Tengai's roots in naturalism. Having become immersed in a scandal and been cut off both emotionally and financially from her family, Hatsuno has moved to the back alleys of the Nezu district of the capital, into rooms on the second floor of the home of an impoverished practitioner of the traditional tea ceremony. If there was one category of housing that was perceived as worse than the private boarding house, it was exactly this kind of temporary rental; a female student living on her own in a building that could conceivably house unrelated men and women is a sure sign that our heroine has hit rock bottom.

Our view of Hatsuno's final quarters is once again mediated by Yoshie, who has made up with her friend, and now "gazed about the room with a faint air of tragedy" (330). Through her eyes, we are given the following description: "It was a six-mat room, and the damage to the *tatami*, the ceiling, the closet doors had been hastily papered over. The hanging scroll in the small alcove gave an air of age. Perhaps it was a trick of the dim lighting, but she could not see a single broken item. The pillar, the tableware, and such were immaculate and orderly. It was clear that the boarder took great care with the room" (330). With its dark tones and general atmosphere of decay, the passage comments on the heroine's fall. Yet even as Yoshie insistently stresses Hatsuno's straitened circumstances, she takes pains to note that everything is in its proper place, orderly at the end as it was in the beginning, emphasizing fastidiousness in equal proportions with decrepitude. This serves to underscore the irony of the novel mentioned earlier: Hatsuno has been brought low less by her own agency than due to the machinations and actions, direct and indirect, of the people surrounding her.

I want to dwell on the implications of this for the representation of the heroine, because it provides a useful counterpoint to the discussion thus far. It provides us with a way to acknowledge the shared narrative conventions and ideological orientation of Tengai's serial novel and the sensationalist press, but to avoid simplistically equating them. Throughout the novel we can find sympathy for the heroine, something that is entirely lacking in the newspaper accounts, which insistently demonized the female student and refused to give her a voice. Tengai, on the other hand, gives his heroine qualities that prevent the reader from vilifying her. Dreaming of "success, fame, and fortune" at the end of the novel as at the beginning, Hatsuno is almost single-minded in her devotion to school and study. The fact that we almost never see her engaged with a book should not lead us to doubt her zealousness, but to acknowledge that reading and note-taking can never be the driving forces of a melodrama.

What causes her to veer from her studies is, of course, love. Hatsuno shares a passionate kiss with Tōgō at the midway point of the novel, but the scene is presented with such voluptuous romanticism that a devoted reader would be hard-pressed not to feast on the language of the scene: "Her body quivered, her heart danced, she thought she would cease to breathe. She felt ecstatic, as if she were flying through a warm dream world" (308). There are whole pages featuring this kind of language. Furthermore, although the novel is rumored to have been prohibited reading at women's schools,[53] the relationship is not nearly as scandalous as the articles in the newspapers (or even most naturalist novels), because, as mentioned earlier, Hatsuno and Tōgō do not engage in sexual relations, preferring instead to create a relationship defined by platonic love.[54] It is true that the courtship clouds Hatsuno's mind, leading her to engage in deception when she learns that Tōgō capitulates to familial pressure, agreeing in the end to marry Yoshie. Yet it is precisely at this moment that Tengai delves into the mind of his heroine, giving us substantive access to her thoughts; we witness Hatsuno struggle with jealousy, love, feelings of friendship, and feelings of betrayal. Indeed, the penultimate chapter is almost entirely a scene of interiority, the reading of which cannot but engender sympathy for a heroine struggling to maintain her moral compass as she is engulfed in a swirl of events beyond her control. This sympathy prevents us from reducing an ideologically complex serial novel inhabited by multiple agendas to the newspaper in which it appeared.

❖

Nonetheless, it is in the end an understatement merely to claim a simple connection between Tengai's blockbuster and scandal journalism of the age. The two forms of writing share fundamental narrative paradigms, representational strategies, ideological orientations, and social anxieties. In demonstrating this, my goal has not been to erase the boundary between literature and the news. Rather, I wish to argue that a flexible historicist criticism capable of moving between text and context is necessary to make sense of literature in the era of print capitalism, a world in which news stories provide the materials for fiction and fiction provides rhetorical tools for framing and presenting the news. For literary study, the serial novel illustrates how the notion of a self-contained text must be exploded. For historical study, what is at stake here is the veracity of a historical archive of journalism that is always already literary.

In order to be successful, the serial novelist must tap into the collective energies and anxieties of the age, turning them into narratives that offer understanding and resolution. As was the case with most novels appearing day after day in the nation's newspapers, the serialization of *Makaze koikaze* was preceded by an advertising campaign. On February 22, 1903, a lengthy advertisement of 24 lines was printed on the first page of the *Yomiuri*; it would appear daily until serialization commenced and can be found in condensed form as far back as February 11. The advertisement promises in its first sentence that the forthcoming novel will "take up the present-day female student as its great theme."[55] Furthermore, it claims a pedagogical function, stating that the forthcoming novel will provide knowledge about this new social actor. The new novel will even cast judgment on the female student: is she "rotten" (*fuhai*) or "pure" (*kōketsu*), "corrupted" (*daraku*) or "redeemable" (*kaikai*)? In this instance, these words have distinct sexual connotations, making the text's promised knowledge erotic. Additionally, this knowledge is fundamentally melodramatic, for it partakes of the logic of the excluded middle, in which only the extremes of a moral continuum are available for representation. There are no gray areas in this stark moral terrain, and the female student will either be a Madonna or a Whore in a story that will make the reader "laugh" (*warai*) or "cry" (*naki*). Furthermore, the advertisement also emphasizes that the forthcoming novel will feature "lessons" (*shugi*), "ideals" (*risō*), and "hot tears" (*netsurui*). Drawing on the sensational escapades of real-life female students, which were even then animating the pages of the scandal sheets, the author underscores the forthcoming novel's didactic intent; this is fiction that will edify readers by alerting them to the dangers confronting society in the form of the independent, socially mobile, and sexually free female student. As we have seen in other instances, this is simultaneously a promise of the salacious. Pleasure and didacticism are conjoined in narratives that provoke anxiety and then reassuringly contain it.

The energies flowing from the scandal page, which featured reportage, and the front page, which is where readers encountered the fictional *Makaze koikaze* each day, are not one-way, however. Even while Tengai's bestseller was appearing in daily installments, the sensational articles about fallen schoolgirls continued unabated. There was, for example, the short piece about Akiba Kaoru, a nineteen-year-old student from Chiba, who, after being caught for theft and spending half a year in jail, attempted to kill herself by jumping into a river in Tokyo; only an alert police officer prevented her death.[56] This appeared on the fourth page while an installment of Tengai's novel appeared on the front page that same day. Nearly two weeks earlier, while Hatsuno's fictional story appeared on page one, the factual account of Katō Kiku, a twenty-year-old student from Ibaraki, appeared on the sixth page. Kiku was apprehended for criminal acts committed with her lover, the twenty-two-year-old Yūkichi.[57] When combined with similar articles appearing in other newspapers, we encounter a dense intertextual web in which it becomes quite impossible to say whether fact inspires fiction or whether a melodramatic bestseller is stoking a demand for real-life scandals. A reader can be forgiven for being suspicious of the veracity of the scandal articles.

Even more striking is an account that appeared in mid-March in 1903, when *Makaze koikaze* was less than a month into its run but when it was already clear that Tengai had galvanized the public's imagination. We are given the story of Uchida Fusa, an eighteen-year-old who earned a reputation as a serious student while in school in her native Kōfu in Yamanashi Prefecture. She was granted permission by her family to further her studies in Tokyo, but once there fell in love with one Iino Seinosuke, age twenty-three, and then became mired in financial problems stemming from her affair: she lied to her family in order to get money and absconded from at least two rooming houses without paying rent. She eventually found herself in such dire straits that she turned herself into the police, confessed to her actions, and was sent home. Young Fusa's feelings were apparently too strong, though: after defiantly expressing a desire to marry Seinosuke, she was disowned by her family. Nothing is known of her fate. Tellingly, as a preface to the piece, the anonymous reporter remarks, "it seems necessary to give the story that follows the headline *Shin [New] makaze koikaze*."[58] Setting aside the fact that Fusa's story does not much resemble that of the fictional Hatsuno in Tengai's tale except at the most general level, it is clear that the journalistic text draws its inspiration from the novel that is being serialized on the front page of the same newspaper and attempts to capture the reader's attention by explicitly affiliating itself with the well-known fictional heroine. Perhaps the factual account of Fusa's adventures has even been embellished to make it more sensational and to make it more closely resemble the fictional blockbuster that was, at least according to anecdotal evidence of the day, noticeably improving the circulation numbers of the *Yomiuri*. There is no way to know in this case, but it is worth emphasizing that once a narrative paradigm emerges, it becomes almost mandatory to alter the facts, however slightly, to better fit the blueprint. It will be recalled, too, that the advertisement for Tengai's melodrama had already claimed that the novel drew its own inspiration from real life. The circulation of social anxiety seems to move in both directions, and, if the demarcation between text and context has become unstable in our historicist reading, so, too, has the line between fact and fiction.

CHAPTER 5

A Genealogy of Failure: Korea, Manchuria, and the Japanese Novel

> At present, for half our population, nay for 80 or 90 percent of it, the means to rise in the world and succeed are outmoded. Go! Go abroad! Abroad! Go!
>
> —Sakamaki Gentarō, *Kaigai risshin annai* (1911)

The novels we have examined thus far have produced heterogeneous, even competing portraits of space as part of their exploration of what it means, in the words of Sakamaki Gentarō, to "rise in the world and succeed" (*risshin seikō hō*).[1] Moreover, each traces the fortunes of a national subject who attempts to close the gap between what he (or sometimes she) is at the beginning of the novel and what he wishes to be. To join circumstances with desire is success; to be unable to do so is failure. Japan's embarkation on a course of territorial expansion complicates these issues. Our basic question in this final chapter is: What does it mean to "rise in the world and succeed" (or fail) in a nation that possesses colonies? Additionally, building on the themes of the preceding chapters, how does imperialism transform the topography of *risshin shusse* and, in turn, the spatial imagination of the novel?

The pursuit of these questions across the waters to continental Asia requires an expansion of the concepts that have informed this study so far, for they move us from consideration of nation-building to that of empire-building. Additionally, such questions present us with the phenomenon of a *national* subject negotiating *colonial* space in his effort to close the gap between circumstances and desire, and this, in turn, entails a consideration of the encounter with and representation of cultural difference. Although we can postpone detailed discussion, the most important addition to the vocabulary of *Struggling Upward* will be drawn from ethnography and its postcolonial critique. Even as we retain the conceptual framework of the preceding chapters, then, we must expand our analytical language for grappling with the discourses on ambition and social mobility, for by the end of the Meiji era such discourses had become embedded in a larger geopolitical context and encompassed a space greater than Japan's own borders.

There is, first of all, the difficult task of coming to terms with the various methods of imperial domination. Whether we distinguish, with Edward Said, between imperialism and colonialism or, as is common in Japanese historiography, between informal and formal empire, or in some other way, we still face difficulties.[2] Japan's imperial ambition encompassed much territory at its height, but even on the eve of the Pacific War, its formal colonial possessions were limited to Taiwan, Korea, Karafuto (southern Sakhalin), the Kwantung peninsula, and Micronesia (the Mariana, Carolina, and Marshall Islands). Having found itself without much forethought or planning with the island of Taiwan after the Sino-Japanese War ended in 1895, the Japanese government used the island to experiment with different methods of rule and scientific management. The Korean peninsula was the object of a far more aggressive acquisitiveness, in a mere fifteen years passing through several distinct forms of indirect control, including the treaty port system, concession politics, and the apparatus of the protectorate, before being annexed in 1910. Japan competed with other powers in Manchuria, and this activity, especially after Russia's defeat in 1905, threatened to turn it into a formal colony. Although it is beyond the scope of this book, it is worth recalling that Japan eventually set up the puppet regime of Manchukuo in northeast Asia in 1932 and established ad-hoc systems of control over large portions of the Chinese coast and the old colonial enclaves of the European powers. In this chapter, I will most often rely on the terms "colonial Asia" and "semicolonial Asia" to refer to this complex geopolitical area, which are terms well established in the field of Japanese Studies. The lands that will most concern us here, because of the use to which they are put in novels after the turn of the century, are colonial Korea and semicolonial Manchuria at the very end of the Meiji era.

The most common way of discussing such lands using a spatial metaphor is to rely on the categories of metropole and colony, but beyond this basic dyad lies a world of daunting complexity. The situation is analogous to the heterogeneity that underlies the basic city-country dichotomy: it is serviceable for certain levels of abstraction, but quickly becomes inadequate when grappling with details. And novels are relentlessly preoccupied with details. The metropole is as filled with divisions and conflicting interests after the acquisition of colonies as it was before, including class and geographical antagonisms, and these differences influence the kinds of people who travel beyond national borders to outlying lands. Nor do they disappear with movement to the colonies; it is simply that they take on new meanings within a fractured settler community there. Furthermore, colonial space is itself complex, consisting of rural areas, metropolitan areas, port cities, and the hybrid cultures of these varied spaces. As I will demonstrate, the metropole-colony dichotomy, with its emphasis on the domination of the colonized, obscures the ethnographic interest in the Japanese expatriate community within the novels of the Meiji era, the study of which can help us add nuance and complexity to our conceptualizations of early colonialism.

In examining this heterogeneity, we will be concentrating once again on the spatial imagination as it manifests in literature. The spatial imagination is inextricably connected to opportunity and its depiction, but in this chapter we investigate this connection in a colonial context. It is worth dwelling for a moment on reality before moving to representation. By the time of Korea's annexation in 1910, census data indicate that there were over 170,000 Japanese on the peninsula, with the vast majority of them crowded into the capital, Seoul, and the bustling port city of Pusan.[3] There were relatively few Japanese in the interior of Korea, though this population increased rapidly after annexation. Most Japanese came from five provinces in western Japan, lured by what they hoped would be better economic conditions on the peninsula. Despite the dreams on the part of officials in Tokyo of turning Korea into an agricultural prefecture of Japan through strategic settlement, the overwhelming majority of immigrants early on were not farmers but adventurers, small entrepreneurs lured by easy money, and carpetbaggers catering to the Japanese military, which had a growing presence with each conflict and international incident. Economic development helped spur the movement of men, material, and goods to Korea, but even here things did not proceed according to the wishes of the authorities. Tokyo was constantly prodding big capital to invest in the colonies, but the reluctance for years of the great entrepreneurs to risk their money in such uncertain ventures left the Japanese government little choice but to fund fully or partially large-scale capital projects on the peninsula, with the railroad being one of the most important. With the establishment of the protectorate, and especially after annexation, most settlers came from the middle and lower-middle classes, a group made up of shopkeepers and small-time capitalists, but farmers, too. Peter Duus deftly conveys the perceived difference here between the early and late arrivals: "The adventurers, carpetbaggers, and penny capitalists who streamed to Korea in 1894–95 and 1904–5 were drawn by the lure of quick money. . . . After the Russo-Japanese War, with the imposition of new regulations and institutions by the residency-general, the days of quick money were on the wane, and the ordinary migrant could no longer hope to be rewarded with miraculous profits."[4] Representations of opportunity in Korea across the spectrum of colonial texts tend to turn on this perceived division between the days of quick money and the days of profits gained solely through hard work and cautious investment.

Looking farther north, the Japanese population in Manchuria in 1910 was roughly 74,000, a relatively small presence that would increase dramatically in the Taishō and Shōwa eras.[5] The image of Manchuria was that of a land of plenty—an image it retained well into the twentieth century, partly because of the widespread perception that the possibility of making it big in Korea was becoming increasingly difficult. Manchuria was portrayed as a kind of wonderland of modern technological development and opportunity, as if Japan were building a "modernist utopia," in Louise Young's words, in the lands north of the Great Wall.[6]

There was a deluge of travelogues, ethnographies, guidebooks, and journalism on colonial Asia. Lurking behind every representation, however innocuous it appears on the surface, is an ideological agenda, and such texts are no exception. Journalism was fixated on colonial settlement as necessary to resolve the continually prophesied food shortages at home, which would supposedly be unavoidable with Japan's Malthusian population increase, thus slyly turning the colonization of Korea into the only possible solution to Japan's very survival in a harsh, unforgiving world. The travelogues and ethnographies tend to waver uncertainly between highlighting the ethnic similarities and shared cultural heritage between Japan and Korea and trumpeting the difference between Japan's modernization and transformation into a civilized nation and Korea's persistent "backwardness." Though seemingly in conflict, these attitudes ultimately coexisted on the agenda of imperialism, with the first being mobilized to represent Japan's annexation of Korea as the reunion of a larger ethnic family tragically separated in the past by arbitrary national borders and the second being used to justify Korea's need for Japanese tutelage in the ways of civilization and modernity. The guidebooks, buttressed by charts and data of dubious authority, portray the peninsula as a site of unrivaled opportunity, where one could find untapped markets that would allow one to get rich—rapidly in the early years, slowly but steadily in later decades.

There was also substantial overlap among these texts, with each new book or article borrowing from and reinforcing the message of its predecessors. Samura Hachirō's *Tōkan no susume* (An Encouragement to Journey to Korea, 1909), for example, moves effortlessly among the personal, the national, and the international as it encourages the reader to stake a claim on the peninsula. Its fluency in these matters makes it the clear beneficiary of its predecessors' efforts. The first chapter is addressed to youth facing poor job prospects and attempts to convince them that the best chance of personal success is to get a fresh start in Korea. The peninsula is undeveloped compared to Japan, Samura suggests, and a youth facing a shrinking job market at home can easily make his fortune across the Tsushima Straits. At the same time, Samura argues that Korea lags behind Japan in its development, and so it is Japan's great responsibility to protect Korea from predatory Western powers and help it achieve independence.[7] Such self-serving rhetoric justifying colonialism was common among the many and varied texts reinforcing the call for an expansive Japanese presence in Asia.

More complex representations are produced in literary works, the primary reason being that the goals of most fiction writers are not the same as those actively promoting colonization of the continent. Fictional works tend to have a greater ethnographic interest in colonial lands than such nonfiction, even if they tend to be preoccupied with Japanese settlers as national subjects. The representation of the colonies as a space of opportunity, however, occupies a place of paramount importance in literature; this is the most crucial point of overlap between fiction and nonfiction. The ebb and flow of economic possibility punctuates Japanese literary texts, but the overarching portrait that emerges tends to cluster around a few paradigms during the final decade of the Meiji era. Interestingly, the two that dominate early on are at odds: colonial lands as a space of adventure or as a destination for those derailed from the pursuit of success on the home islands. Beginning with these two paradigms, this chapter offers a context for understanding them and a genealogy of the earliest colonial fiction in Japan up to the end of the Meiji period. Such stories are marginal to the main action of fictional works until the annexation of Korea in 1910. After this key moment in modern history, writers began increasingly to utilize the colonies as the main stage for a story. An investigation of these issues is important for this book because opportunity is one of the many manifestations of the larger discourse on *risshin shusse*, fusing capitalism and social mobility, and opportunity is the chief motive driving people—real and fictional—to the colonies.

The Margins of Japan, the Margins of the Novel

There was once a time when the fifty-year-old Japanese empire, though as rapacious as any, was deemed too short-lived to have had a lasting impact on the culture of the metropole or on literary production in colonial Asia. How times have changed! As a result of historiography since the 1990s, Japan's very modernization is now widely viewed as being inextricably connected to its emergence as an imperial power, not just to its sudden feeling, after 1853, of backwardness and belatedness in relation to the West.[8] Within the field of literary study, especially after 2000, scholarship on both sides of the Pacific has shed light on a plethora of transnational literary venues across colonial Asia and uncovered an imperium comprising a dynamic circulation of literary texts.[9] There is now a healthy questioning of the meaning and boundaries of "Japanese literature," which creates a welcome disjunction between literature and the national.

I wish to highlight the achievements of recent scholarship because the findings in this chapter support its conclusions to some extent, while also going against the trend in other ways, especially by scrutinizing the textual preoccupation with the Japanese national subject in colonial texts. In fact, we risk serious distortion of the archive in our rush to cast the national into the dustbin of history. After all, colonial and semicolonial lands were rare spaces in Japanese literature during the Meiji period.[10] Part of this is because the colonies were new spaces in the era, but Meiji literature is preoccupied with the national, even, I will argue, when its setting is outside Japan. Indeed, it would be surprising if it were otherwise. The rapid creation of national subjects who identify with the nation and its projects and who can help fortify the country in a dangerous imperialist world was a major effort of the officials and ideologues of the era.

Even if little Meiji literature is set outside Japan, colonial and semicolonial Asia gradually encroached upon the margins of many Meiji-era novels set in the metropole. At the time of the Russo-Japanese War, this ghostly (semi-) colonial presence was not crucial to the development of plot, but as if by unspoken agreement among metropolitan writers, the colonies gradually acquired a particular set of narrative functions. This newfound literary use for colonial lands can be found throughout the oeuvre of Shimazaki Tōson. In Tōson's *Ie* (The Family, 1910), the head of the titular Koizumi family, after being twice arrested for business dealings of questionable legality, has been shipped off to Manchuria by his younger brothers in something of familial coup d'état; after all, the siblings cannot allow the carefully cultivated family business to be ruined by the profligate eldest brother. These men have spent some time in Asia, and the second brother's ties to Korea are as extensive as they are mysterious. Japan's imperial reach is certainly not the centerpiece of the novel, which mostly focuses on the protagonist, Koizumi Sankichi, and his experiences as a newly married man and father. However, as Michael Bourdaghs has astutely observed, "The colonies serve in Tōson's fiction as a sort of dumping ground for problematic family members, those who have committed some violation that makes it impossible for them to remain at home."[11] What I would add to this important observation is that, in the case of Tōson's *Ie*, semicolonial Asia has this meaning for the ostensible family head, Minoru, yet it simultaneously has a different meaning for his upstart younger brother, Morihiko, for whom it is a space of business connections and valuable managerial experience. In one instance, it is a space of profit, in the other a destination for incorrigibles. This minor plot line, almost beyond the pale of novelistic interest in *Ie*, harbors differing connotations, and I want to suggest that the reason for the differing connotations is that Asia itself has been inscribed ambivalently within the domestic ideology of *risshin shusse* by the end of the Meiji era.

By focusing attention on such marginal elements of the Meiji novel, we can uncover a larger world of ambition and desire centered on colonial and semicolonial Asia, which similarly encroach on the edges of many of Natsume Sōseki's late novels. As in Tōson, these territories function as a narrative "dumping ground" for difficult or troubled family members, but even more, as a destination of last resort for characters unable to succeed in the home islands. To return to a novel discussed in chapter 3, consider *Mon*, published in the same year as Tōson's *Ie*, 1910. As we have already observed, Sōseki's novel focuses on the tragic history and current circumstances of Sōsuke and his wife Oyone. Yet within this resolutely domestic tale, the assassination of Itō Hirobumi by a Korean nationalist is a topic of discussion within the family, and there is talk of sending young Koroku to Korea or Manchuria to make a start in life if the resources to put him through university cannot be secured. Here the colonies would function as a kind of poor man's college. Fukatsu Ken'ichirō has noted that the Sōseki family member who tends to go abroad is the second son, who inherits neither the patriarchal mantel nor the family fortune.[12] Colonial Asia is represented as a space that, however undesirable relative to opportunity at home, may allow young Koroku to get some traction on a career, or at the very least acquire some business connections that may prove profitable in the future. Nonetheless, in keeping with the ambivalent quality of portraits of colonial Asia within the corpus of Meiji fiction, the hesitant, hopeful possibility of Koroku making a life overseas is undercut when Sōsuke's wealthy landlord, Sakai, refers pejoratively to these outlying lands as spaces fit only for "adventurers," which Sōseki writes using the Japanese *bōkensha*, glossing it with the English term.[13] In *Mon* use of this word expresses the landlord's exasperation with his own younger brother, who went overseas to make his fortune because he either would not or could not succeed in Japan. Colonial Asia occupies an additional dramatic function, for, toward the end of the novel, after years spent in Manchuria and even Mongolia, the landlord's brother returns to Tokyo accompanied by Yasui, the very man whom Sōsuke and Oyone betrayed in their youth.

To underscore an earlier point, it is important to keep in mind here that we are dealing with representations, not reality, but actual, historical conditions inform the various portraits of the emerging imperium within Meiji literature. To rehearse a point from chapter 3, many novels, such as *Mon*, reveal their rootedness in a specific historical situation: in the wake of the financial panic of 1907 and the subsequent recession, university graduates found it increasingly difficult with each passing year to find employment commensurate with their education, and even when they did, they were often confronted with falling wages. Consequently, many works dealing with youth at the end of the Meiji era, like most discussed in this chapter, dwell on poor job prospects.

Along with the inclusion of such specific contemporary references and anxieties, there is a larger, more fundamental picture to bring into focus. The reality of an emerging empire makes available new spaces for the literary imagination, and those spaces can be put to varied uses within narrative. I take this to be the most important lesson in Edward Said's influential book on *Culture and Imperialism*. Using a term coined by Raymond Williams, Said argues that novels, plays, and poems create a "structure of feeling" that supports the project of imperial expansion and the maintenance of that empire. As an expansive instrument of the imagination, the novel in particular provides a form in which "outlying territories are available for use, at will, at the novelist's discretion, usually for relatively simple purposes such as immigration, fortune, or exile."[14] Power is implicated in any representation, but even more basically for Said, dominated lands are taken for granted as simply being there. Similarly, Meiji authors will, more often than not, utilize such space as a dumping ground whenever the plot makes it necessary or compelling to do so. Yet the periphery can also function as an off-stage space from which characters such as Yasui can be brought into the narrative at dramatic moments.

The basic narrative function of the frontier does not change significantly during the Meiji era, even after we begin to see this territory become the center of attention in some fiction from the period. Consider Nakamura Seiko (1884–1974), a minor, largely forgotten writer associated with Japanese naturalism, who published a short story "Chōsen e, Chōsen kara" (To Korea, from Korea) in *Waseda bungaku* (Waseda Literature) in 1909. There is little in the way of plot in this brief, undistinguished tale. A narrator recounts select memories of two friends from his days in university, Kobayashi and Kurasawa. The title is a reference to these two men: the former is the one who goes to Korea and the latter the one who returns to Japan from the peninsula.[15]

The story opens with an unnamed first-person narrator recollecting a surprising letter he once had from a friend named Kobayashi, who had written, "Fate has temporarily brought me to this place."[16] "This place" is, of course, Korea, and we learn from the envelope that the specific locale is Wŏnsan, a small port town in the northeast. The letter, dated November 1908, gives rise to reminiscences about the Akita-born Kobayashi, who, though a university graduate, never settled into stable employment after leaving school. The story is not explicit on this point, but we are probably supposed to interpret Kobayashi's decision to go to Korea as an act of desperation stemming from an inability to find a reputable position at home after his graduation in 1907. In his letter, Kobayashi states that he plans to spend five or six years on the Korean peninsula and two or three years elsewhere (presumably Manchuria), which means that he would return to Japan a decade after his departure—with luck, as a wealthy man (2). Those plans have gone horribly awry. The narrator once tried to send some letters and packages to his old schoolmate at the address specified on the envelope, but they were returned. Kobayashi, it seems, has not merely changed his address; having gone to Korea to seek his fortune, he has vanished. The narrator then states, with some sense of resignation, that with the passing of the years, "eventually I forgot about him completely" (6).

The event that forces Kobayashi back into the narrator's thoughts is the return to Tokyo of another friend, Kurasawa. We learn that Kurasawa graduated from university around 1900 and, after passing through a number of unsatisfying jobs, departed Japan for Korea in either 1906 or 1907. After a period of silence, Kurasawa arrives out of the blue at a reunion in January 1909 of his university classmates, who have spent much of their time at the party boasting about their burgeoning careers since graduation. The mood is festive, until everyone notices the arrival of the dour Kurasawa; he has just returned to Japan from Seoul. The author is typically circumspect here, so we do not get much in the way of detail, but Kurasawa's somber mood suggests strongly that he has returned to the home islands out of a sense of resignation, having been unable to make his fortune on the peninsula. The narrator cannot help but notice that Kurasawa's fate seems ominously to foreshadow that of the younger Kobayashi. The implicit question at the heart of the story is: Will Kobayashi, too, return to Japan many years hence, a mere shadow of his former self like Kurasawa? Perhaps Kobayashi has already returned, unbeknownst to anyone, and is now living a hardscrabble life in Tokyo. The story concludes with the narrator noting that he never saw Kurasawa again after that day.

Nakamura thus overlays the story of the person who went to the peninsula with that of the person who just returned in order to make a larger statement about the bitter fate of those who go overseas in the hope of somehow making a success of themselves, thereby producing a very different portrait of the colonies than the journalistic discourse we examined earlier. The fate of his former university friends is a mere stimulus for the egotistical narrator, and the story is ultimately about his own anxiety:

> Kobayashi was confident in his letter: "I'll spend five or six years here [in Korea], then travel about for a couple years, before returning to Tokyo." But, thinking of Kurasawa's situation, I couldn't help but wonder about Kobayashi. It seems dangerous for people to have great expectations for the future. I began to grow fearful about my own fate. (12)

The overriding emotion here is fear: fear of the future and fear of failure. The narrator here inserts himself into a larger context with his two friends—the fate of youth after 1907—and glimpses a premonition of his own destiny in theirs.

Natsume Sōseki uses similar colonial references and a similar mood of suspense about a disappearance in the first part of his *Higan sugi made* (To the Spring Equinox and Beyond, 1912), an experimental novel consisting of interlinked stories focused on a central protagonist, Keitarō, who is a recent university graduate trying to find his way in life. He is thus at a similar age and confronting a similar dilemma about his future prospects as the narrator of Nakamura's story. The lands outside of Japan occupy an important place only in the first of the six stories, which concerns the relationship between Keitarō and Morimoto, a fellow boarder at our hero's rooming house. Morimoto leads a cheerfully dissolute existence, moving continually from one unconventional occupation to another, never holding onto any position for long. Such drifting holds a certain appeal for Keitarō, who dreams of post-graduation adventures. Mostly, though, Keitarō is attracted to the older man's command of the storyteller's art. Ever the consummate artist, Morimoto turns himself into something worthy of another's story (which then turns out to be the first part of our novel) when he disappears without a word. As Komori Yōichi has observed, the tropes of detective fiction dominate the entire text of

Higan sugi made.[17] Disappearance in the colonies, in particular, was an appealing tool for Meiji writers; at a practical level, the colonies can be put to dramatic use, but, because they are outside the narrative proper, there is no need to provide explanation. Characters can be dispatched from the story and then suddenly brought back into its pages, successful, broken in spirit, or anything in between. Certainly this is the case in Sōseki. After several months, Keitarō finds an envelope on his desk without the sender's name; opening it, he discovers that it is from Morimoto—he is now in Manchuria. After leaving Japan, Morimoto found employment in Dalian, a coastal city on the Kwantung peninsula, at a place with the fantastic name "Electric Park" (*Denki kōen*), suggesting that all the wonders of modern industry and entertainment are on display in one of Japan's most important overseas concessions.

Morimoto's lengthy letter relating his reasons for leaving Japan includes an ebullient coda in which he tries to coax Keitarō to northeast Asia. The crucial part, at least for our purposes, comes at the end of the letter:

> Manchuria is a fine place, especially Dalian. A talented youth like yourself could really develop this area. Why not just set aside all your obligations and come? I've made a lot of connections since arriving here, especially among the people at the South Manchuria Railway, so I can see that you're taken care of when you get here.[18]

Morimoto has disappeared and reappeared, like Kurasawa in Nakamura's story, but Morimoto's Manchuria, as a place of adventure and upward mobility, is the opposite of the Korea that appears in Nakamura's tale. Morimoto's Manchuria is a seductive, virginal place awaiting development by the ambitious youth of Meiji Japan. This is certainly consonant with Manchuria's dominant representation in Japan as a realm of modern wonder par excellence, the "modernist utopia" described by Louise Young. The difficult job situation for university graduates shadows Sōseki's characters, too, but Morimoto's is a tale of someone who goes to the colonies and succeeds.

Whether imagined as a space of danger or as a space of opportunity (and it tends to be one of these two), the key to understanding such representations is *risshin shusse*. In Nakamura's story, the Korean peninsula is made available within the literary imagination as a destination of last resort for those unable to succeed on the home islands. Yet it is also imagined as a space that manifests a false promise, as the fate of Kurasawa implies. The fact that Kobayashi disappeared once he reached Korea magnifies the ominous portrait of the peninsula and the narrator's skeptical assessment of the chances of success there. This portrait of the emerging empire is reversed in Morimoto's enthusiastic letter to Keitarō. Here Manchuria's promise is that of the open horizon, with the vast prairies of northeast Asia functioning as metaphors for untapped potential and unlimited possibility. The emerging empire on the continent is once again made available to the literary imagination in the context of *risshin shusse*; the difference is that in the latter it is a place in which society's restless dreamers have the hope of finding the life unavailable to them in the straitlaced home islands after the Russo-Japanese War.

What are we to make of these two representations, of the peninsula as a space of danger and of the continent as a space of adventure? It would be rash to hastily equate Korea with anxiety and Manchuria with enticement in Meiji Japan; a broader perspective shows that the collective portrait of colonial and semicolonial Asia does not break so evenly across old borders, for the representations could just as easily have been swapped or given still other overtones, depending on the author and the text. We recall that Samura Hachirō's *Tōkan no susume* is an exuberant treatise on the supposedly unbounded opportunities on the Korean peninsula, and this encouragement came mere months after Itō Hirobumi had been assassinated while overseas. Unsurprisingly, texts that try to encourage Meiji youth to start a new life in the colonies tend to equate Korea and Manchuria—using the portmanteau words "Mankan" or "Manchō"—and to distinguish them from other settler destinations, such as Taiwan, Micronesia (Nan'yō), Hawaii, and the countries of South America (Nanbei). Korea does not simply signal failure and Manchuria success. We are in a better position if we allow for a complex portrait of a space that can harbor both trepidation and adventure to different degrees.

Colonial and semicolonial lands are portrayed as the destinations of two fairly distinct character types. The first is well represented by Kurasawa and Kobayashi. Kurasawa has made it through all the hurdles of the educational system, even graduating from university, but lacks the talent, the connections, and perhaps even the drive to brave the Darwinian struggle, secure a good position, and thereby advance in society. His failure manifests itself physically, for in the narrator's description, Kurasawa "draped his threadbare uniform over his thin body, always had his hair cropped short, and, though his haggard face couldn't be called ugly, his pale countenance left little impression on others" (2). Kobayashi is sketched with "unkempt hair, left dry and scraggly," and a "frightfully emaciated face" (9). The second personality type is well represented by Morimoto, the boisterous, slothful figure for whom the workaday world with its schedules and tedium is anathema. An incorrigible bachelor, past thirty and still living in a rooming house, Morimoto is the antithesis of the ambitious youth of the Meiji era. Yet, there is also a seductive aura of mystery around him, and rumors of his having had several short-lived relationships with women make him, if anything, even more of an interesting figure for the still inexperienced Keitarō. For Morimoto, the lack of stable employment is something to boast about, and he regales Keitarō with stories of "the world's most carefree life"—in other words, his own. Morimoto is the heedless adventurer (the word is used in *Higan sugi made*, where it has more positive connotations than it does in the landlord's mouth in *Mon*), whereas the Kurasawa-Kobayashi type is the untalented, feckless youth. What accounts for the bullish portrait of Manchuria and the bearish representation of Korea? Quite simply, Morimoto went to the former and Kobayashi to the latter. Had their destinations been swapped, the representations would undoubtedly have been reversed accordingly. Wherever these two character types venture in the growing Japanese imperium, they are protagonists of different narratives, with Kurasawa-Kobayashi living the life of failed expectations, in contrast to Morimoto, who seems ready to strike out on any adventure. I will call the first paradigm a colonial tragedy and the second a colonial romance.[19]

These two narratives, inhabited by different character types, are complexly positioned in relation to the chronotope of success; they compel us to account for the way empire impacts this chronotope. As we have seen in the previous chapters, Tokyo was placed at the center of a series of hierarchical concentric circles stretching from the capital to the hinterlands of Japan. By the end of the Meiji era, after successive wars with Qing China and imperial Russia, a new ring had been added to this series of imaginary circles: an emerging Japanese empire. It is clear from the texts examined thus far that (semi-) colonial Asia is at the bottom of the hierarchy of these imaginary spaces. In terms of the temporal axis of narrative, the youth who strikes out for the outlying territories is one whose smooth life course to success has been interrupted, his dreams of fortune deferred. His only hope is to leave the home islands and attempt to make a go of things overseas. This time spent in the colonies becomes something of a liminal time. If a character achieves success on the continent, we are in the narrative archetype of the colonial romance; if he fails in this endeavor, we are confronted with a colonial tragedy. The continent is an important narrative space for the unfolding of these two archetypal narratives because of its structural ambivalence: it is ideologically incorporated as part of the nation even as it is kept separate as a space of the Other.

Before Japan's annexation of Korea in 1910, literary narratives only gestured toward these outlying lands, putting such territories to limited imaginative use. Even Nakamura's story is more concerned with the narrator's fears than with the peninsula itself. The Kobayashis and Morimotos of late Meiji fiction are not the protagonists; they merely haunt the margins of the narrative universe, barely affecting the development of the plot. The tales of these drifters and adventurers are left without the finishing details, and so their narratives remain potential stories, which the writers chose not to flesh out in detail. This does not mean that they do not serve a purpose. The primary function of these two character types must be attributed to a particular novelistic need: to make available figures who allow for comparison and contrast with the upwardly mobile metropolitan heroes who are the main focus of the narratives of Meiji. But in a clear example of the impact of politics on literature, Japanese writers found greater potential narrativity in the emerging imperium after Korea's annexation and began filling out these possible stories by taking the reader across the waters to colonial Asia itself.

The Novel's Travels in Korea and Manchuria

Takahama Kyoshi's *Chōsen* (Korea) is among the earliest metropolitan novels set in the colonies. The first half was serialized in seventy installments in both the *Tokyo nichi-nichi shinbun* and its Kansai cousin, *Osaka mainichi shinbun*, from June 19 to August 27, 1911. After a one-day hiatus, the second half, also in seventy installments, appeared only in the Tokyo paper from August 29 until November 25. Then, after significant revisions and alterations, including the excision of many scenes, a shorter book version consisting of forty-eight chapters of widely varying lengths appeared in February 1912, in the waning months of the Meiji emperor's reign. The book was published by Jitsugyō no Nihon Sha, whose flagship magazine, *Jitsugyō no Nihon* (Entrepreneurial Japan) was, along with *Seikō* (Success), one of the major nodes in the expanding Meiji media culture from which the discourse on *risshin shusse* was disseminated. This is, to be sure, an unorthodox publication history. The usual explanation is that the novel was not popular, so the newspaper tried to cut its losses by serializing the second half only in the market with the greater population. This is certainly plausible, especially considering that *Chōsen* is a wearying read at times, particularly the second half, but the readership of serial novels is extremely difficult for literary criticism to measure.

Kyoshi (1874–1959) was a major literary talent in his day and remains a canonical figure even now. More so than his fiction, however, his reputation rests on his haiku and, still more, on his successful stewardship of the literary magazine *Hototogisu* (The Cuckoo) after the death of cofounder Masaoka Shiki in 1902. In his capacity as head of a prominent literary journal during the first half of the twentieth century, Kyoshi was a major arbiter of taste in prewar poetry and in prewar literature more broadly, especially among the majority conservative stream of modern haiku. (His estranged friend and former colleague, Kawahigashi Hekigōtō [1873–1937], stands at the head of the minority experimental stream.) For a short time at the end of the Meiji era and during the early 1910s, Kyoshi, still uncertain that poetry was his true calling, was experimenting with fiction writing, in imitation of his friend Natsume Sōseki, much of whose early work had appeared in serialized form in *Hototogisu*.[20] Among Kyoshi's most experimental works of this period of his literary career was *Chōsen*.[21]

We are interested here less in Kyoshi's personal authorial stamp, and still less in judgments about the quality of the novel, than in the way he inherited and modified the colonial tropes uncovered in the previous section. With the publication of *Chōsen*, the colonies move from a marginal space filled with potential stories to the main stage of novelistic action and thus a story in itself. Things become more complicated with this historic movement of narrative action, but much remains the same. *Chōsen*, in fact, directly inherits the two character types we examined and includes them both in its pages. The Kurasawa-Kobayashi type, who haunts the colonial tragedy, is embodied in the sullen figure of Tsurumi Keinosuke, who shadows the narrator throughout the tale. Keinosuke exists at the extreme fringe of literary and artistic culture, and we first encounter him as a member of an itinerant theatrical troupe, which moves about the peninsula, entertaining the Japanese expatriate community wherever it can find them (387–88). Keinosuke specializes in female roles in these old-fashioned Kabuki-style plays, further emasculating him (398–99). Despite his marginal position, he dreams of cutting his teeth on the peninsula, gathering novel artistic material, and returning to Japan to become a famous writer. This desire is simply the literary equivalent of those of Kurasawa and Kobayashi, and the reader is given no indication that Keinosuke has the talent to fulfill his dreams. Quite the opposite: the aspiring writer asks the narrator-protagonist to critique his manuscript and gets back pages overflowing with critical ink (399). The message here is clear: Keinosuke has no future as a writer, an actor, or anything else. The Morimoto type, who stars in the colonial romance, is embodied in the figure of Ishibashi Gōzō. Kyoshi keeps Ishibashi an enigma, but there are plenty of hints that he is engaged in adventures of a political kind on the peninsula. He is often called a *shishi* (man of high purpose), a word used to refer to those romanticized imperial loyalists who were instrumental in bringing down the Tokugawa shogunate. Ishibashi is a wanted man on the home islands and has thus come to Korea to continue his subversive activities (409). Like Keinosuke, Ishibashi drifts in and out of the narrative, but his activities are described as "secret" (475, 477). With his slothful figure, obsession with games of strategy (especially *go*), boisterous laughter, steady drinking, and bon vivant personality, he is the very figure of the colonial adventurer, like Morimoto, but he is given a slightly dangerous mien. Kyoshi was apparently well read in the kind of fiction we examined in the previous section, for toward the end of the novel, after all the characters have relocated to P'yŏngyang, he includes the narrator's musings about Ishibashi and Keinosuke in a way that seems to link his own work directly to previous fiction: he hyperbolically contrasts Ishibashi, "who as a *shishi* bore responsibility for the realm on his shoulders," and Keinosuke, "the passive type leading a drifter's life" (478). Kyoshi fills in some of the potential stories surrounding these two character types, but still keeps much a mystery and continues the motifs of disappearance and reappearance from earlier fiction.

As different as they are, each functions as the narrator's doppelganger, embodying alternative fates for him; and the improbable reappearance of both characters every time the narrative shifts to a new locale on the peninsula serves to convey an image of the three as being fatefully connected. Changes between the serialized and book versions, however, complicate the matter. In the serial version, the opening installment specifies that the narrator and his wife have lost their child, but the statement that they decided to leave Japan because of grief on the tenth anniversary of the incident fails to convince as a motivation for traveling to Korea.[22] Why Korea, after all? Perhaps Kyoshi was aware of this, for in the book version he excised the references to the death of the child.[23] There is another, more convincing explanation for the narrator's trip to Korea in the serial version: the narrator is a novelist who has lost the recognition for his work within the *bundan* or in society at large and has traveled to the peninsula because of his growing disillusionment with the literary life:

> Could it be that I've simply lost all interest and pride in literature? Even if the world had enthusiastically greeted my newer work, as they had in the past, would I still have lost my interest and pride in literature? Regardless, it's perhaps only natural that the current society would not embrace my novels. I'm completely separated from society now.[24]

In other words, in keeping with the representation of the peninsula in fiction, Korea is also a dumping ground for failed writers. This is far more interesting as a motivation for travel, for it means that Ishibashi's adventures might have the capacity to provide materials for a captivating narrative and that Keinosuke can function as a reminder of what might happen if the novel fails to capture an audience. However, the scenes in which the narrator discusses his background as a writer and his doubts about his talents and his position in the world of letters back home were dramatically reduced or excised completely from the book version. With little explicit motivation given in the book, the only available explanation for the narrator's travels is to gather materials for a forthcoming novel of the colonies, which then turns out to be the one we are reading.

As this discussion of the three major male characters hints, there is little in the way of plot in Kyoshi's novel, which simply features a narrator-protagonist traveling through the peninsula, seeing the sights in Japan's latest colonial acquisition, observing cultural differences between Japan and Korea, and falling into the orbit of a handful of eccentric characters: Tsurumi Keinosuke and Ishibashi Gōzō, of course, but also the maid Okyō, the geisha Ofude, the *kisaeng* (courtesan-entertainer) Sotan, the "native informant" (fluent in Japanese) referred to as Kō-san (Hong in Korean), and an assortment of minor characters, mostly Japanese. The sights include restaurants and teahouses in the backstreets of Seoul, mountain temples on the outskirts of the capital, the natural sights around the northern city of P'yŏngyang, and old battlefields from the Sino-Japanese War, among other locations. If there is not much in terms of plot, there is even less in the way of character development, and Kyoshi relies on coincidence in an ostentatious way, as the entire cast of characters keeps disappearing and reappearing with each change of locale, their motives and itinerary left largely to the reader's imagination. With few hints as to character motivations in either version, any discussion of the matter is pure speculation—that is, until we notice that Kyoshi has folded all of these characters into a larger narrative of the Japanese settler community, which does receive detailed attention. It will be our focus here, and my reading of Kyoshi's novel will turn on how to interpret this group as a whole.

What *Chōsen* adds to the fiction we examined in the previous section is the direct confrontation with and representation of cultural and ethnic difference on foreign soil. Because of this, there is an inevitable interest in description of the foreign culture, that is, a need to document and catalogue difference. To this concern we can add the issue of novelistic form, for such texts tend to take on the dimensions of a travelogue when the stage is an unfamiliar place, and this, of course, is closely related to the ethnographic interest of colonial novels. I am by no means the first to note these two elements, though I hope to contribute to this discussion through an examination of Japanese texts. What an analysis of Kyoshi's work tellingly contributes to colonial studies is yet another ethnographic interest: a desire to document the lives of the Japanese settler community in colonial Asia and to catalogue the similarities and differences between them and those at home. If we stipulate that ethnography produces figures of alterity, such figures cannot be limited to national, racial, or ethnic Others, but also includes domestic Others. When Japanese fictional works begin to take the colonies as their setting, they inevitably become ethnographic in important ways, but while their attention is drawn to ethnic and cultural difference, such novels are equally, if not even more, concerned with fellow countrymen in colonial lands. Here, too, the key to understanding the multiple ethnographic designs of the colonizer's fiction lies in the discourse on *risshin shusse* and especially in the ways in which Japanese settlers are coded as failures within that discourse.

We can begin by drawing on the resources of previous critical work. Kyoshi's novel has been the subject of only a half dozen essays, but such work has gained increased sophistication with the maturation of postcolonial theory in the past two decades in Japan (as far as I know, *Chōsen* has never before been discussed in English). Because *Chōsen* reads like a travelogue as much as a novel, with descriptions of postcard-like venues around the peninsula prominent, the most common way to approach it is through the lens of *shasei*, the technique of sketching we examined in chapter 1. This is not an arbitrary critical strategy, for Kyoshi was, in fact, a strong advocate of *shasei* and even extended the theorization of it begun by Shiki. Takane Nakayuki, in his reading of *Chōsen*, suggestively links Kyoshi's interest in sketching to Japan's expanding empire by arguing that *shasei* requires new territory to artistically conquer, and thus the colonies make for an important new venue.[25] Noting that Korea's politics are emphasized in the novel and that minor characters such as Ishibashi are engaged in mysterious political activities, Mizuno Tatusrō reads *Chōsen* as perched between the imperatives of *shasei* and the inheritance of the political novel from an earlier generation.[26] In an essay published that same year, Mitani Norimasa similarly interprets the novel as being pulled between *shasei* and romance (here meaning adventure).[27] Even with their varying approaches to literary criticism, all three scholars see Kyoshi's novel as being uneasily poised between sketching and something else.

The reason for this similarity of views is that all three rely on Kyoshi's explanation of his novel, which he penned for *Hototogisu* in January 1912, presumably in order to garner attention for the book version, which was due out the following month. This "preface" or "introduction" (not in the book version) consists merely of two short paragraphs, suggesting that Kyoshi did not invest much time in his task. The first paragraph reveals that *Chōsen* was based on Kyoshi's own experiences on the peninsula the previous year, thus promoting the authenticity of the novel's portrait of Korea. The second discusses the writer's craft:

> I would also like to say a word about technique. While being aware of the incompatibility between the objectivity of *shasei* [sketching] and the subjectivity of the *shōsetsu* [novel], I also believed that relying solely on objective depiction could never yield an art of a great subjectivity. In this sense,

the work that will be published is part of the story of the battle between *shasei* and the *shōsetsu*.[28]

Kyoshi had inherited Shiki's concern with the importance of *shasei* in haiku and had even turned it into something of a dictate for his own followers. At the same time, he was turning his attention (temporarily as it turned out) to fiction. He contrasts the two forms using the ideas of objectivity and subjectivity respectively, but he hints that his larger objective is some kind of higher interpretive perspective (which he confusingly calls "great subjectivity," or *daishukan*). We can gain a little clarity by noting that he seems to be following Tayama Katai here, who had argued for a similar dialectic in his critical writings and had even coined the phrase *daishizen no shukan* (subjectivity of great nature) in 1901 to indicate such a higher-order perspective.[29]

The "preface" is hardly a well-articulated or convincing piece of literary theory, and readers can be forgiven for thinking that Kyoshi was cynically trying to promote the book version of an unsuccessful serial novel among readers of the high-minded *Hototogisu* by grasping onto some of the key terms within the literary debates in the wake of Japanese naturalism. Rather than dismiss this important paratext, much less insinuate that previous critics are wrong to focus on it, I would like to suggest that through recourse to claims of objectivity and subjectivity Kyoshi was trying to write something that was beginning to appear as a practice all around the imperial world at the turn of the century, including that of Japanese in Korea, but which he is unable to name in 1912: an ethnography.[30] At the same time, he is trying to further his ambitions as a novelist and promote his ideal of *shasei*, here in prose rather than verse.

In a comparative study of the novelist Joseph Conrad (1857–1924) and the anthropologist Bronislaw Malinowski (1884–1942), James Clifford writes, "Ethnographies are both like and unlike novels. But in an important general way the two experiences [of Conrad and Malinowski] enact the process of fictional self-fashioning in relative systems of culture and language that I call ethnographic."[31] Clifford is thus able to bring the two forms together through recourse to the postcolonial critique of ethnography by drawing on the notion (at the time new, now widely accepted) that writing the other is also the writing of the self and that figures of alterity are, in fact, extremely useful, even necessary, for self-definition and self-fashioning.

In another essay, Clifford argues that ethnography, as it emerged in the late nineteenth century and became a formal methodology by the early 1920s (and before it was subjected to postcolonial critique beginning in the 1970s), is characterized by the paradigm of "participant-observation." He elaborates:

> "Participant observation" serves as a shorthand for a continuous tacking between the "inside" and the "outside" of events: on the one hand grasping the sense of specific occurrences and gestures emphatically, on the other stepping back to situate these meanings in wider contexts. Particular events thus acquire deeper or more general significance, structural rules, and so forth. Understood literally, participant observation is a paradoxical, misleading formula, but it may be taken seriously if reformulated in hermeneutic terms as a dialectic of experience and interpretation.[32]

Inside and outside, participant and observer, experience and interpretation: these are alternative ways for describing exactly what Kyoshi is attempting to formulate in his preface as a dialectic of novelistic (subjective) and sketching (objective) techniques, with the goal of illuminating a wider context (*daishukan*). Like previous Japanese critics, I, too, will read *Chōsen* as split, but split like all ethnography between participation and observation. Kyoshi's product could be called an ethnographic novel exhibiting *shasei*-style description. The presence of a first-person narrator is crucial here, for the "I" (*yo*, the classic personal pronoun of *shasei*) who is the subject of narration experiences life on the peninsula and attempts to interpret that experience within "relative systems of culture and language." Connecting Kyoshi's anthropological leanings with the discourse on ambition, we would have to call the novel an ethnography of failure—that is, an ethnography of the losers in the Darwinian struggle of *risshin shusse*, and an analysis of that which was left unarticulated in the fiction we examined in the previous section: the colonies as a dumping ground within the cultural imaginary.

If we are to read Kyoshi's novel as inhabited by an ethnographic imagination, we need to know what informs that imagination. A recent monograph by E. Taylor Atkins on the anthropological work that began in earnest in Korea upon annexation can provide us with a horizon of expectations with which to take the measure of Kyoshi's text. The crucial difference between Japanese colonial ethnography and that of most imperial powers is that the Japanese in Korea could not convincingly rely on race as a figure of difference. Instead, Japanese ethnographers concentrated on a subordinate feature of Western ethnography and predicated difference in time, whereby Korea represented a place of racial and ethnic similarity, but one that was located at an earlier temporal stage in the development of civilization. The task of ethnography was to reconcile similarity of race and ethnicity with difference in time; the result of these efforts was an assertion that "a primordial 'Japan' survived on the Korean peninsula, and could be rediscovered, perhaps even 'salvaged' through anthropological diligence."[33] Atkins calls this construction the "primitive self." As anthropologists of the past twenty years have convincingly demonstrated, ethnography is also always auto-ethnography, generating self-representations through recourse to figures of difference.

Kyoshi is preoccupied with such figures. Since race is unavailable to Japanese in colonial Korea as a marker of difference, the narrator is especially careful to note other exterior markers, especially hairstyle and clothing, with particular attention devoted to the predominance of white clothing among Koreans. As Atkins notes, this was a sartorial obsession among early Japanese ethnographers working on the peninsula, precisely because it was the most visible sign of difference. In addition, Kyoshi relies heavily on the trope of the "primitive self" by having his narrator-protagonist note that many of the cultural rituals that occur in Korea are reminiscent of Japan's distant past. Read against the larger anthropological record, we can see that Kyoshi's novel shares much terrain with the colonial ethnographies, but it is important to note that the work is attuned to heterogeneity as well, for the narrator is eager to note class and regional differences within the Korean population.

The narrator is also deeply interested in the Japanese on the peninsula. He is quick to discern in the landscape the presence of Japanese homes mixed in with the native dwellings, and his eye effortlessly picks Japanese nationals out of the Korean crowds. He notes the differing regional accents of his fellow Japanese and, like an anthropologist in the field, invariably inquires into the circumstances that brought such people to Korea, making some parts of the narrative sound like transcripts of oral interviews. At the same time, the narrator is invested in discovering forms of cultural hybridity. One of his favorite words is *Chōsenka*, which he uses to indicate how Japanese settlers gradually become more like Koreans when living amongst them. Both the dialogue and the narrative discourse utilize Japanese words with Korean language glosses (including pejoratives) with increasing frequency as the novel proceeds. To add to this list, female figures are available to yield an erotic tinge to the ethnographic gaze, and we have the *kisaeng* Sotan and the geisha Ofude filling this role for Korea and Japan respectively, both of whom are tantalizingly held out as being sexually available.

The most effective way to illustrate Kyoshi's twin interests in Korea and the Japanese who live there is to examine in some detail the movement of the narrator-protagonist through the peninsula, for his travel through the territory of the ethnic Other is, in a colonial situation, always travel through territory already inhabited by Japanese as well. Both the book version and the serialized version of the novel begin in Shimonoseki, a port city on the southwestern tip of Japan's main island of Honshū, with the protagonist and his wife waiting for the ship that will ferry them across the straits to the peninsula. Because of its proximity, this city was the major point of embarkation for Japanese going to Korea, but it also occupies a prominent place in the history of imperialism in East Asia, and this adds layers of meaning to the locale. Before the Meiji Restoration, the city was part of Chōshū domain, the home of many samurai who were not sympathetic to the Tokugawa regime's attempt to accommodate the Western powers and their efforts to open Japan up to trade. In the summer of 1863, antiforeign Chōshū activists attacked foreign ships passing through the Shimonoseki Straights between Honshū and Kyūshū and were in turn bombarded by a coalition of British, French, and Dutch ships in a series of altercations during June.[34] In the modern era, the city was the site for the signing of the treaty that ended the Sino-Japanese War in 1895. Not only did the treaty formally cede Taiwan to Japan; it also demanded that China recognize the independence of Korea, thus beginning the process of Japanese encroachment on the peninsula, which would eventually result in annexation fifteen years later.[35] It is from such a storied place that *Chōsen* launches.

Whereas the first installment of Kyoshi's novel is set at this symbolic port in the home islands, the second installment (and second chapter) moves us quickly to Pusan, a major port city on Korea's southern coast and one that had seen a Japanese trading presence since the mid-fifteenth century. By the time of Korea's annexation it had become a sizable city and the primary disembarkation point for Japanese traveling to the peninsula; indeed many never moved on, and it is estimated that in 1910 half the population of the city was Japanese.[36] On the third day of serialization (which corresponds to the third chapter), Kyoshi has whisked us by train to Taegu, a large regional market town that was an important destination for Japanese commercial goods.[37] The reader is allowed to pause in Taegu for several installments before Kyoshi has moved us on again, this time to the Korean capital, with the train ride occupying the seventh installment (the book's brief fourth chapter) and our arrival at Seoul opening the eighth (chapter 5 in the book version). By 1910, Seoul had the largest Japanese settlement on the peninsula, with most of the Japanese population concentrated at the foot of Mount Namsan, where the Japanese governor-general's offices were located, or in the Honmachi district downtown.[38] Although we do follow the protagonist on some sightseeing excursions to nearby areas, the novel's action remains based in Seoul for the remainder of the first half. We spend most of the second half in P'yŏngyang, where all the characters have relocated for the novel's second act (the seventy-first installment in the newspaper, the twenty-ninth chapter of the book). P'yŏngyang was an important northern base for the Japanese military and also housed a sizable civilian population, which had initially settled there to provide those troops with services and grew from there.[39] The action remains based in P'yŏngyang and its pictorial outskirts until the final installment (and the final chapter in the book version), in which we are given two letters from Ofude addressed to the narrator. She has traveled north with Keinosuke and Ishibashi, leaving the narrator and his wife behind in P'yŏngyang. The first letter was written at Sinŭiju, a small Korean town in the far northwest on the Yalu River, the second in Andong, on the Manchurian side of the border; Ofude reports that she is planning to get on a train the next day and travel to Mukden (Shenyan), thereby leaving the Korean peninsula far behind for the interior of northeastern China.

We should take note of the geographical boundaries of the text, which are confined to the Korean peninsula, but bookended by a port city in Japan and the border between Korea and Manchuria. The narrative begins in familiar Japanese territory, passes through most of the major Japanese communities on the peninsula, and concludes with the departure for a place that in 1912 would have been sparsely inhabited by Japanese migrants. Whereas the action unfolds within this carefully circumscribed physical boundary and sense of place, what we might call the text's geographical imagination is not so circumscribed. The protagonist and several of the minor characters keep repeating a particular mantra, "kita e, kita e" (to the north, to the north; 388, 440, 480, 499, 500), almost as if motion itself were the main point of the novel. Indeed, as if to make this subtext more explicit, in a few places in the serialized version the phrase is "Manshū e, Manshū e" (to Manchuria, to Manchuria). Furthermore, as we noted, Kyoshi does not provide us with significant motivations for the travels of any of the characters, except for Ishibashi and Keinosuke, the former because of political activities, the latter moving with his troupe, but even these are vague. We can be excused for thinking that, whatever few words Kyoshi may put in the mouths of his characters as motivating their travel to and movements throughout Korea and into Manchuria, from a formal perspective, his primary interest seems to be to map the Japanese presence in Asia, to document the hybrid culture resulting from the intertwining of cultures, and to see how far north one can travel before the literary imagination is unable to encompass the geography of imperial ambition.

Importantly, this journey also follows a route of industrial development, for once we as readers arrive on the peninsula, we travel with the protagonist by train to each succeeding place, and it is the train that carries Ofude beyond the Korean border and beyond the narrative proper into Manchuria. The train is given significant symbolic weight early in the novel, where the narrator describes his first impressions of the quintessential colonial vehicle as he departs Taegu for Seoul: "I was thrilled by the train, violently shaking as it traveled further and further north. I thought of the power of postwar Japan [post-Russo-Japanese War], which had built these iron tracks for speed and strength" (389). The train itself receives similar reveries: "It was something that had to be called colonial—completely practical, without decoration or amenities, just a gigantic iron shell" (389). Later, as the protagonist and his wife board the train for P'yŏngyang, it is described as "a weapon" that was "ever running north" (440). As Steven Ericson has discussed, the train in Japan, as in other industrializing lands, became a powerful symbol of technological progress and industrial prowess; the railroad was also much more than symbolic, for it facilitated social and national integration, both in reality, through the movement of goods and people, and as a form of imagined community.[40] Within the colonies, the train was also a potent symbol of might and of Japan's self-perceived mission of modernizing the peninsula and other parts of Asia. Furthermore, the locales for the action of the novel are hardly chosen at random: Pusan, Taegu, Seoul, P'yŏngyang, Sinŭiju, Andong, and Mukden all lie on the newly developed rail network connecting Korea and Manchuria.

Peter Duus, in his thorough study of the Japanese encroachment on Korea, has observed that "few projects excited the imperialist imagination more than railway construction."[41] Through a combination of luck and persistence during the early twentieth century, Japan managed to wrest control of the concessions for the peninsula's major lines. These included the Seoul-Inch'ŏn line (completed in 1900), connecting the capital to the nearby port city on the west coast (which does not appear in Kyoshi's novel), and the Seoul-Pusan line (1904), which a Japanese conglomerate, financed by public and private funds, completed on the eve of the war with Russia. The third major artery was the Seoul-Ŭiju (or more properly, Sinŭiju) line (1906), which connected the Korean capital to the Manchurian border to the north.[42] Once Japan's encroachment on northeast Asia began in earnest, Manchuria also became the site of frenetic railway development through the auspices of the South Manchuria Railway, which occupied an unusual position between a public company and a government agency. The organization was established in 1906 and was built on the infrastructure inherited as part of Japan's victory over Russia the previous year, thereafter becoming a highly visible agent of the colonization of northeast Asia, a prime example of what many term "railway colonialism." The main line connected Xinjing in central Manchuria to the port city of Dalian in the Kwantung territory (Morimoto's destination in *Higan sugi made*), but also important was the ancillary line connecting Mukden and Andong, which lay just across the Yalu River from the Sinŭiju terminus of the trunk line traversing the Korean peninsula. The Mukden-Andong route was laid over the military's temporary light rail and was completed in 1911 (which Ofude explicitly mentions), thereafter connecting Manchuria and the entire Korean peninsula.[43] While these train lines excited the imperialist imagination, it is also important to underscore the novelty of the project; after all, at the time of annexation, the trunk line traversing the peninsula, supported by branch lines connecting the main artery to the major port cities on the eastern and western coasts, was still quite new.

What excites the imperialist imagination is also bound to excite the literary imagination when the stage is the colonies. As we saw, Japan's growing empire allowed for the literary use of outlying territories as a narrative dumping ground whenever it was convenient. The development of a rail network throughout colonial Asia allowed the literary imagination to turn the colonies to still other ends. The train symbolizes the freedom of movement within colonial Asia on the part of the protagonist of Kyoshi's novel and blurs the boundaries between formerly sovereign areas. Ofude memorably dramatizes this by her choice of wording in describing her move across the Yalu River into Manchuria: "At last, a foreign country" (*Iyoiyo mō gaikoku ne*, 500). The train thus helps construct an image of the colonies as a singular territory unified under the Japanese banner through industrial development, even as it still retains traces of older national boundaries and of the older national cultures inhabiting them. In the imagination of this novel, Korea is already part of Japan; now it is semicolonial Manchuria that defines Japan's new national border.[44]

Kyoshi's treatment of the train exemplifies an aspect of imperial travel writing uncovered by Simon Gikandi in his study of how the culture of Englishness depends on colonial figures of alterity. Gikandi points out that imperial touring is always a "re-touring," for the traveler from the metropole cannot but see the colonies otherwise than through the lens of sedimented discourses and inherited ideologies. Travel, in fact, more typically confirms those preexisting ideas than unsettles them, and thus the typical colonial adventurer reassuringly "returns home" (both physically and mentally) by traversing the colonies. Even when a travelogue seems to challenge stereotypical representations of the colonies, it is still enmeshed in other metropolitan ideologies.[45] We might acknowledge, for example, that Kyoshi's protagonist avoids caricature with his attention to the heterogeneity of Korean culture and that he seems more willing to be "unsettled" than his English counterpart, but Kyoshi's treatment of the railroad shows that he does not escape the dominant ideologies of his day, for both the train and the industrial infrastructure that makes its movement possible are always represented as exemplifying Japan's growing power, technological prowess, and ingenuity. Korea becomes, in this representation, the logical extension of Japan's modernization. Even if Kyoshi can be credited with a more nuanced view of peninsular culture than the broader journalistic discourse in Japan, his celebratory treatment of the train is ultimately an affirmation not just of nationalism but of "railway colonialism," too; and the perpetual northward movement of the novel's action along its rails symbolically appropriates the entire peninsula as Japanese territory. Indeed, the mantra of perpetual northward movement threatens to figuratively bring all of northeastern China into the Japanese imperium, thereby implicating the literary imagination in the acquisition and maintenance of empire in the ways Gikandi, Said, and others have highlighted.

On another level, there is a kind of mimicking of the protagonist's northward journey in the phenomenon of serialization, which allows us to draw connections between imperialism and media culture. If we are readers encountering the work day-in and day-out as it appeared in the pages of either the Osaka or Tokyo newspaper, we never quite know when we will pack our metaphorical bags and travel with the protagonist to a new destination farther north. Indeed, the text has conditioned us in this respect by whisking us to a new location in almost every installment early on. We may not know when we will move farther north, but we know it will happen, probably repeatedly. Furthermore, given that there is little in the way of plot and that the main interest of the text seems to lie in ethnographic description, there is nothing formally preventing the text from proceeding north forever. The fact of empire has provided an entirely new space available for literary exploration, and newspaper serialization has ensured that this exploration could potentially continue without end. The only things limiting the serial expansion of the text to match Japan's imperial expansion are the boundaries of the empire, which does indeed have limits in 1912, amorphous though they may be, and perhaps the interest of the newspaper's readers, which is probably confined to the areas of Asia populated by Japanese settlers. Still, serialization is closely allied to the imagining of empire and to the literary service provided by that empire. The mantra of continual northward motion is linked to the promise, inherent in serialization, to expect a new installment of the story the next day; in the process, the novel will periodically move the reader to a new and exotic location farther north, which, coupled with the ethnographic interest of the novel, promises to yield new insights into Japan's colonial territories and its inhabitants, further naturalizing the imperialist mission.

To engage in our own slight detour, it is interesting that each installment of the novel during its serialization was accompanied by either an illustration or a photograph, and sometimes by a combination of the two. (The 1912 book includes no photographs and only an occasional illustration.) The presence of both types of images in a single ongoing narrative was certainly unusual for the time. As was customary in the case of serialized novels, the illustrations allude to specific characters or events in the narrative. These illustrations are often meant to serve an ethnographic function by giving the reader a sense of the customs, clothing, architecture, and other sights that would be unfamiliar to most. They quite literally illustrate things that may be difficult to visualize solely through description, in addition to depicting key moments in the story. The photographs, however, are somewhat different. They are invariably generalized images of specific places. For example, the first installment of the serial version includes two photographs of Shimonoseki, including an image of its busy harbor. The fourth installment includes a photograph of the bustling market at Taegu. The eighth installment, which sees our protagonist's arrival at Seoul, includes a photograph of a train arriving at Namdaemun Station in the capital, as well as an illustration of rickshaw drivers. The ninth installment has a photograph of the Japanese settlement area in Seoul. Photographs are far less frequent after that, perhaps because the narrative action remains anchored in Seoul, so illustrations accompany most of the text thereafter. But later excursions in the vicinity of the capital do include photographs of the places visited. The photographs do not so much illustrate the events unfolding in the narrative proper as document each new location by providing an iconic visual reference. In addition to being pictorial representations of exotic locations that would be unfamiliar to most readers, the photographs communicate a distinctive message to the reader: the story may be fictional, but it is overlaid on real places, of which the photographs, being indexical, are supposed to function as indisputable proof. An ethnographic novel is granted authority through photographs, supplementing Kyoshi's own emphasis on authenticity when he relates, in the "preface" examined earlier, how his experiences in Korea informed the novel.

Focusing on such images highlights the text's ethnographic interest in the colonial population, whereas its interest in the Japanese settler community can be brought into focus by examining the novel's paratextual elements—that is, the elements produced by the author or his accomplices, those elements that supplement the text and prescribe the desired way of relating to and consuming it.[46] The advertisement for *Chōsen* appeared in the Tokyo paper on two consecutive days, June 13 and 14, 1911. The same advertisement appeared in the pages of the paper's Osaka cousin on June 15 and 16. It is unclear who authored the advertisement, but it was common for authors to promote their own novels, as Sōseki generally did. Whether by Kyoshi or not, the ad is short enough to quote in full:

> Having lost their beloved child, a writer and his wife flee to Korea filled with grief. The lives of the Japanese on the peninsula are reflected through this couple's eyes. We will see the mournful Korean courtesans and heartless missionaries. There are pleasure seekers who drift aimlessly through life, like the smoke from a pipe. We will encounter government functionaries working for the glory of the nation and traveling merchants working ceaselessly for profit. Taking Korea as its stage, this work examines present-day society and the lives of the Japanese in a story that is captivating, detailed, and true to life. The author himself has traveled to the peninsula and examined conditions there. His novel will create a vivid and lasting impression on the reader.[47]

The signals here have become familiar. With its emphasis on Kyoshi's own experiences on the peninsula earlier in the year, the advertisement highlights the authenticity of the portrait in the upcoming work, even as it labels that work a novel and thus fiction. The advertisement promises an authoritative ethnographic account of an exotic place that would be unfamiliar to the vast majority of readers, while it encourages the reader's identification with that space by emphasizing that the novel will focus on the lives of a wide swath of Japanese living in Korea. The novel will thus have an auto ethnographic dimension.

Because the advertisement promises so much, it is easy to overlook the fact that Kyoshi tends consistently to focus on a certain group, albeit generally in a comparative context and with full view of the larger mise-en-scène of empire. We get a hint of this in the very beginning of the novel, as the inquisitive and observant narrator-protagonist takes note of his fellow Japanese waiting at Shimonoseki for the ship that will carry them to the peninsula. Among them are an older couple and their pale-faced, malnourished daughter. The father is balding, with his unkempt hair and dirty beard yielding a distinct impression of poverty and dishevelment. His wife is so thin she appears about to disappear (383). The narrator encounters a similar ragtag group of Japanese upon arrival in Pusan, but he then travels to Taegu to spend some time with an aunt and uncle.

We may not get explicit motivations for the major characters in the novel, but we get strong indications of the movements of the Japanese settlers in Korea as a collective body in these moments when the narrator takes note of his fellow Japanese. Furthermore, the narrator-protagonist attempts to comprehend the situation of the Japanese settler community through the prisms of capitalism, in general, and of *risshin shusse*, more specifically. The experience of the relatives of the narrator's wife in Taegu is exemplary. The narrator learns that even though they look like a prosperous family relative to other Japanese on the peninsula, they came to Korea because they were unable to succeed in Japan and that their real economic situation is far more tenuous than appearances would suggest. This leads to one of the narrator's many ruminations about the Japanese on the peninsula:

> The failures at home had been able to cross over to the colonies and succeed before there were many Japanese coming here. Once other Japanese, with greater talent, begin moving here, those original settlers once again lost out in the competition. In fact, they were merely people used as an advance front in the settlement of the colonies. (388)

In part, this description relies on the standard depiction of Korea—opportunity and easy money before 1905, the difficulty of both after the Russo-Japanese War—but now with a bleaker view. The narrator's relatives—these "failures at home" (*naichi de no shippaisha*)—traveled from Japan to Pusan to open a business. Unable to compete with the Japanese who came after them, they had to close up shop and reopen it farther north in Taegu. As the novel finds its way there, they are once again feeling the pressure from newcomers displaced from Pusan to Taegu and are considering moving their business once again—this time to Seoul (388). A pessimistic vision of the colonies comes into view early in the novel: they are the destination of the failures and losers in a larger capitalist competition on the archipelago, but almost before they can establish themselves on the peninsula and start a new life, they come under pressure from another wave of unfortunate immigrants in a perpetual cycle of displacement.

Far from depicting triumphant return to the home islands, the novel portrays a defeated population, forever journeying northward in an effort to establish itself outside of the realm of the Darwinian competition that characterizes capitalism. In this sense, there is no need for Kyoshi to detail the specific motivations of the individual characters, for he clearly illuminates the larger social canvas. The itinerant actors, adventurers, low-ranking geisha, hungrily opportunistic merchants, and tea stall operators who rarely see a customer—through them we are given a startling portrait of what Zygmunt Bauman, in a study of contemporary society but one that reaches back to the nineteenth century, has bluntly called "human waste," whose sole hope comes from their country's very possession of outlying colonial lands and ever expanding tracts of territory. Bauman makes clear the link between a superfluous and redundant humanity and imperialism: "The disposal of human waste produced in the 'modernized' and still 'modernizing' parts of the globe was the deepest meaning of colonization and imperialist conquest."[48] Kyoshi himself anticipates this connection.

This portrait takes on morbid dimensions when the narrator relates his discussion with a priest, who discloses that after presiding over the funeral services of many in Korea, he has noticed that middle-aged Japanese constitute the vast majority of deaths (411). Irrespective of actual historical conditions, Kyoshi's colony is populated by middle-aged Japanese from the lowest stratum of domestic society. Connecting this fact with his earlier observations, the narrator concludes that these men and women are so close to the margins in the colonies that the death of either the husband or wife leaves the survivor in desperate circumstances (411–12). This is, of course, the tragic narrative figure examined earlier writ large to cover almost the entire settler population in Korea. Even here, though, the narrator takes note of a discernible minority in the colonies: the young romantic who, having somehow gotten his hands on some money, wanders through colonial lands in pursuit of an unconventional life (412). Once again, the literary imagination relies on the stock types from earlier fiction, adding new character types, such as the colonial administrator with his ill-conceived plans of turning isolated and dusty P'yŏngyang into a major tourist destination in Asia, and female characters possessing an erotic charge.

In such moments, we see the mechanism by which real geography becomes an imagined geography of *risshin shusse*. The home islands constitute the space of authentic success, and the newly acquired colonies become an outlying territory into which stream the "failures at home." Tokyo is at the center of domestic space, with the villages and towns of the countryside, regardless of their actual physical proximity to the metropolis, positioned as lesser spaces. The colonies, too, are no simple dumping ground, for those who make the journey there are under perpetual pressure from recent arrivals, with the losers in this new struggle on colonial territory forced to pack up and move farther north, sometimes repeatedly. The ragtag group at the extremities of empire constitutes the truly desperate, at least in the representational system of this novel. The imagined geography that takes shape in *Chōsen* is fully dependent on notions of proximity and distance. The space of success on the home islands consists of concentric circles with Tokyo at its center, with the colonies added in late Meiji as an outer ring and the destination of failures and adventurers, as in the novels we examined in the previous section. Once colonial and semicolonial lands were moved from offstage to the main site of novelistic action after annexation, that outer ring of success was in turn subdivided into still more discreetly coded rings to account for ever finer distinctions of failure, all connected by the railroad.

❖

Examination of the midpoint of the novel allows some final observations of the importance of the Japanese settler community for the work's ethnographic impulse. In the last installment of the first half of *Chōsen* (number 70; chapter 28), the minor characters have left Seoul, and the narrator and his wife are on the platform waiting to board the train that will take them, too, away from the Korean capital. Eventually everyone will be reunited in P'yŏngyang, but we do not yet know this, and thus the final installment of the first half feels very much like an ending of sorts, with a new beginning and a new place awaiting us in the next installment in this drama of serial expansion. Awaiting departure at Namdaemun Station is the train that will carry the couple north: it is described, once again, as both a practical vehicle and as a weapon (440). As the narrator strolls the platform by the third-class (the lowest) passenger car before boarding, he notices an older man, his wife, and their daughter. Astonishingly, this is the same family he had seen at the beginning of the novel, when they boarded the third-class section of the ship departing Shimonoseki for Pusan. Surprised to see them again, he asks where they are headed; they reply that they are now traveling to Mukden, where their son resides (440). Everyone, it seems, is heading north to Manchuria, even the minor characters.

With this the first half ends, but there is a fascinating and instructive paragraph appended to this installment, which is not in the book version of the novel. Though unsigned, the note's self-effacing rhetoric of the pen being unable to go where the authorial will directs it suggests that it is by Kyoshi himself. He states that one of the novel's goals is to "depict the entirety of the situation of society in Korea," thereby invoking once more ethnography as a chief concern of writing the work. Despite this claim to totality, however, the author reveals a narrower, auto-ethnographic concern as he elaborates: "I wished to write about the failures [*haibokusha*] on the home islands [*naichi*] and those who strayed from the normal course, who went to Korea and then to Manchuria and even farther afield, thereby becoming pioneers in the development of national strength."[49] He might as well have named Keinosuke ("the failures on the home islands") and Ishibashi ("those who strayed from the normal course")—that is, the two major character types of early colonial fiction. The word used here, *haibokusha*, is different from the typical word for a failed individual in the novel, *shippaisha*. *Haibokusha*, meaning "the defeated," is typically used to designate the side routed in battle—the vanquished rather than the victor. In *Chōsen*, the term indicates someone who has retreated from the home islands because he has lost out in the Darwinian struggle for social advancement. Interestingly, *haibokusha* means literally a person who retreats to the north and contains within itself the character that is such a key term in the novel: *hoku* (here in aspirated form *boku*, also pronounced *kita*), meaning "north."

It is significant that the note comes immediately after the reappearance of the family from the first chapter. But the terms of the note actually refer to all Japanese in the colonies, each of whom is, from the perspective of those in Japan proper (for example, readers in Tokyo or Osaka), a "loser" or a "failure" within capitalist modernity. The demarcation between the home islands (*naichi*) and colonial Asia allows a distinction to be made between Japanese nationals in the two lands. This difference is important from an ideological perspective, for those who for whatever reason are unable to make a success of their lives in Japan travel to Korea or Manchuria to start over. The division allows a Japanese in the colonies to function as a figure of alterity for a Japanese in the home islands. Nonetheless, such figures are simultaneously recouped for another ideological purpose in the note. Failures they may be, but by traveling to colonial and semicolonial Asia, they contribute to the "development of national strength" (*kokusei no hatten*). Moreover, the author characterizes them as people who "pioneer" (*senku o nasu*) this development. These failures have been slyly turned into heroes in the span of a single sentence. The note appears only in the serial version, but we can easily argue that something similar happens in the book version, too, for the simple reason that these characters together constitute the subject of the novel, its "protagonist," with the "plot" being the perpetual northward movement of this collective body. The paratext has practiced a kind of rhetorical magic on the reader, for it has rescued the losers and failures on the home islands and transformed them, as agents of empire, into winners in the development of national power as they struggle up the new social ladder in the colonies. Viewed from the perspective of *risshin shusse*, the settler is the Other of the normative, upwardly mobile metropolitan subject, but, viewed from the perspective of national identity, the same expatriate figure is a Japanese subject, the same as the national subject on the home islands. The text's continual, ambivalent oscillation between identity and difference yields a clear explanation for the fact that the preponderance of attention in early colonial fiction is given to the national subject rather than the colonial subject.

It is now a commonplace, though important enough a point to underscore here once again, that Japan's modernization and transformation into a nation-state cannot be divorced from its increasing imperial possessions, which allow for self-definition through recourse to figures of difference. What we have uncovered in this chapter suggests that this important and invigorating scholarship is itself missing something crucial unless it references the discourse of social mobility. An examination of early colonial fiction has revealed that alterity is not constructed exclusively from national, cultural, or ethnic Others, but also (and, I would argue, more importantly) from the Others of *risshin shusse*. Representations of the national subject in the Meiji era and beyond most certainly rely on its colonial others for self-definition, but it also relies on a steady stream of Japanese nationals lighting out for the territories to start a new life, men and women who are coded ambivalently as failures and pioneers.

CONCLUSION

Modern Japanese Literature and the Public Sphere

> The public that read and debated this sort of thing read and debated about itself.
>
> —Jürgen Habermas, *The Structural Transformation of the Public Sphere*

Once the nation-state has ceased to be a self-evident entity, and we begin to see it instead as the product of an insistent, sustained work of the imagination, as Benedict Anderson has taught us, there are a number of ways to handle this new knowledge of the quintessential form of modern sociopolitical organization. A common scholarly response is to turn to the past in an effort to demonstrate that the borders of the nation have always been permeable and that localities have always been situated in transnational conduits. This is laudable work, and it has the salutary effect of demystifying the rhetoric that posits the nation as entirely natural and self-contained. This approach also has potential pitfalls, however, for it can sometimes project our own globalized world anachronistically into the past, thereby flattening the differences between our highly interconnected present and a past that may also have been interconnected, but in a qualitatively different way. A second approach stemming from awareness of the contingent nature of the nation—and the approach utilized in this book—entails investigating the specific mechanisms by which the nation-state is constructed and maintained within the imagination of its subjects and in the culture more broadly.

As many have noted, literature plays a crucial role in this endeavor; and the imagination is the special provenance of literary study. There is a danger in this second approach, too: we may end up homogenizing these mechanisms, thereby reducing the richness, complexity, and ambiguity of literature to a mere support mechanism for a particular form of political community. The novels examined in *Struggling Upward* belie such unity; they exhibit heterogeneous and sometimes even directly competing visions of social and national space as part of their exploration of worldly success. Once we have learned Benedict Anderson's basic lesson about the novel, we need to move from an account of how literature imagines the nation to one that shows how literature engages in a dialogue about the nation.

I develop in this conclusion a framework for conceptualizing how novels participate in an emerging public sphere in modernity, one in which the chief concerns of such fiction are, broadly speaking, the present and future of the Meiji polity. While I believe this is applicable to many literary works of the era, my focus here is debate about the place of the individual desire for advancement within this larger collective. The novels considered in this book map the emerging nation-state and new relations of power and authority by staging dramas in which the protagonist tries to close the gap between circumstances and desire. A fictional character who negotiates a space shaped by social mobility into hierarchically concentric circles centered on Tokyo is, at the same time, navigating a different kind of hierarchically organized space, in which the state is a centralizing authority. The drama of these novels rests, in part, on an awareness of the complex intertwining of the forces shaping the imagination of space in modern Japan.

Jürgen Habermas is the inevitable starting point for any serious thinking about the public sphere in modernity. He defines the institution as follows:

> The bourgeois public sphere may be conceived above all as the sphere of private people come together as a public; they soon claimed the public sphere regulated from above against the public authorities themselves, to engage them in debate over the general rules governing relations in the basically privatized but publicly relevant sphere of commodity exchange and social labor. The medium of this political confrontation was peculiar and without historical precedent: people's use of their reason.[1]

The public sphere, in Habermas's social-historical account, is neither an organ of state authority nor the private world of family and commerce. Rather, it is the space between society and the state, thus bridging the public and private. Habermas traces the emergence of this new institution in eighteenth-century Europe and its transformation in our own time. In this account, we see how the public acquired a critical voice in matters of government through the use of the faculty of reason, with which matters of state policy that affect the private world were debated and discussed. Because the state must pay some heed to this emergent public voice of the citizenry and even draw on it for justification of its policies, the public sphere is a space in which some measure of accountability is demanded of the state by its own subjects.

Habermas places particular emphasis on economic concerns. As he stresses repeatedly, the desire of private citizens to influence state policies regarding commerce is the most fundamental impetus for the emergence of the public sphere in Europe. On the other hand, precisely because this public uses the human faculty of reason to debate matters of state, the individuals who constitute this public have two personas, "the role of property owners and the role of human beings pure and simple."[2] This ultimately lays the foundation for conceptions of belonging and citizenship. Eventually, a public debating matters of commerce sees more and more of its interests at stake in politics, and thus the public sphere is instrumental, in this view, in the formation of the bourgeois democracies of Europe and North America: "The constitutional state as a bourgeois state established the public sphere in the political realm as an organ of state so as to ensure institutionally the connection between law and public opinion."[3] If the public sphere began as a space between the state and society in which debate about commerce was central, it evolved into a space that helped align state policy and public opinion with regard to a wide range of issues that affect the citizenry of a polity.

In his emphasis on the public use of reason, Habermas draws heavily from the European Enlightenment tradition, and this provides a link between his sociohistorical work and his philosophical interests in legitimation and communicative action. When Habermas's story reaches contemporary times, he gives us a portrait of a fallen society in which a valorized public sphere of debate has degenerated into a squabble among competing interest groups. There is thus a direct connection between his conception of the public sphere in his path-breaking book and in his essay "Modernity, an Incomplete Project," in which he attempts to retrieve and revitalize the Enlightenment ideas against postmodernity. A full discussion of this matter is beyond the purview of this book, but even this brief juxtaposition allows us to see that there is a degree of idealism at the heart of Habermas's account of the public sphere. This has provided an opening for critics of his concept, who focus on the relationship between marginalized social groups and the public sphere. Because he places the public use of reason at the heart of the institution, Habermas avoids acknowledging that the marketplace of ideas is, despite appearances, ridden with class and other interests that produce convenient rationalizations as frequently as (and probably more often than) they do carefully considered action about the public good.

Though written in the early 1960s, Habermas's seminal book was not rendered into English for some time. Once translated, however, it had, and continues to have, a profound influence in a variety of disciplines, including history, religion, and many of the social sciences. In the new millennium, the concept of the public sphere has even seen a growing use in literary studies. In formulating my ideas about Japan, I have found the books on Caribbean studies, trans-American studies, and what is coming to be called New World studies to be of the greatest interest because they are the most conscious of national borders, the making of those borders, and their unmaking and crossing. I would like to briefly take up two of them, Anna Brickhouse's *Transamerican Literary Relations and the Nineteenth-Century Public Sphere*, from 2004, and Raphael Dalleo's *Caribbean Literature and the Public Sphere*, published in 2011. Both books are admirable in their dexterous treatment of literature's participation in transnational arenas of public debate about political matters in multiple languages. Both are admirable, too, for the way they account for multiple intersecting and interacting public spheres by drawing on a variety of materials in the historical archive, not just literature. My emphasis here on the weaknesses of their shared framework is not meant to devalue this important scholarship, but to understand both the opportunities and the challenges of appropriating the concept of the public sphere for literary studies.

Brickhouse's most characteristic strategy in each chapter is to read one or more literary texts with transnational currency together with journalistic discourse within the United States in order to show that the literary texts challenge the public sphere in the United States and its global (or at least hemispheric) pretensions and ambitions. In making her case, the number of such oppositional public spheres quietly proliferates—there are francophone, hispanophone, abolitionist, anti-colonial, and transamerican public spheres, among others—and they are usually pitted against a larger public sphere that is characterized as a dominant U.S. public sphere or an anglophone public sphere or sometimes as a northeastern anglophone public sphere.[4] Brickhouse is surely right to seek "a plurality of competing and often mutually antagonistic public spheres," and this sentiment accords well with the Bakhtinian spirit of my own approach.[5] Nonetheless, in practice, her conceptualization tends toward unity of language or ideological agenda, often both. Allowing for the fact that oppositional public spheres tend to be quite unified precisely because they are oppositional and face a larger, more powerful opponent, when linguistically and ideologically homogeneous public spheres proliferate to the extent they do in Brickhouse's book, the emphasis on debate, persuasion, and the public use of reason in Habermas's original conception disappears. For Brickhouse, the oppositional public spheres are transnational and tend to be represented as sharing a single perspective and a unified ideological agenda, which is pitted against "dominant opinion," which is also generally represented as homogeneous, but becomes national, or sometimes regional, rather than transnational. At the regional and national levels, however, the characterization of a public sphere as having a unified perspective on any matter is unpersuasive.

Something similar happens in Dalleo's stimulating and ambitious study. Drawing primarily on conceptualizations of a black public sphere in the United States, Dalleo rightly stresses that relations of power enable some to speak to and for the public and to have their opinions heard and treated seriously, whereas others lack such a voice. His most common strategy for critical utilization of the public sphere concept is to showcase a variety of "counterpublics" (a term also used by Brickhouse, though less frequently than "oppositional public spheres") in relation to the normative public sphere of the colonial and postcolonial metropole; this, too, is the portrait of smaller public spheres offering a unified critical perspective on dominant public opinion.[6] Although many of Dalleo's criticisms of Habermas's idealism are entirely valid, his emphasis tends to fall exclusively on the critical voices forming a counterpublic. Given his interest in revealing anti-colonial critique and its suppression, this tendency to pit a valorized counterpublic against a vilified dominant public sphere is understandable, but it is susceptible to the same critique as Brickhouse's approach.

To retain its utility, the concept of a public sphere must embrace genuine debate, handle a range of views greater than just opposition, and encompass a more complex conceptualization of power, persuasion, and identification, even as we also acknowledge that opposition is a genuine and important position in the public sphere. In short, a useful concept of a public sphere must be dialogic in both theory and practice—a Bakhtinian public sphere. In the work of Dalleo and Brickhouse, the interest in transnational, oppositional public spheres tends to occlude such a dialogic formulation. The public sphere requires an investment in or identification with a community, a feeling that the speaker represents and is authorized to speak for that community, and the dissemination of a message to readers. Identities are not exclusive (as both Brickhouse and Dalleo acknowledge in theory, if not always in practice), but flexible and overlapping. In Meiji Japan, with the collapse of the early-modern status system, national identity was becoming the cornerstone of individual identity. We witness a protracted struggle to create a higher-order identity of nationalism, which can encompass, harmonize, or subordinate competing identities, whether regional, class, religious, gender, or others. Whereas Brickhouse and Dalleo stress the transnational, I would stress instead the old-fashioned national in any study of the nineteenth and twentieth centuries.

Here I follow recent efforts to conceptualize the public sphere in Japan. Kyu Hyun Kim has extended Habermas's idea in a revisionist history of the parliamentary movements during the first two decades of the Meiji era. In this account, the Freedom and People's Rights Movement (*Jiyū minken undō*) of the 1870s, which is typically seen as a failure and as having had limited impact on subsequent political developments, is viewed as instrumental in the establishment of a public sphere in Japan, that is, the space between the state and society in which matters of shared concern are debated by private individuals come together as a public.

In drawing on Habermas's theories, Kim notes that the public sphere in Meiji Japan cannot be convincingly conceived as a category of bourgeois society, because such a class did not yet exist in the early decades of the era. Instead, Kim shifts the discussion to the nation-state and conceptions of national identity. Because the central concern of an emergent public is the present and future (and even, early on, the legitimacy) of the new polity, Kim calls the institution in Japan a "national public sphere."[7] The story Kim tells for Meiji Japan, then, is different from Habermas's story for Europe in important ways:

> The public sphere in early Meiji came into being in conjunction with the very invention of Japan as a modern nation-state. The narrative of the "public" emerging through its participation in parliamentary discourse and the parliamentarian movement was itself the story of the construction of Japan's "citizen-subjects" within the new framework of the state-society relationship. The public in early Meiji went beyond such class identifications as "ex-samurai" or "bourgeoisie," and increasingly constituted itself as "citizen-subjects," even though class consciousness certainly remained a factor.[8]

Though Kim does trace the roots of this public sphere in the preceding period of Tokugawa rule, the crucial move here is to show how old identities become unmoored and new ones are formed in modernity. The new citizen-subject constitutes and is constituted by a public sphere and a nation-state in the making. This shifts the focal point for an analysis of the public sphere away from political economy and social class (though Kim does acknowledge these as important factors) toward the creation of the nation-state and the national subjects who populate it and contemplate its future.[9] Equally important, Kim grants agency to the new polity's subjects, which is a welcome retort to histories that stress the overwhelming power of the Meiji government, a power that the historical record shows it did not possess until at least the third decade of the era, if it ever did.

Still, we would do well to heed Mary Elizabeth Berry's caution against conflating a developing public sphere and a popular movement toward democratic government. She shows that suspicion of popular, republican politics was widespread among the elite in Meiji Japan and that many of those contributing to the public sphere were as firmly committed to elite rule as those in government. For Berry, early participants in the public sphere in Japan saw their role as safeguarding good government and disciplining those in positions of authority through vigilant scrutiny, merciless critique, and, when necessary, political agitation. Here, too, the public sphere is invested in the welfare of the nation, even in relation to an authoritarian state. In fact, because the public sphere had "gradually decoupled birth from rightful power"—a process that began in the Tokugawa period, as Berry points out[10]—the public sphere in Meiji is constituted by individuals who had adopted the identity of citizen-subjects in a nation-state, even if they were not advocates for fully democratic government.

The reformulation by historians of Japan of Habermas's galvanizing concept around the problems of the nation-state and the critical voice of the citizenry provides an opening for situating Meiji literature in relation to an emergent public sphere in the late-nineteenth and early twentieth centuries. Rather than utilize models of the European novel, which tend to portray this literary form as a bourgeois genre, one that functions rather like a mirror reflecting class values back to that social group,[11] the Japanese novel of the Meiji era can be seen as participating in the representation and imagination of the nation and the upwardly mobile national subject. It then becomes a mirror reflecting national identity as much as class identity back to citizen-subjects in the making. If we have learned anything from the rich scholarship on the era from a variety of disciplinary perspectives, it is that the Meiji period sees the rapid emergence of the nation-state and the construction of a national identity.[12] The public sphere emerged as an institution for debating these new, and by no means uncontested, forces in modernity. Utilizing Kim's emphasis on the nation and Habermas's brief but suggestive comments on literature, we can call this institution a national literary public sphere.

The crises engendered by rapid change and foreign encroachment before and after the Restoration authorized writers to take up social issues and cast their views in narrative form in ways that could never have been done in the Tokugawa era. At the same time, we witness the efforts of novelists to raise the status of fiction to a serious art form. These two threads come together in the figure of the novelist penning fiction that engages serious ideas about the modernizing polity. Even if Tokugawa fiction can sometimes be read as referencing contemporary social and political matters (which it most certainly does at times, often in veiled ways due to the threat of censorship), we do not see a widespread feeling that the writer is authorized by the society to address such issues or to speak on behalf of a larger public or attempt to persuade it. The novel in the Meiji era is a form preoccupied with the national subject and the destiny of the new polity, and this public engagement is historically specific. Even if Taishō-era (1912–1926) fiction exhibits an "inward turn," as has long been argued (with quite circular reference to the inward turning *shishōsetsu* [personal novel or I-novel] and little or no discussion of the national allegories so prominent in popular fiction of the interwar era), such a swerve away from public suasion would itself be part of the larger history of literature's engagement with or retreat from the public sphere. Such a history has yet to be written. My efforts in this conclusion are directed toward beginning such a project by using the discourse on social mobility and the imagination of space as focal points.

The media context of Meiji is crucial to understanding the difference between early-modern and modern literature and theorizing modern literature's interest in social critique. New media forms in Meiji made writers aware of the larger national collective and increasingly allowed the writer to reach vast segments of the public. Readers will have undoubtedly observed that most of the major narratives examined in *Struggling Upward* were serialized in newspapers or magazines, a common way of publishing fiction in modern Japan, as in so many other countries. Print media is a crucial component of the public sphere for both Habermas and Kim. For Habermas, it is arguably even more important than the coffee houses and other venues in which people debated public matters, especially when his story reaches the nineteenth century. Similarly, Kim highlights a diverse array of institutions—such as metropolitan intellectual associations (153–90), the lecture circuit (224–54), satiric cartoons (312–18), and the emergence of political parties (379–442)—but underscores the importance of institutionalized media, with particular attention given to newspapers, which both contest the authority of the state and help form a reading public with national concerns (86–98, 139–53). Print media is not the sole component of the public sphere, but it is perhaps the most important. Certainly it is central to any consideration of modern literature.

Nagamine Shigetoshi has discussed the maturation of print culture in the third decade of Meiji (almost coterminous with the 1890s) and observed a qualitative shift in the relationship between people and print at the turn of the century; to describe the phenomenon, he has proffered the term "reading nation," his English rendition for his own concept of *dokusho kokumin*.[13] Concentrating on the spread throughout Japan of print media, the proliferation of libraries and other types of public reading spaces, and the growing habit of citizens to read on trains, streetcars, and buses while en route to destinations, Nagamine shows that print capitalism and new reading habits had penetrated deep into the culture at large during the ten-year period leading up to the twentieth century. These practices had become routine by the end of the Meiji era.

The book had become increasingly familiar and commonplace during the early-modern era, especially during the second half of the eighteenth century. The stunning expansion of print culture in the Tokugawa period has been made increasingly clear in literary and historical scholarship, culminating in Mary Elizabeth Berry's designation of this massive body of print as "the library of public information."[14] There is no need to deny the existence of this burgeoning early-modern print culture and the nascent national identities it helped create to see that there is something qualitatively different in the late nineteenth century. Nagamine highlights two aspects of the phenomenon: one is that reading newspapers, magazines, novels, and other forms of print media became a daily habit for an increasingly literate population, occupying a significant, predictable, even measurable portion of each person's day; the other is that the population's sense of national identity emerged from this proliferating print media and the infrastructure that supports reading. Nagamine is, of course, drawing on Benedict Anderson's account of nationalism as an "imagined community" that is impossible, ultimately, without an all-encompassing print culture, with the daily newspaper being singled out by Anderson for special attention; but Anderson also discusses novels and other forms of print culture in forming national identity.[15] A print culture of sufficient magnitude and social penetration is necessary to link, on a vast scale, writers and readers across an entire nation, from the capital to the provinces and the colonies. Even this expanding world of print would see a qualitative increase in the 1920s and 1930s and once again in the 1950s and 1960s.

The reader in a world in which newspapers, magazines, and books are ubiquitous does not encounter fiction in isolation, but in relation to other discourses in numerous publications. Writers pen their fiction in such a media context. Whether it is a novel by Sōseki or Shinsen, such works exhibit one of the chief characteristics of the novel as theorized by Mikhail Bakhtin: the ability, even the need, to absorb surrounding discourses and genres into itself.[16] Recent scholarship on modern literature has observed that these discourses come from the surrounding columns and pages of the publications in which the novels and stories appear.[17] The fiction column in a newspaper or magazine, for example, is inextricably connected to other components of the serial, as shown in my own readings of Tengai's *Makaze koikaze* and Shinsen's *Ase no kachi*. Yet serialization is only the most apparent way in which literature can be situated in relation to debates within society. A novel that appears as a book on the market, such as Katai's *Inaka kyōshi* or the many *risshi shōsetsu* published independently of serialization, takes its place in a large and burgeoning media field and can be considered a salvo in larger debates taking place in print within an emergent public sphere in the Meiji era, even if it is not concerned with politics narrowly defined. In the era of full-blown print capitalism, a fictional text cannot be convincingly read as a self-contained literary work, but is more properly considered as a text that echoes, supports, or contests other discourses in the media field. Functioning primarily as socially symbolic acts, literary texts participate in debates on Japanese modernity along with the many nonfictional books, essays, and editorials at the time. My emphasis on the juxtaposition of texts from different culturally demarcated zones arises from this conviction about literature's role as a bearer of ideas and its centrality to public debate in modern Japan.

Literature participates in its own unique way, typically relying on symbolic structures and metaphoric language, and its didactic intent is mediated by the contingencies and conventions of storytelling. To understand literature's participation in the public sphere, we can return to Shinsen's ambition novels. They are manifestly rags-to-riches stories. Yet a close reading also reveals both a latent concern with the ravages being wrought on the countryside by the forces of urbanization and industrialization and a form of wish-fulfillment by means of which such problems are resolved within the literary imagination. A novel such as *Ase no kachi* does more than just tell a story: it presents an argument in narrative form for relocating an authentic and meaningful success to the countryside. The text shows the reader a utopian nation that would result from this, albeit a fictional one. Furthermore, as we saw, the novel argues—and explicitly tells the reader—that the fate of the nation hinges on society's adoption of its utopian program, even if its ultimate vision of a Japan without cities is clearly a fantasy.

Katai's novel is a naturalist critique of society and is implicitly opposed to the vision put forth by Shinsen in his *risshi shōsetsu*. There is no evidence that Katai is directly responding to Shinsen's ambition novels, though, given the prominence of such narratives after the Russo-Japanese War, it is difficult to believe that he was unaware of them. In contrast to Shinsen's modern provincial utopias, Katai offers a pessimistic portrait of the provinces as a space unable to fulfill the promise of modernity for the ambitious individual. Using the trope of revelation, the text rhetorically splits a homogeneous countryside into the natural world and provincial community, thereby rescuing nature from a countryside that can signify only social inertia. Regardless of whether or not he knew of Shinsen's work, Katai's novel offers an opposing view.

In other cases, the texts examined herein explicitly argue against each other. When, in *Mon*, Sōsuke peruses the magazine *Seikō* in the dentist's office, he dismisses the entire ideology advocated by the magazine and, by extension, of the message of Shinsen's novels; after all, whatever issue Sōsuke picked up would have included a short story or a section of a longer serialized work by Shinsen himself, even if Sōseki does not openly name this fiction. In this case, Sōseki is responding directly and forcefully to the very media network in which the genre of the ambition novel was central, thereby rejecting the fiction serialized therein.

Some of the novels discussed herein reinforce and extend the tropes of earlier works. Takahama Kyoshi's novel, for example, inherits the basic character types and narrative paradigms from his predecessors' accounts of Korea and Manchuria, supplementing these archetypes with an ethnographic impulse. In other ways, however, Kyoshi's novel departs from its predecessors. The earliest fiction treating Korea and Manchuria—before the peninsula's sovereignty was dissolved—frequently rejoin the drifters to the national body on the home islands, some of whom return as successes while others return broken and dispirited. Not so Kyoshi's *Chōsen*, which does not rejoin the displaced individual to the national collective, but instead gives the reader a portrait of the failures retreating farther and farther north, thereby forming a marginal group whose very livelihood depends upon the poaching of outlying territories and who assist the process of imperial expansion. Before annexation, the "protagonists" of the colonial romance and the colonial tragedy were generally brought back to Japan (and brought back to the narrative) because their primary function was to provide a contrast to the upwardly mobile youth who is the protagonist of the novel. In Kyoshi's novel, however, in which the main stage of novelistic action has shifted to the colonies, competing ideological needs—representing such figures as failures and representing them as crucial to spreading national power—requires that they keep pressing north rather than return home.

There are multiple portraits of the city, as well, which is rarely represented as an entirely desirable space. In *Sorekara*, Natsume Sōseki reveals an atomized urban world in which social relations are instrumentalized for personal advancement, consequently producing the city as a space of ennui and alienation. Kosugi Tengai's melodramatic blockbuster mobilizes the discourse of the dangerous city in its portrait of its heroine's ambitions, even as it features a covert acknowledgment of the city as a seductive site of self-fashioning within modernity, especially for women.

With these novelistic debates in mind, we can now add the public sphere to the nation-state, the discourse on social mobility, and the modern novel as the group of phenomena that all emerge at the same historical moment, as I suggested in the introduction. The dialogic interaction among novels and between a novel and its media context can be plotted in any number of ways in relation to these four entities. If participation in the public sphere can serve as a general guiding principle for studying Meiji fiction (without insisting that each and every novel is so concerned), can we be more specific about how this engagement is intertwined with the discourse on *risshin shusse*, the subject of this book?

To answer this question, let us return to the most important tool in this study: Bakhtin's concept of the chronotope and, in particular, what we have called the chronotope of success, which has served as a heuristic device for reading Meiji literature. Modern novelists writing at the turn of the century confront a widespread belief that a meaningful and socially significant life involves upward mobility, from birth to the attainment of success, and the new socioeconomic system made it an imperative impossible to dismiss. Even novels critical of the discourse on *risshin shusse,* such as those of Katai, nonetheless give us protagonists who orient their lives around this ideal—and this despite its skeptical representation. The discourse on social mobility may not have become so powerful as to be invisible, but the new conception of the socially significant human life had become largely naturalized by the end of Meiji. It is accepted as truth by both canonical writers, such as Tokutomi Roka, whose *Omoide no ki* we briefly examined in the introduction, and popular writers, such as Horiuchi Shinsen. The ideal of social mobility provides the basic temporal framework for many of the novels of the Meiji era.

Further examination of the temporal axis of the chronotope of success would surely yield its own insights, but I have instead concentrated on the way the Meiji novelists engage in a vigorous exploration of its spatial axis. At some level, space and time must be thought together, but the utility of the concept of the chronotope is that it allows one to usefully pry apart the representation of time and space for analysis and, simultaneously, to see the interaction between them in the representational system of a novel. Focusing on the spatial axis of the chronotope of success will allow us to address the question of why Meiji writers would be so preoccupied with the topography of social mobility and why space became such a contested category within the national literary public sphere of Meiji Japan.

Even as *risshin shusse* propagates a single narrative of the socially meaningful life, the discourse allows for multiple paths to the desired destination. Worldly success depends on the differentiation of spaces within the nation (and eventually the colonies) and the placement of these locations within a spatial hierarchy that, I have suggested, is best captured by the metaphor of concentric circles. Indeed, ambition is a form of desire that thrives precisely on the tension between a single narrative of a successful life and differentially coded spaces. Opportunity, after all, is not uniformly distributed through this space. To return once again to Nancy Armstrong's conceptualization, desire is inscribed as a "supplement" or "rhetorical additive" in a character; that character attempts to close the gap between circumstances and desire, according to a modern social contract. In an industrializing nation that is still mainly rural, the character's effort to close the gap and conform to a unitary narrative of a successful life entails the traversal of a spatial hierarchy. This hierarchy is built, in part, on a simple dichotomy of center and periphery. But this antinomy is flexible enough so that the center and periphery shift depending on where one happens to be standing. In a small community in the distant provinces, the center may be the provincial capital. From the standpoint of such mid-size communities, the larger regional city, such as Osaka or Nagoya, is the center. Yet Tokyo is the apex of the spatial imagination of upward mobility, the center of the ring of concentric circles. And from its perspective, everything outside the capital is the periphery.

This is an alternative way of conceptualizing modernity, one that goes beyond narrowly conceived political categories and accounts for the impact of capitalism and social mobility on the imagining of the nation. In her widely cited historical work, Tessa Morris-Suzuki examines the Tokugawa and Meiji orders and concludes that the modern nation-state "allowed difference to be transposed from the realm of space to the realm of time."[18] According to this view, difference in early-modern Japan was conceived as "foreignness," which increased the farther one moved away from the center of Tokugawa rule, whereas, in distinct contrast, difference became temporal in the Meiji era, functioning as a way to differentiate Japan's spatially demarcated and unified civilization from the "backwardness" of other nations in Asia. It is enticing to think about the transition from Tokugawa to Meiji as a "transfer of difference from geography ('foreignness') to history ('backwardness')," as Morris-Suzuki does.[19] Yet even if we concede the centrality of the spatial imagination to the maintenance of Tokugawa authority, the study of Meiji literature through the lens of worldly success suggests that modern social, economic, and political orders rely as extensively on spatial differences as premodern regimes. Furthermore, Morris-Suzuki notes that the spatial imagination that informed early-modern conceptions of difference depended on Chinese conceptions of concentric circles, "in which barbarism (*i*) increases the farther one moves away from the settled and civilized center (*ka*)."[20] It is this spatial system that is allegedly replaced by fixed national borders. But this framework, too, is unconvincing when modern Japan in viewed from the perspective of social mobility, for *risshin shusse* creates its own system of hierarchical concentric circles within the nation, even as it blurs those national borders in the era of imperialism.

We are better off thinking of the transition from Tokugawa to Meiji as being a passage from one spatio-temporal order to another. Stefan Tanaka, for example, has emphasized that modern temporality was put in the service of naturalizing a particular space: the geographical space occupied by the nation, as we examined in chapter 2.[21] We must think of this new spatio-temporal order of modernity as both political (the nation-state) and economic (capitalism). A study of the discourse on *risshin shusse* provides a way to think about the nation beyond the narrow conceptualization of a politically controlled territory without reducing it to purely economic spatial projection. A successful model must account for the fact that the nation-state and capitalism are attempting to appropriate and exert authority over a particular space; their efforts are sometimes coordinated and sometimes exist in a state of tension.

Kären Wigen has demonstrated how modernity replaces one spatial order with another in an analysis that accounts for the political and economic in a more satisfactory way than Morris-Suzuki. Here we can build on the discussion of her work begun in the first chapter. Wigen has pointed to the transformation of a heterogeneous countryside into a periphery and the concomitant subordination of this new periphery to Tokyo, the new center. By focusing on the Ina Valley in the Japan Alps region between Tokyo and Nagoya and taking a cross section from the mid-eighteenth to the early twentieth centuries, thereby traversing the Tokugawa-Meiji divide, Wigen reaches the following conclusion:

> Over the course of the Tokugawa period, the Ina Valley was slowly knit into a cohesive economic region, only to be unraveled and reworked into a very different fabric when the Japanese countryside was incorporated into a globalizing economy and a centralizing state. . . . As Shimoina was subsumed, it was also subordinated, reconfigured as a periphery within this larger politico-economic universe.[22]

This conceptualization adds weight to the inherited view that, even acknowledging the existence of some continuity between Tokugawa and Meiji, the two eras represent profoundly different orders. As we saw in the first chapter, Wigen calls the remaking of a relatively autonomous region into an economic and political periphery in modernity a "regional inversion." In her case study of how this process unfolded in the Ina Valley, Wigen places as much emphasis on manufacturing and trade as the new political regime. Wigen's work is also suggestive of how political and economic transformations implicate the imagination and conceptions of identity, both local and national.[23] Additionally, Wigen not only shows how coherent premodern regions are remade into modern peripheries and subordinated to a centralizing state power, but also extends the discussion to demonstrate how this process is crucial to Japan's emergence as a regional power within East Asia, and one with extensive economic ties to the rest of the globe, as well. The suggestive implication is that the colonies were eventually incorporated as a new periphery for Japan in much the same way as the archipelago's provinces were subordinated within Japan proper, even as that periphery is itself the center when viewed from the perspective of the colonized.

Wigen's book successfully accounts for the way the emerging nation-state exerts power over the space of its domain to accomplish its program of centralization, which, more often than not, facilitates capitalist development. She writes, for example: "The conversion of Edo to Tokyo . . . gave the new rulers unprecedented power to mobilize the resources of the archipelago."[24] The way power works to mobilize resources suggests a fundamental violence at the heart of the project of modernization. The archipelago must be forcibly remade, from one thing into another. Henri

Lefebvre's reworking of the fundamental Marxian conceptual apparatus from the perspective of space is suggestive here. Lefebvre writes: "Sovereignty implies 'space,' and what is more implies a space against which violence, whether latent or overt, is directed—a space established and constituted by violence."[25] Why is force necessary to the project of modernization? The new Japanese nation-state in Meiji relies like any other on ideas of fixed national borders, beyond which lie other nation-states. National identity, as a higher-order identity, can take root inside those borders in a space coded as homogeneous. In reality, however, the claim of national unity is challenged, even undermined, by class, gender, geographical, and other persistent divisions. *Risshin susse* also operates in a space differentially coded and shaped into concentric circles by capitalism, meaning that opportunity, too, is unevenly distributed in space, although the official rhetoric of the modern social contract does not admit it.

To understand the gap between rhetoric and reality, Lefebvre points to a "metaphorization" of space, which involves "a space where violence is cloaked in rationality and a rationality of unification is used to justify violence."[26] Working sometimes together with capitalism, at other times at odds with its demands, the modern nation-state appropriates a particular space, a process that involves violence of some kind, always discursive and often accompanied by the use of force. This violence is cloaked in a rhetoric of collective unity and national purpose in order to mask the reality of a strategically fragmented and hierarchically situated national space.

For Lefebvre, the space shaped by political hegemony and capitalism has three contradictory dimensions: it is global ("the space of sovereignty"), fragmented ("a space that locates specificities, places or localities, both in order to control them and in order to make them negotiable"), and hierarchical ("ranging from the lowliest places to the noblest, from the tabooed to the sovereign"), all at the same time.[27] Yet the fissure between the rhetoric of unity and universality and the reality of fragmentations and hierarchy is always visible to those who would look. Looking is what Meiji novelists do best.[28]

This book has endeavored to understand the implications of a particular context in which the modern novel, the ideology of upward mobility, and the modern nation-state emerge at the same historical moment. *Struggling Upward* has sought answers in Meiji-era conceptualizations of space. Social mobility always implies the traversal of differentially coded and hierarchically situated spaces shaped by new economic and political regimes. By the end of that era, these spaces had become implicated in and complicated by a colonialist enterprise in which an official rhetoric of unity across old national borders is belied by a preoccupation with hierarchically conceived ethnic differences. By sending their protagonists across such stratified landscapes in their effort to close the gap between circumstances and desire, Meiji novelists explore the complex intersections and contradictions between a space shaped by social mobility and a nation-state in the making. This is not a literary geography, however, even if the novels herein reference specific places. Rather, the new discourse on worldly success provides a way for writers to scrutinize how space is coded in different ways within the larger context of the centralization of national and economic power in Tokyo and the peripheralization of the countryside and the colonies. To draw on Lefebvre's categories, *risshin shusse* gives Meiji writers a specific, concrete handle with which to grapple with a seeming contradiction: a national space imprinted by centralization and shaped by capitalism and industrialization is not only homogeneous and unified, but also, paradoxically, fragmented and hierarchical.

The study of the relationship between the Meiji novel and social mobility—or, more broadly, between narrative form and social discourse—helps redraw the map of Meiji literature, which is too often cast as a story of writers careening from one literary movement to another—Romanticism, Naturalism, and such—with each European wave that crashed onto Japanese shores. It is too often a story of a handful of writers, which ignores two of the most pivotal events of the era: the emergence of a reading public and a public sphere. Turning our sights to these new social phenomena helps us see literature's participation in an emerging public sphere of debate about the present and future of the nation and a social hierarchy that belies a national rhetoric of unity. Placing social mobility at the center of an analysis of the modern novel allows us to take a step away from the staid framework of literary history and its artificial separation of canonical literature from its larger literary and historical context. At the same time, this study has suggested an alternative framework for conceptualizing the passage to modernity in Japan.

Notes

Introduction

1. My information about this image is drawn from Morse, *Reinventing Tokyo*, 83. For more on the building, see Seidensticker, *Low City, High City*, 7–8, 70–73.

2. In addition to using the Japanese term, I draw on a range of English phrases for stylistic variation, including social/upward mobility, ambition, (worldly) success, and so on.

3. The discourse on *risshin shusse* has been a local yet important component of many studies of Meiji works: Walker, *The Japanese Novel of the Meiji Period*, 16–29 (in relation to individualism); Fujii, *Complicit Fictions*, 94–95 and 216–17 (in readings of *Hakai* and *Arakure*, respectively); Torrance, *The Fiction of Tokuda Shūsei*, 56–81 (in readings of *Arajotai* and *Ashiato*); Mertz, *Novel Japan*, 195–211 (in a reading of political novels); Reichert, *In the Company of Men*, 36–64, esp. 60–64 (in a reading of *Sawamura Tanosuke*); Ueda, *The Concealment of Politics*, 115–43 (in a reading of *Tōsei shosei katagi*); Ito, *An Age of Melodrama*, 140–87 (in a reading of *Chikyōdai*); and Saito, *Detective Fiction*, 91–92 (in readings of Kuroiwa Ruikō's detective stories, both original and translations). This list could be expanded greatly by noting Japanese sources, but, because of their number, I will reference them in the body of the book.

4. Takeuchi, *Risshin shusse shugi*, 9–11.

5. Thomas M. Huber's analysis of the Meiji Restoration is suggestive here. He sees the Restoration as a service intelligentsia revolution, in which the agents are motivated both by a personal, class investment in elevating those of talent and by a concern for the public welfare. See Huber, *The Revolutionary Origins of Modern Japan*, 209–31.

6. Asao, "Mibun shakai no rikai," 141.

7. Howell, *Geographies of Identity*, 20–44.

8. Fukaya, *Edo jidai no mibun ganbō*, 7.

9. This basic narrative arc of *risshin shusse*, beginning with disaffected samurai and then spreading outward to the general population around the turn of the century, was first described by Kinmonth in *The Self-Made Man*.

10. Hirakawa, *Ten wa mizukara tasukuru mono o tasuku*, 5.

11. Hirota, *Fukuzawa Yukichi*, 107.
12. Takeuchi, *Risshin shusse shugi*, 11 (section title).
13. Armstrong, *How Novels Think*, 3.
14. Lefebvre, *The Production of Space*, 54.
15. Bakhtin, "Forms of Time and of the Chronotope," 84.
16. Ibid., 243.
17. The subtitle to Bakhtin's book-length essay—"Notes toward a Historical Poetics"—hints at this tendency. It is also apparent in a related essay, "The *Bildungsroman* and Its Significance."
18. Ladin, "Fleshing Out the Chronotope," 219. Graham Pechey makes a similar point: "We cannot speak of *a* chronotope unless there is at least one other to choose" (*Mikhail Bakhtin*, 86; italics in the original).
19. Ladin, "Fleshing Out the Chronotope," 230.
20. Ibid., 224.
21. Especially as described by Moretti in *The Way of the World*.
22. "In an anthropological spirit, then, I propose the following definition of the nation: it is an imagined political community—and imagined as both inherently limited and sovereign" (Anderson, *Imagined Communities*, 5–6).
23. Brennan, "The National Longing for Form," 49.
24. Hampton, *Inventing Renaissance France*, 110–11. Italics in the original.
25. For the diversity of the domestic debate on the war, see Shimazu, *Japanese Society at War*. Shimazu is especially good at shattering any lingering illusions that Meiji Japan was a monolithic entity with a single, common, uncontested purpose.
26. Komori, "Kinsei shōsetsu kara kindai shōsetsu e," 80.
27. Levy, *Sirens of the Western Shore*, 29–32.
28. Maeda, *Kindai dokusha no seiritsu*, 112–14.
29. The English translation by Strong renders the title *Footprints in the Snow*.
30. An important exception is Fujii, *Complicit Fictions*, 45–102, who deftly treats the relationship among the three. *Struggling Upward* builds on this important precedent.

Chapter 1. Desire and Deferral

1. Kobayashi, *Shizenshugi sakka*, 47.
2. Tayama, *Jūemon no saigo*, 307. I use my own translations throughout and indicate the page number of the original in parentheses in subsequent citations. A fine English translation is included in Henshall, *The Quilt and Other Stories*, 97–147.
3. Though the only title of Turgenev the narrator mentions is *Sketches from a Hunter's Album* (1852), he also gratuitously drops the names of Rudin, from the work of that name (1857), and Bazarov, the protagonist of *Fathers and Sons* (1862).
4. Iwanaga has detailed the changes and argued that the basic materials were shaped by Katai's desire to create a naturalist work in the spirit of the European writers he so admired. See his *Shizenshugi ni okeru kyokō*, 204–19.
5. The most important of these is Shimamura Hōgetsu's "Bungei jō no shizenshugi" (1908), which divided Japanese naturalism into an early, Zola-esque phase and a later, confessional phase.
6. For a fuller discussion, see Fujii, *Complicit Fictions*, 52.

7. For more, see Hijiya-Kirschnereit, *Rituals of Self-Revelation*, 21–24.

8. This is the face of naturalism emphasized in Kataoka, *Shizenshugi kenkyū*, 7. Hill has argued that Japanese naturalism was part of a larger international movement that explored the "modern maladies" afflicting all the "civilized" societies, with special emphasis on neurasthenia. See his "The Naturalist Novel," 72.

9. Rubin, *Injurious to Public Morals*, 55–107.

10. Nakamura Mitsuo argued that *Futon* marked the point at which the necessary critical distance between author and protagonist collapsed, leading to a distorted realism that finds its ultimate expression (lamentably, in Nakamura's view) in the *shishōsetsu*. See his *Fūzoku shōsetsu ron*. It is also important to underscore that Nakamura's view of the trajectory of the modern Japanese novel has been severely criticized over the years, though it remains influential to this day.

11. Suzuki, *Narrating the Self*, 87–88.

12. Link, *The Vast and Terrible Drama*, 1–20.

13. Den Tandt attempts to include such elements as romanticism, the gothic, and the sublime in his own theory of American naturalism. See his *The Urban Sublime*.

14. Suzuki, *Narrating the Self*, 69–82.

15. An important exception to the critical neglect of naturalism's treatment of nature is Sōma, *Nihon shizenshugi ron*, 12–21. See also Fujii, *Complicit Fictions*, especially the chapters on Tōson and Shūsei.

16. Miyauchi has noted the prevalence of the "provincial-born" (*chihō shusshinsha*) within the naturalist movement in Japan. See his *Tayama Katai ronkō*, 58.

17. For details, see Platt, *Building and Burning*.

18. For more, see Dodd, *Writing Home*, 27–31.

19. Ibid., 72–75.

20. See Kobayashi, *Shizenshugi sakka*. He is especially persuasive when examining how Katai conceived of success for the writer as literary fame.

21. Yoshida Morio discovers a narrative discourse that straddles objectivity and subjectivity and relates it to Katai's theories. See his "Hayashi Seizō ni iru fūkei."

22. Kobayashi, *Shizenshugi sakka*, 119–20. The way Katai used the diary has thoroughly dominated discussions of the novel in Japanese criticism to the detriment of other approaches, and I will not pursue the matter here. The best accounts can be found in Kobayashi, *Tayama Katai*, 9–31, or Iwanaga, *Shizenshugi ni okeru kyokō*, 265–90.

23. Sōma memorably refers to Seizō's life as "a youth spent missing the train" (*noriokurete iku seishun*). See his *Nihon shizenshugi saikō*, 119.

24. Tayama Katai, *Inaka kyōshi*, 192. I use the Japanese paperback here rather than the version in the *zenshū* (Complete Works). The page numbers for all further references to the novel will be given in parentheses. The translations are my own. For a superb rendition of the novel into English, see Henshall, *Country Teacher*.

25. The most interesting reading along these lines is offered by Fujimori, *Katari no kindai*, 67. Fujimori links the representation of Tokyo to the visual arts of its day to argue that the panoramic view is itself a critique of the city.

26. The most recent iteration of this view can be found in Kishi, *Tayama Katai sakuhin kenkyū*, 104. Kishi interprets the protagonist as a sacrifice (*giseisha*) of society because his family is poor, thus necessitating his leaving school to support them and foreclosing other opportunities for advancement. For an alternative reading, one that critiques the

common ideals/reality dichotomy and instead interprets the novel as an "affirmation of the self" *(jiko kōtei)*, see Nagai Kiyotake, "Inaka kyōshi no fukushū."

27. Interestingly, Katai took a fair amount of heat in the contemporary reviews of his novel, primarily because he added a fictional series of visits to a brothel, which is not at all part of the diary of the real-life Kobayashi Shūzō. Katai was clearly interested in pursuing the sexual theme.

28. Kamei, "Tayama Katai, *Inaka kyōshi*," 52–58.

29. The characterization of *Myōjō* as "idealist" is the narrator's. We would now call it "romanticist," with emphasis on modern romantic love, decadence, and self-dramatization. See Morton, *Modernism in Practice*, 14–17.

30. Fujimori, *Katari no kindai*, 38.

31. See Ueda, *The Concealment of Politics*, 44–48.

32. See Karatani, *Nihon kindai bungaku no kigen*, 7–43.

33. Etō, *Riarizumu no genryū*, 7–43.

34. Karatani, *Nihon kindai bungaku no kigen*, 25–36.

35. Kajiki, *Shasei no bungaku*, 50–51.

36. Tsubouchi Toshinori, *Masaoka Shiki*, 130.

37. Brower, "Masaoka Shiki and Tanka Reform," 399–400. See also Keene, *The Winter Sun Shines In*, 94–102.

38. Masaoka, "Jojibun," 247.

39. Ibid., 241.

40. See Derrida, *Of Grammatology*, 141–64. The supplement is both a surplus that is cumulative and accumulative and a substitute or proxy. Furthermore, "this second signification of the supplement cannot be separated from the first. . . . Whether it adds or substitutes itself, the supplement is *exterior*, outside of the positivity to which it is superadded, alien to that which, in order to be replaced by it, must be other than it" (145).

41. Tsubouchi Toshinori, *Masaoka Shiki*, 158. Morris, speculating on Shiki's likening of sketching to painting, notes that haiku for Shiki would take as its object "small-scale scenes and individual objects in nature." See his "Buson and Shiki: Part Two," 280.

42. Masaoka, "Jojibun," 247.

43. Morris, "Buson and Shiki: Part Two," 281–83.

44. Dodd, *Writing Home*, 91–95.

45. Shimazaki, "Shasei," 33.

46. Ibid., 34.

47. Shimazaki, "Kumo," 259.

48. A genealogy of this idea might reveal another indebtedness to Zola. Berg notes that "Zola's literary theories express his belief that the eye could embrace, within the act of seeing, the faculties of cognition and imagination required of scientific analysis and literary creation" (*The Visual Novel*, 60).

49. For examples of his descriptive power, see Ruskin, *Modern Painters*, 93–113.

50. Masaoka, "Kumo," 253.

51. For example, Hiraoka, *Nichiro sengo bungaku*, 1:333–38. Katai stated he was moved by the tragedy of a youth who died on the same day that Japan celebrated its victory over Russia, but this can also be interpreted as Katai being attuned to the irony of that juxtaposition. See Tayama, *Tōkyō no sanjūnen*, 271–79.

52. Wigen, *The Making of a Japanese Periphery*, 296. Italics in the original.

Chapter 2. A Utopia of Self-Help

1. This project has been compellingly discussed in Ortabasi, *The Undiscovered Country*.

2. See, for example, Najita, *Ordinary Economies in Japan*, 163–64.

3. Irokawa, *The Culture of the Meiji Period*, 287–93.

4. Yanagita, "Inaka tai tokai no mondai," 38–39.

5. Ibid., 46.

6. See Bourdaghs, *The Dawn that Never Comes*, 77–113, esp. 91–92.

7. For characteristic works of Horatio Alger, see *Ragged Dick and Struggling Upward*.

8. Recent works in this vein include Ito, *An Age of Melodrama*, and Zwicker, *Practices of the Sentimental Imagination*.

9. Jameson, *The Political Unconscious*, 77.

10. The known information about Horiuchi Shinsen is compiled from various sources in *Nijū-seiki Nihonjin jinmei jiten*, 2: 2257. Information about Shinsen's literary output was compiled from the collection at the National Diet Library, Tokyo. For information on Rohan and the ideology of social advancement, see Maeda, *Kindai Nihon no bungaku kūkan*, 134–52.

11. Among the most thorough and informative of these are: in Japanese, Takeuchi, *Nihonjin no shussekan*, 106–33, and Ameda, "Kindai Nihon no seinen," 259–320; and, in English, Kinmonth, *The Self-Made Man*, 166–205.

12. For basic information on the American magazine *Success*, see Richard Huber, *The American Idea of Success*, 153–54.

13. The circulation figures are from Nagamine, *Zasshi to dokusha no kindai*, 102, 108.

14. Takeuchi, *Nihonjin no shussekan*, 106–9.

15. *Kokkei shinbun*, July 20, 1907. The spread matches twenty-one magazines and their readers.

16. See the exhaustive research into the "Letters to the Editor" column of *Seikō* conducted by Ameda Ei'ichi in his "Kindai Nihon no seinen," 269–84.

17. Kinmonth, *The Self-Made Man*, 171–72.

18. I borrow the phrase "self-help type" (*jijoteki jinbutsu*) from Takeuchi, *Nihonjin no shussekan*, 116–17.

19. Kinmonth, *The Self-Made Man*, 10. Kinmonth also notes that the self-help message in *Seikō* centered more on educational achievement than Smiles's text (178).

20. These observations come from an investigation of the large number of *risshi shōsetsu* held in the collections of the National Diet Library in Tokyo and Waseda University.

21. See the advertisement in *Seikō* 23, no. 4, August 1, 1912, and 29, no. 5, August 1, 1915.

22. Ito, *An Age of Melodrama*, 19–20. Both *Hototogisu* and *Konjiki yasha* had an extensive afterlife on stage and screen as well.

23. Komori, *Shōsetsu to hihyō*, 27–33.

24. "I have termed this general enterprise—study of the collective making of distinct cultural practices and inquiry into the relations among these practices—a poetics of culture." Greenblatt, *Shakespearean Negotiations*, 5.

25. See, for example, Kan, *Media no jidai*, Naitō, "Media toshite no *Meian*," and the foundation of all such work, Maeda Ai's classic *Kindai dokusha no seiritsu*.

26. This particular advertisement is from *Seikō* 23, no. 4, August 1, 1912.

27. Wada, "'Risshi shōsetsu' to dokusho mōdo." See also his follow-up essay, "'Risshi shōsetsu' no yukue." To my knowledge, this is the only previous scholarship on this genre of fiction. The fact that *Seikō* featured fiction attracted no attention in previous historical or sociological studies of the magazine.

28. Takeuchi, *Nihonjin no shussekan*, 120–23.

29. *Seikō* 15, no. 3, January 1, 1909, and in many other issues as well.

30. *Seikō* 19, no. 6, December 1, 1910.

31. Ibid.

32. I use the definitions of "scene" and "summary" in Genette, *Narrative Discourse*, 94.

33. Kinmonth, *The Self-Made Man*, 166–205.

34. *Seikō* 18, no. 2, April 1, 1910, 34–35.

35. *Seikō* 19, no. 2, September 1, 1910, 9–10.

36. *Seikō* 19, no. 6, December 1, 1910, 21–22.

37. *Seikō* 18, no. 5, June 1, 1910, 41–43.

38. Havens, *Farm and Nation*, 84–85.

39. Shōji, *Kin-gendai Nihon no nōson*, 34–36.

40. This is the major point in Waswo, "The Transformation of Rural Society."

41. Shōji, *Kin-gendai Nihon no nōson*, 41.

42. Waswo, "The Transformation of Rural Society," 590–91.

43. Najita, *Ordinary Economies in Japan*, 104–74.

44. Etori, *Nihon sonraku shakai*, 399–462; Havens, *Farm and Nation*, 25–27, 41–49.

45. Tsutsui, "The Impact of the Local Improvement Movement," 60; Pyle, "The Technology of Japanese Nationalism," 53; Waswo, "The Transformation of Rural Society," 571–72.

46. Partner, "Peasants into Citizens?," 179–209.

47. One of the state's earliest efforts to "nationalize" the countryside was the new educational system. For an excellent study of this effort, including rural resistance to the state's educational initiatives, see the later chapters of Platt, *Burning and Building*.

48. See specifically *Seikō* 17, no. 5, January 1, 1910; 17, no. 6, February 1, 1910; 18, no. 6, July 1, 1910; 19, no. 1, August 1, 1910; and 19, no. 2, September 1, 1910.

49. Horiuchi, *Ase no kachi*. All citations from *Ase no kachi* are henceforth given parenthetically in the body of the chapter.

50. Midoro, *Ninomiya Sontoku*, 2.

51. Ibid., 6.

52. Ibid., 18–24, 35–40. Midoro's book is a popularization of Sontoku's thought and does not do justice to his hero's ideas of the relationship between long-term plans (*shihō*) and budgeting (*bundo*). A discussion is in Najita, *Ordinary Economies in Japan*, 125–37.

53. Midoro, *Ninomiya Sontoku*, 8–9.

54. Tanaka, *New Times in Modern Japan*, 144.

55. *Shimin* 2, no. 10, October 1, 1907, 27–32.

56. See Najita, *Ordinary Economies in Japan*, 163–73.

57. Jameson, *Archaeologies of the Future*, 1–9.

58. Horiuchi, *Kannondō*. Page numbers for citations are hereafter given in parentheses in the text.

59. Bloch, *The Utopian Function of Art and Literature*, 107.

60. There is an even more obvious reason for their lack of inclusion in the canon: these genre staples feature hastily written prose, formulaic plots, and two-dimensional characters. They also rely heavily on coincidence, a major fault from the perspective of literary modernity. One of the small pleasures of reading these works in their original format is that we have the marginalia of previous readers, both sympathetic and unsympathetic. For example, after a breathtaking string of coincidences brings the hero of *Ase no kachi* to the verge of his inevitable success, one jaded reader wrote in the margins of page 286 of the copy of the novel held by the National Diet Library in Tokyo, "His luck is so good it's irritating" (*amari un ga yosugiru iya ari*).

Chapter 3. Topographies of Value

1. Natsume, *Mon*, 414. I have added italics for emphasis. The translations are my own, but there is a fine new rendition by the late William F. Sibley.

2. For a partial list, see Maeda, *Kindai dokusha no seiritsu*, 172.

3. Maeda, *Toshi kūkan no naka no bungaku*, 346. Maeda sees much symbolism in the fact that the couple resides in "a place that cannot be named" (347).

4. The three novels were released in a single volume in 1914, published by Shun'yōdō. It includes a preface stating that they were written as a "trilogy" (*sanbu shōsetsu*), but have been considered as separate novels in the past, a situation that can be rectified by the new edition. See *Sōseki zenshū*, 27:477–78.

5. Thomas, *Reconfiguring Modernity*, 164.

6. Michio Nagai, "Herbert Spencer in Early Meiji Japan," 55.

7. Takeuchi, *Risshin shusse shugi*, 16–21.

8. Natsume, *Sanshirō*. 273–92. There is a spirited translation by Jay Rubin.

9. Takahashi, "Chishikijin no kunō," 55.

10. Kenmochi, "Natsume Sōseki *Sorekara* to Danantsio *Shi no shōri*," 82.

11. Yoshida, "Daisuke no kansei," 117.

12. An old essay by Kamei Katsuichirō comes close to situating the characters in the context of social mobility, but it does not, in the end, reference *risshin shusse*. See his "Nagai Daisuke," 9–11.

13. Karatani, *Sōseki ronshūsei*, 282.

14. I use another's translation in this chapter: the superb rendition by Norma Moore Field. The page numbers for citations are in parentheses, and I also include the page numbers from *Sōseki zenshū*, abbreviated SZ.

15. Takahashi sees Daisuke's characterization as forming the template for novels stretching through the entire twentieth century. See his "Chishikijin no kunō," 59–62.

16. Ichiyanagi, "Tokkenka sareru 'shinkei,'" 42.

17. Simmel, "The Metropolis and Mental Life," 410.

18. Ibid., 410.

19. Ibid., 412–13.

20. Sōseki also uses the word in French/English in his original outline for the novel. *Sōseki zenshū*, 20:89.

21. The most sophisticated of these efforts to think about the novel through the lens of degeneration (*taikaron*) is Ubukata, "Atarashii otoko no shintai."

22. Similarly, there is a tradition of linking the representation of nature to the psychology of the protagonist. This lineage goes at least as far back as Ochi, *Sōseki shiron*, 166.

23. Simmel, "The Metropolis and Mental Life," 410.

24. My discussion of color is indebted to an influential essay by Ino Kenji, "*Sorekara* no shiso to hōhō." He concludes that the symbolism of the flower and color are fundamental structuring devices in the novel (18–19). I will offer an alternative of what fundamentally structures the novel in the next section.

25. In the advertisement for *Sorekara*, penned by Sōseki himself, the author suggests the title has three meanings: (1) it moves beyond its predecessor's university setting; (2) the protagonist will be at a more mature stage of life; (3) the new novel will end on a note of suspense such that the reader will ask "and then [what happened]?" See *Asahi shinbun*, June 26, 1910, or *Sōseki zenshū*, 16:285.

26. Uchida Michio, *Natsume Sōseki*, 149. Ochi Haruo also points out how the plot of *Sorekara* follows the unfolding of the seasons. See Ochi, *Sōseki shiron*, 166–67.

27. Rubin, "Sanshirō and Sōseki," 153. Takai Yūichi reaches similar conclusions, calling *Sanshirō* a novel of light and *Mon* a novel of darkness. See his "Tokyo no hikari to kage," 97. Takai's schematic paradigm leaves little room for *Sorekara*.

28. Miyoshi Yukio made the point long ago that *Sanshirō* cannot really be considered a *bildungsroman* (as it was commonly conceived in the earliest critical essays) because most of its action takes place over a mere three and a half months. The same can be said for *Sorekara* and *Mon*. See Miyoshi, *Sakuhin ron no kokoromi*, 20–21.

29. Bakhtin, "Forms of Time and of the Chronotope," 248. Lisa Eckstrom has used the chronotope of the threshold in a perceptive reading of Henry James, with whose novels Sōseki was familiar. See Eckstrom, "Moral Perception and the Chronotope."

30. Watanabe, *Risshi no Tokyo*. The preface is unnumbered. I will include page numbers in parentheses in future citations. The translations are my own.

31. See Ishii, *Nihon no sangyō kakumei*, 194–212. This historical context appears frequently in Sōseki's oeuvre. For a sustained analysis of how it is thematized in *Sanshirō*, see Takeuchi, *Risshin shusse shugi*, 96–109.

32. Ambaras, "Social Knowledge, Cultural Capital, and the New Middle Class," 2–3.

33. For Sōseki and social Darwinism, see Komori, *Seikimatsu yogensha*.

34. Simmel, *The Philosophy of Money*, 392. Simmel had earlier used essentially the same phrasing in his "Metropolis and Mental Life," 414.

35. Komori, *Sōseki o yominaosu*, 141–55.

36. Komori Yōichi, for one, has asserted, "The women portrayed by Sōseki always appear together with money" ("Sōseki no onna-tachi," 27).

37. Ishihara Chiaki shifts attention from the burgeoning love affair of the odd-numbered chapters, which are the preoccupation of most critics, to the even-numbered chapters, which center on Daisuke's relations to his family, to produce a bravura psychoanalytic reading of the text. However, he overlooks the fact that money and its circulation join all chapters. See Ishihara, *Hanten suru Sōseki*, 205–39.

38. See Saitō Hideo's impeccably argued essay, "Shinjū no yubiwa," which first placed the pearl ring at the center of debates on the novel. Saitō also connected this to the narrative present and past and even suggested that money creates connections among characters, thus paving the way for my own narratological discussion. Komori Yōichi extends

several of Saitō's observations and further cleared a route for my own reading in his "Sōseki no onna-tachi," 35–40. He elaborates further in his *Sōseki o yominaosu*, 155–64. Though my conclusions differ, I have also profited from Takemori, "Tegami to shisha," in which he shows, among other things, how letters serve to build novelistic relationships among characters and advance the plot.

39. Vincent, *Two-Timing Modernity*, 90.

40. Mizumura, "Resisting Women," 33.

41. Mauss, *The Gift*, 49.

42. Ibid., 59–60.

43. If this seems farfetched, consider that Claude Lévi-Strauss notes that Mauss is writing at around the same time as the structural turn in linguistics. Lévi-Strauss essentially makes Mauss a precursor figure for structuralism in the social sciences. See Lévi-Strauss, *Introduction to the Work of Marcel Mauss*, 38–44.

44. Jakobson, "Two Aspects of Language," 119.

45. See, in particular, Maeda Ai's writing on the genre of the so-called "account of prosperity" in Edo and Meiji. Maeda, *Toshi kūkan no naka no bungaku*, 96–117.

46. See Tucker, *The Marx-Engels Reader*, 319–29.

47. Simmel, *The Philosophy of Money*, 84.

48. Appadurai, "Introduction," 16–29.

49. Bourdieu, *The Logic of Practice*, 105.

50. For this aspect of Sōseki's fiction, see Yiu, *Chaos and Order*.

51. Simmel, *The Philosophy of Money*, 79.

Chapter 4. Winds of Scandal

1. For details, see Shindō, *Besutoserā no yukue*, 91–93.

2. *Waseda bungaku*, June 1, 1906. In subsequent citations, I include the page number in parentheses in the text.

3. *Shinshōsetsu* 6, no. 1, January 1, 1901, 27.

4. Kosugi, *Hayari uta*, 77.

5. The *Yomiuri*'s circulation in 1903, the year when Tengai's *Makaze koikaze* was serialized, was only 21,500; at the time, the circulation of the most successful dailies approached 100,000. See Huffman, *Creating a Public*, 386–87.

6. *Waseda bungaku*, February 1, 1906, 141–46.

7. See Honda Yasuo, *Shinbun shōsetsu no tanjō*, 75–121, 204–32.

8. Huffman, *Creating a Public*, 89–94, 235, 268.

9. Zwicker, *Practices of the Sentimental Imagination*, 171–72.

10. Baba, "Kosugi Tengai *Makaze koikaze*," 85–89.

11. Kosugi, *Makaze koikaze*, 289. Though old, this edition preserves the orthography of the original serial work. All further citations from and references to the novel will be given parenthetically in the body of the essay. The translations are my own.

12. A short list from the Meiji era would include the heroines from Kimura Akebono's *Fujo no kagami* (Mirror of Womanhood, 1889), Higuchi Ichiyō's "Warekara" (Split Shell, 1896), and Kikuchi Yūhō's *Chikyōdai* (Sisters Suckled at the Same Breast, 1903), among a handful of other works.

13. Tosa, "*Makaze koikaze* kō."

14. Although the context is very different, I have drawn inspiration from Ohmann's discussion of serial fiction's role in alleviating social anxiety and generating narratives of social reconciliation in early twentieth-century America. See his *Selling Culture*, 287–339.

15. *Yorozu chōhō*, June 3, 1902.

16. Recent scholarship has begun to show how women utilized the circumscribed realm of the home in order to assert citizenship, which Marnie Anderson has called "citizenship through the household." See her *A Place in Public*, 18, 146, and 191.

17. As defined in "Jogakusei no setsu," *Yorozu chōhō*, November 16, 1902.

18. Honda Masuko, *Jogakusei no keifū*, 88.

19. Sano, *Jitensha no bunkashi*, 171, 164.

20. Ibid., 173–74.

21. Kan, *Media no jidai*, 132–33.

22. The scene just quoted appeared in the *Yomiuri* on March 9, 1903. The receipt for the pawnshop appears in the illustration for this day, even though it does not appear in the text proper until the next day. This is one of many instances of foreshadowing of upcoming plot elements through pictures, thus indicating close collaboration between Tengai and his illustrator. See Seki, *Shinbun shōsetsu no jidai*, 242–43.

23. Shindō, *Besutoserā no yukue*, 99–103. Shindō also adds the act of overhearing as an important motif in the novel.

24. Kan has analyzed this passage and its accompanying illustration, which shows frontal nudity. See her *Media no jidai*, 133–36.

25. Brooks, *Body Work*, 99.

26. Freud, "Three Essays on Sexual Theory," 169–70. The new translation replaces the older "instinct" with "drive" for knowledge, which is the preferred rendition of almost all commentators nowadays. In most respects, however, the translations are nearly indistinguishable. For the previous version, see *The Standard Edition of the Complete Psychological Works of Sigmund Freud* [*SE*], 7.

27. In addition to the 1905 "Three Essays," see, for example, Freud's "On the Sexual Theories of Children" (1908, *SE* 9) for the primacy of the "origins" question. For the emphasis on the perception of anatomical difference, see "Leonardo DaVinci and a Memory of His Childhood" (1910, *SE* 11), "The Infantile Genital Organization" (1923, *SE* 19), and the third footnote to "Some Psychical Consequences of the Anatomical Distinction between the Sexes" (1925, *SE* 19).

28. Moi, *What Is a Woman?*, 367.

29. Brooks, *Body Work*, 105–6.

30. Ito, *An Age of Melodrama*, 5–6.

31. *Yomiuri shinbun*, October 5, 1902.

32. Inagaki, *Jogakkō to jogakusei*, 4–39.

33. For example, *Yorozu chōhō*, October 12, 1902.

34. For example, *Yorozu chōhō*, March 27, 1902.

35. Genette, *Narrative Discourse*, 162.

36. For details on the paper, with a focus on political scandal, see Kōno, "Sukyandaru jānarizumu," 22–24. See also Huffman, *Creating a Public*, 243–44. This orientation toward the salacious made the paper one of the most successful in the era; Huffman notes that its circulation was 87,000 in 1903 (386–87).

37. *Yorozu chōhō*, June 12, 1902.

38. *Yorozu chōhō*, July 29, 1902. This article, incidentally, is the one that Tosa, cited earlier, believes to have been the inspiration for *Makaze koikaze*, though he also admits to many discrepancies between news story and fictional story.

39. *Yorozu chōhō*, March 7, 1902.

40. In using the term "liminality," I follow Judge, *The Precious Raft of History*, 72–81. In examining the reasons why female Chinese students evoked social anxiety in their own milieu, she points to their "social, gender, and sexual liminality" (77). There is much overlap between the two countries at the turn of the century.

41. Silverberg, "The Modern Girl as Militant."

42. Loose sexuality was an important component in attacks on Hiratsuka Raichō and others, but it was not the only threatening aspect of their activities. More fundamental were their claims to personhood and their efforts to call attention to the arbitrary division of men's and women's spheres. See Reitan, "Claiming Personality."

43. For the serialized stories of *dokufu*, see Marran, *Poison Woman*, 36–64.

44. For the whole lineage, see Miller and Bardsley, eds., *Bad Girls of Japan*. This book includes Czarnecki's short essay on the degenerate Meiji schoolgirl (49–63). It covers some of the same territory as my own work, although I did not discover Czarnecki's piece until after I had completed this chapter. I thank Amanda Seaman for the reference.

45. Inagaki, *Jogakkō to jogakusei*, 122.

46. Ōtsuki, *Shinsen Tokyo joshi yūgaku annai*, 3.

47. Sakai, *Tokyo yūgaku annai*, 1 (this is the first page of the "Joshi no bu" [Women's Section] of the book).

48. Quoted in Inagaki, *Jogakkō to jogakusei*, 123.

49. Inagaki, *Jogakkō to jogakusei*, 129.

50. Ōtsuki, *Shinsen Tokyo joshi yūgaku annai*, 4–5.

51. *Yomiuri shinbun*, June 27, 1902.

52. *Yorozu chōhō*, October 1, 1902.

53. As Patessio observes, discussing such texts is fraught terrain because of the lack of lists with titles in the archive. However, novels that were lascivious, immoral, or emotionally heightened were the most typical targets for prohibition in the schools. See her "Readers and Writers."

54. Saeki, *'Iro' to 'ai' no hikaku bunka shi*, 150–57.

55. *Yomiuri shinbun*, February 22, 1903.

56. *Yomiuri shinbun*, July 23, 1903.

57. *Yomiuri shinbun*, July 12, 1903.

58. *Yomiuri shinbun*, March 11, 1903.

Chapter 5. A Genealogy of Failure

1. Quoted in Duus, *The Abacus and the Sword*, 321.

2. Said, *Culture and Imperialism*, 9. For Japanese historiography, see Duus, "Introduction," xiv–xix.

3. Robinson, *Korea's Twentieth-Century Odyssey*, 37.

4. Duus, *The Abacus and the* Sword, 320. The information on Japanese immigrants is drawn from the chapter "Dreams of Brocade" (289–323). While noting the importance

of the image of the self-made man, Jun Uchida argues for the shift from "subaltern migrants" to "subimperialists." See his *Brokers of Empire*, 93.

5. Matsusaka, *The Making of Japanese Manchuria*, 414. The remarks that follow are culled from the introduction to the book (1–16).

6. Young, *Japan's Total Empire*, 241.

7. Samura, *Tōkan no susume*, 6–42.

8. In addition to the books by Duus, Matsusaka, Uchida, and Young, cited above, see especially Tanaka, *Japan's Orient*.

9. See, for example, Kleeman, *Under an Imperial Sun*, Thornber, *Empire of Texts in Motion*, and, in Japanese, Kawamura, *Ikyō no Shōwa bungaku*.

10. Anderer, *Other Worlds*, 9.

11. Bourdaghs, *The Dawn that Never Comes*, 96.

12. Fukatsu, "'Yamanote no oku' no shinzō chiri," 42.

13. Natsume, *Mon*, 550, 552, 562.

14. Said, *Culture and Imperialism*, 74.

15. I came across this story quite by chance when looking through *Waseda bungaku* for other materials. I later discovered that it has been discussed in Nakane, *"Chōsen" hyōshō no bunkashi*, 77–78. Nakane's analysis centers on the dichotomy of civilization and barbarism, whereas my own analysis will offer an alternative reading.

16. Nakamura, "Chōsen e, Chōsen kara," 2. In subsequent citations, I include the page number in parentheses in the text. The translations are my own.

17. Komori, "Sōseki bungaku to shokuminchi shugi," 59–60.

18. Natsume, *Higan sugi made*, 36.

19. My inspiration for these terms comes from Frye. It is not an exact correspondence, but there is some resonance between these archetypes and the terms "tragedy" and "romance" as used in Frye, *Anatomy of Criticism*, 186–223. McClure, drawing on a tradition of literary criticism directly concerned with imperialism and colonialism, has used the term "imperial romance," defined as a fictional world "apparently divided into zones of order and disorder; adventurers caught up in projects of exploration, conquest, and conversion; and legitimizing discourses (themselves romances) that valorized these ventures." See McClure, *Late Imperial Romance*, 2.

20. Keene, *Dawn to the West*, 2:109.

21. Takahama, *Chōsen*. I include the page numbers in parentheses in the text for all citations. I also consulted the original 1912 book and will have occasion to refer to it. When citing the serialized version, I include footnotes with the relevant information.

22. The opening lines of the serial version are: "Having lost our only child, my wife and I decided at last to cross over to Korea" (*Osaka mainichi shinbun*, June 19, 1911). The narrator goes on to note that the child would have been ten years old at the time. There are further references to the child in later installments.

23. This excision had the unfortunate side effect of rendering incomprehensible a saccharine scene near the end (495–97), when the narrator and the geisha, Ofude, stroll back to the inn pretending to be husband and wife. Ofude invents a child, Satoko, for the "couple," and the characters speculate that Ofude may have had a child by that name.

24. *Osaka mainichi shinbun*, June 27, 1911. Subsequent substantial references to being a disillusioned writer include July 4, July 6, and July 18.

25. Takane, *"Chōsen" hyōshō no bunkashi*, 172.

26. Mizuno, "'Shasei' no kyōkai." Incidentally, translations and adaptations of Japanese political novels were popular in Korea early in the twentieth century. For details, see Thornber, *Empire of Texts in Motion*, 146, 158–61.

27. Mitani, "Takahama Kyoshi no shōsetsu hō."

28. Takahama, "Shōsetsu *Chōsen* jijo," 5.

29. See Tayama, "Sakusha no shukan."

30. For early examples of Japanese ethnography and ethnology in Korea, which date at least as far back as the protectorate era, see Walraven, "The Natives Next Door."

31. Clifford, *The Predicament of Culture*, 110.

32. Ibid., 34.

33. Atkins, *Primitive Selves*, 58. Using slightly different language, Uchida notes the need to simultaneously "stress affinity" and "deny coevalness." See Uchida, *Brokers of Empire*, 200–201.

34. Auslin, *Negotiating with Imperialism*, 98–102.

35. For details, see Beasley, *Japanese Imperialism*, 55–68.

36. Duus, *The Abacus and the Sword*, 328–29.

37. Ibid., 332–33.

38. Ibid., 325–27.

39. Ibid., 331–32.

40. Ericson, *The Sound of the Whistle*, 53–57, 92.

41. Duus, *The Abacus and the Sword*, 136.

42. For details, see ibid., 136–57 and Uchida, *Brokers of Empire*, 52–54. The dates are from Robinson, *Korea's Twentieth-Century Odyssey*, 8.

43. Matsusaka, *The Making of Japanese Manchuria*, 142. Among other benefits, this book also offers an entire history in miniature of the South Manchuria Railway up to 1931. See also Young, *Japan's Total Empire*, 243–47.

44. As a side note, the rapid shift in the geopolitical balance of power in East Asia beginning in the late nineteenth century spurred a number of competing claims to Manchuria. Even some segments of Korean society were, through recourse to notions of ancient boundaries between Korea and China, making claims to Manchuria for Korea. See Schmid, *Korea between Empires*, 226–36.

45. Gikandi, *Maps of Englishness*, 90–105.

46. For a full articulation, see Genette, "Introduction to the Paratext."

47. *Osaka mainichi shinbun*, June 15, 1911.

48. Bauman, *Wasted Lives*, 6.

49. *Osaka mainichi shinbun*, August 27, 1911.

Conclusion

1. Habermas, *The Structural Transformation of the Public Sphere*, 27.

2. Ibid., 56.

3. Ibid., 81.

4. Brickhouse, *Transamerican Literary Relations*, 29.

5. Ibid., 27–28.

6. Dalleo, *Carribean Literature and the Public Sphere*, 2–8.

7. Kim, *The Age of Visions and Arguments*, 9.

8. Ibid., 444.

9. It is also important to recognize that economic matters did eventually become important within the public sphere. Although Gordon does not use Habermas's term, he essentially uncovers the labor movement's involvement in the public sphere in the era 1905–1937. See his *Labor and Imperial Democracy.*

10. Berry, "Public Life in Authoritarian Japan," 158.

11. The classic statement connecting the modern (British) novel and the rise to prominence of the bourgeoisie can be found in Watt, *The Rise of the Novel*, 35–59.

12. This rich vein of scholarship is too extensive to exhaustively list, but some of the most important, representing different disciplines, are the following: Gluck, *Japan's Modern Myths*; Fujii, *Complicit Fictions*; and Gerow, *Visions of Japanese Modernity.* The effort to trace the roots of this national identity in the preceding Tokugawa period is now well under way. See, for example, Burns, *Before the Nation* and Berry, *Japan in Print.*

13. Nagamine, *Dokusho kokumin no tanjō*, v.

14. Berry, *Japan in Print*, 15.

15. See Anderson, *Imagined Communities*, 22–36.

16. Bakhtin, "Epic and Novel," 33.

17. For a superb recent example, see Naitō, *Teikoku to ansatsu.*

18. Morris-Suzuki, *Re-Inventing Japan*, 28.

19. Ibid., 29.

20. Ibid., 15.

21. Tanaka, *New Times in Modern Japan*, 27–53.

22. Wigen, *The Making of a Japanese Periphery*, 267.

23. In her second monograph, *Malleable Maps*, Wigen demonstrates how power impacts the imagining of locality, even the acceptance by the inhabitants of a region's own peripheral status.

24. Wigen, *The Making of a Japanese Periphery*, 297.

25. Lefebvre, *The Production of Space*, 280.

26. Ibid., 282.

27. Ibid., 282.

28. There is some precedent for the approach I develop in this monograph. Fujii draws on Bakhtin and Foucault in a study of novels that are contemporaneous with the ones in this book. In his chapters on Tōson and Shūsei, in particular, Fujii demonstrates how social tensions such as class and gender were articulated and explored within the city-country dichotomy, and Fujii devotes some attention to social mobility as well. See Fujii, *Complicit Fictions*, chapters 2, 3, 6, and 7.

Bibliography

Periodicals

Asahi shinbun
Kokkei shinbun
Osaka mainichi shinbun
Seikō
Shimin
Shinshōsetsu
Waseda bungaku
Yomiuri shinbun
Yorozu chōhō

Other Sources

Alger, Horatio. *Ragged Dick and Struggling Upward*. Edited by Carl Bode. New York: Penguin Books, 1985.

Ambaras, David. "Social Knowledge, Cultural Capital, and the New Middle Class in Japan, 1895–1912." *Journal of Japanese Studies* 24, no. 1 (Winter 1998): 1–33.

Ameda Ei'ichi. "Kindai Nihon no seinen to 'seikō,' gakureki." *Gakushūin Daigaku Bungakubu kenkyū nenpō* 35 (1989): 259–320.

Anderer, Paul. *Other Worlds: Arishima Takeo and the Bounds of Modern Japanese Fiction*. New York: Columbia University Press, 1984.

Anderson, Benedict. *Imagined Communities: Reflections on the Origins and Spread of Nationalism*. London: Verso, 1983.

Anderson, Marnie. *A Place in Public: Women's Rights in Meiji Japan*. Cambridge, MA: Harvard University Asia Center, 2010.

Appadurai, Arjun. "Introduction: Commodities and the Politics of Value." In *The Social Life of Things*, edited by Arjun Appadurai, 3–63. Cambridge, UK: Cambridge University Press, 1986.

Armstrong, Nancy. *How Novels Think: The Limits of Individualism from 1719–1900*. New York: Columbia University Press, 2005.

Asao Naohiro. "Mibun shakai no rikai." In *Asao Naohiro chosaku shū*, edited by Fujii Jōji, Mizumoto Kunihiko, and Yokota Fuyuhiko, 7:138–61. Tokyo: Iwanami Shoten, 2004.

Atkins, E. Taylor. *Primitive Selves: Koreana in the Japanese Colonial Gaze, 1910–1945*. Berkeley: University of California Press, 2010.

Auslin, Michael R. *Negotiating with Imperialism: The Unequal Treaties and the Culture of Japanese Diplomacy*. Cambridge, MA: Harvard University Press, 2004.

Baba Nobuhiko. "Kosugi Tengai *Makaze koikaze* o meguru media teki toposu." *Kōnan Joshi Daigaku kenkyū kiyō, bungaku bunka hen* 43 (March 2007): 79–90.

Bakhtin, Mikhail. "The *Bildungsroman* and Its Significance in the History of Realism (Towards a Historical Typology of the Novel)." In *Speech Genres and Other Late Essays*, translated by Vern W. McGee, edited by Caryl Emerson and Michael Holquist, 10–59. Austin: University of Texas Press, 1986.

———. "Epic and Novel: Toward a Methodology for the Study of the Novel." In *The Dialogic Imagination: Four Essays*, edited by Michael Holquist, 3–40. Austin: University of Texas Press, 1981.

———. "Forms of Time and of the Chronotope in the Novel: Notes toward a Historical Poetics." In *The Dialogic Imagination: Four Essays*, edited by Michael Holquist, 84–258. Austin: University of Texas Press, 1981.

Bauman, Zygmunt. *Wasted Lives: Modernity and Its Outcasts*. Cambridge, UK: Polity, 2004.

Beasley, W. G. *Japanese Imperialism, 1895–1945*. Oxford, UK: Oxford University Press, 1987.

Berg, William J. *The Visual Novel: Émile Zola and the Art of His Times*. University Park: Pennsylvania State University Press, 1992.

Berry, Mary Elizabeth. *Japan in Print: Information and Nation in the Early Modern Period*. Berkeley: University of California Press, 2006.

———. "Public Life in Authoritarian Japan." *Daedalus* 127, no. 3 (Summer 1998): 133–65.

Bloch, Ernst. *The Utopian Function of Art and Literature: Selected Essays*. Translated by Jack Zipes and Frank Mecklenburg. Cambridge, MA: MIT Press, 1998.

Bourdaghs, Michael. *The Dawn that Never Comes: Shimazaki Tōson and Japanese Nationalism*. New York: Columbia University Press, 2003.

Bourdieu, Pierre. *The Logic of Practice*. Translated by Richard Nice. Stanford, CA: Stanford University Press, 1986.

Brennan, Timothy. "The National Longing for Form." In *Nation and Narration*, edited by Homi Bhabha, 44–70. London: Routledge, 1990.

Brickhouse, Anna. *Transamerican Literary Relations and the Nineteenth-Century Public Sphere*. Cambridge, UK: Cambridge University Press, 2004.

Brooks, Peter. *Body Work: Objects of Desire in Modern Narrative*. Cambridge, MA: Harvard University Press, 1993.

Brower, Robert. "Masaoka Shiki and Tanka Reform." In *Tradition and Modernization in Japanese Culture*, edited by Donald Shively, 379–418. Princeton, NJ: Princeton University Press, 1971.

Burns, Susan L. *Before the Nation: Kokugaku and the Imagining of Community in Early Modern Japan*. Durham, NC: Duke University Press, 2003.

Clifford, James. *The Predicament of Culture: Essays in Anthropology, Literature, and Art.* Cambridge, MA: Harvard University Press, 1988.

Czarnecki, Melanie. "Bad Girls from Good Families: The Degenerate Meiji Schoolgirl." In *Bad Girls of Japan*, edited by Laura Miller and Jan Bardsley, 49–63. New York: Palgrave Macmillan, 2005.

Dalleo, Raphael. *Caribbean Literature and the Public Sphere: From the Plantation to the Postcolonial.* Charlottesville: University of Virginia Press, 2011.

Den Tandt, Christopher. *The Urban Sublime in American Literary Naturalism.* Urbana: University of Illinois Press, 1998.

Derrida, Jacques. *Of Grammatology.* Translated by Gayatry Chakravorty Spivak. Baltimore, MD: Johns Hopkins University Press, 1997.

Dodd, Stephen. *Writing Home: Representations of the Native Place in Modern Japanese Literature.* Cambridge, MA: Harvard University Asia Center, 2004.

Duus, Peter. *The Abacus and the Sword: The Japanese Penetration of Korea, 1895–1910.* Berkeley: University of California Press, 1995.

———. "Introduction: Japan's Informal Empire in China, 1895–1937: An Overview." In *The Japanese Informal Empire in China, 1895–1937*, edited by Peter Duus, Ramon H. Myers, and Mark R. Peattie, xi–xxix. Princeton, NJ: Princeton University Press, 1989.

Eckstrom, Lisa. "Moral Perception and the Chronotope: The Case of Henry James." In *Bakhtin in Contexts: Across the Disciplines*, edited by Amy Mandelker, 99–116. Evanston, IL: Northwestern University Press, 1995.

Ericson, Steven J. *The Sound of the Whistle: Railroads and the State in Meiji Japan.* Cambridge, MA: Council on East Asian Studies, Harvard University, 1996.

Etō Jun. *Riarizumu no genryū.* Tokyo: Kawade Shobō, 1989.

Etori Itsuo. *Nihon sonraku shakai no kōzō.* Tokyo: Kōbundō, 1976.

Freud, Sigmund. "The Infantile Genital Organization." In *The Standard Edition of the Complete Psychological Works of Sigmund Freud*, edited by James Strachey, 19:139–45. London: Hogarth Press, 1995.

———. "Leonardo DaVinci and a Memory of His Childhood." In *The Standard Edition of the Complete Psychological Works of Sigmund Freud*, edited by James Strachey, 11:57–137. London: Hogarth Press, 1995.

———. "On the Sexual Theories of Children." In *The Standard Edition of the Complete Psychological Works of Sigmund Freud*, edited by James Strachey, 9:209–26. London: Hogarth Press, 1995.

———. "Some Psychical Consequences of the Anatomical Distinction between the Sexes." In *The Standard Edition of the Complete Psychological Works of Sigmund Freud*, edited by James Strachey, 19:248–60. London: Hogarth Press, 1995.

———. "Three Essays on Sexual Theory." In *The Psychology of Love*, translated by Shaun Whiteside, 111–220. New York: Penguin Books, 2006.

———. "Three Essays on the Theory of Sexuality (1905)." In *The Standard Edition of the Complete Psychological Works of Sigmund Freud*, edited by James Strachey, 7:123–245. London: Hogarth Press, 1995.

Frye, Northrop. *Anatomy of Criticism: Four Essays*. Princeton, NJ: Princeton University Press, 1957.

Fujii, James A. *Complicit Fictions: The Subject in the Japanese Prose Narrative*. Berkeley: University of California Press, 1993.

Fujimori Kiyoshi. *Katari no kindai*. Tokyo: Yūseidō, 1996.

Fukatsu Ken'ichirō. "*Mon*: 'Yamanote no oku' no shinzō chiri." *Meiji Daigaku Nihon bungaku* 26 (June 1998): 38–46.

Fukaya Katsumi. *Edo jidai no mibun ganbō: Miagari to ueshita nashi*. Tokyo: Yoshikawa kōbunkan, 2006.

Fukuzawa Yukichi. *Gakumon no susume*. In *Fukuzawa Yukichi chosaku shū*, vol. 3. Tokyo: Keiō Gijuku Daigaku Shuppan Kai, 2002.

Futabatei Shimei. *Ukigumo*. In *Futabatei Shimei zenshū*, edited by Togawa Shinsuke and Yasui Ryōhei, 1:3–176. Tokyo: Chikuma Shobō, 1984.

Genette, Gérard. "Introduction to the Paratext." *New Literary Theory* 22, no. 22 (Spring 1991): 261–71.

———. *Narrative Discourse: An Essay in Method*. Translated by Jane E. Lewin. Ithaca, NY: Cornell University Press, 1980.

Gerow, Aaron. *Visions of Japanese Modernity: Articulations of Cinema, Nation, and Spectatorship, 1895–1925*. Berkeley: University of California Press, 2010.

Gikandi, Simon. *Maps of Englishness: Writing Identity in the Culture of Colonialism*. New York: Columbia University Press, 1996.

Gluck, Carol. *Japan's Modern Myths: Ideology in the Late Meiji Period*. Princeton, NJ: Princeton University Press, 1985.

Gordon, Andrew. *Labor and Imperial Democracy in Prewar Japan*. Berkeley: University of California Press, 1991.

Greenblatt, Stephen. *Shakespearean Negotiations: The Circulation of Social Energy in Renaissance England*. Berkeley: University of California Press, 1988.

Habermas, Jürgen. "Modernity, an Incomplete Project." In *The Anti-Aesthetic: Essays on Postmodern Culture*, edited by Hal Foster, 1–15. New York: The New Press, 1988.

———. *The Structural Transformation of the Public Sphere: An Inquiry into a Category of Bourgeois Society*. Translated by Thomas Burger. Cambridge, MA: MIT Press, 1991.

Hampton, Timothy. *Inventing Renaissance France: Literature and Nation in the Sixteenth Century*. Ithaca, NY: Cornell University Press, 2001.

Havens, Thomas R. H. *Farm and Nation in Modern Japan: Agrarian Nationalism, 1870–1940*. Princeton, NJ: Princeton University Press, 1974.

Hijiya-Kirschnereit, Irmela. *Rituals of Self-Revelation*. Cambridge, MA: Council of East Asian Studies, Harvard University, 1996.

Hill, Christopher. "The Naturalist Novel and the Boundaries of Japanese Literature." *PAJLS: Proceedings of the Association of Japanese Literary Studies* 9 (2008): 71–75.

Hirakawa Sukehiro. *Ten wa mizukara tasukuru mono o tasuku: Nakamura Masanao to Saikoku risshin hen*. Nagoya: Nagoya Daigaku Shuppan Kai, 2006.

Hiraoka Toshio. *Nichiro sengo bungaku no kenkyū*, 2 vols. Tokyo: Yūseidō, 1985.

Hirota Masaki. *Fukuzawa Yukichi*. Tokyo: Asahi Shinbunsha, 1976.

Honda Masuko. *Jogakusei no keifū: Saishoku sareta Meiji*. Tokyo: Seidōsha, 1990.

Honda Yasuo. *Shinbun shōsetsu no tanjō*. Tokyo: Heibonsha, 1998.

Horiuchi Shinsen. *Risshi shōsetsu: Ase no kachi*. Tokyo: Seikō zasshi sha, 1911.

———. *Risshi shōsetsu: Hito no ani*, 2 vols. Tokyo: Seikō Zasshi Sha, 1905–6.

———. *Risshi shōsetsu: Kannondō*, 2 vols. Tokyo: Seikō Zasshi Sha, 1908.

———. *Risshi shōsetsu: Tada ikki*, 2 vols. Tokyo: Seikō Zasshi Sha, 1912.

Howell, David. *Geographies of Identity in Nineteenth-Century Japan*. Berkeley: University of California Press, 2005.

Huber, Richard M. *The American Idea of Success*. New York: McGraw-Hill, 1971.

Huber, Thomas M. *The Revolutionary Origins of Modern Japan*. Stanford, CA: Stanford University Press, 1981.

Huffman, James L. *Creating a Public: People and Press in Meiji Japan*. Honolulu: University of Hawaii Press, 1997.

Ichiyanagi Hirotaka. "Tokkenka sareru 'shinkei': *Sorekara* ichimen." *Sōseki kenkyū* 10 (May 1998): 34–44.

Inagaki Kyōko. *Jogakkō to jogakusei: kyōyō, tashinami, modan bunka*. Tokyo: Chūō Kōron Sha, 2007.

Ino Kenji. "*Sorekara* no shiso to hōhō." In *Sōseki sakuhin ronshūsei*, edited by Ōta Noboru, Kimata Satoshi, and Manda Tsutomu, 6:16–30. Tokyo: Ōfūsha, 1991.

Irokawa Daikichi. *The Culture of the Meiji Period*. Princeton, NJ: Princeton University Press, 1985.

Ishihara Chiaki. *Hanten suru Sōseki*. Tokyo: Seidosha, 1997.

Ishii Kanji. *Nihon no sangyō kakumei*. Tokyo: Asahi Shinbunsha, 1997.

Ito, Ken K. *An Age of Melodrama: Family, Gender, and Social Hierarchy in the Turn-of-the-Century Japanese Novel*. Stanford, CA: Stanford University Press, 2008.

Iwanaga Hiroshi. *Shizenshugi ni okeru kyokō no kanōsei*. Tokyo: Ōfūsha, 1968.

Jakobson, Roman. "Two Aspects of Language and Two Types of Aphasic Disturbances." In *On Language*, edited by Linda R. Waugh and Monique Monville-Burston, 115–33. Cambridge, MA: Harvard University Press, 1990.

Jameson, Fredric. *Archaeologies of the Future: The Desire Called Utopia and Other Science Fictions*. London: Verso, 2005.

———. *The Political Unconscious: Narrative as a Socially Symbolic Act*. Ithaca, NY: Cornell University Press, 1981.

Judge, Joan. *The Precious Raft of History: The Past, the West, and the Woman Question in China*. Stanford, CA: Stanford University Press, 2008.

Kajiki Gō. *Shasei no bungaku*. Tokyo: Tanka Shinbunsha, 2001.

Kamei Hideo. "Tayama Katai, *Inaka kyōshi*: Chihō/bungaku seinen no sōshutsu." *Kokubungaku: Kaishaku to kyōzai no kenkyū* 39, no. 7 (June 1994): 52–58.

Kamei Katsuichirō. "Nagai Daisuke: Gendai bungaku ni arawareta chishikijin no shōzō." In *Sōseki sakuhin ronshūsei*, edited by Ōta Noboru, Kimata Satoshi, and Manda Tsutomu, 6:9–15. Tokyo: Ōfūsha, 1991.

Kan Satoko. *Media no jidai: Meiji bungaku o meguru jōkyō*. Sōbunsha Shuppan, 2001.

Karatani Kojin. *Nihon kindai bungaku no kigen*. Tokyo: Kōdansha, 1980.

———. *Sōseki ronshūsei*. Tokyo: Daisan Bunmei Sha, 1992.

Kataoka Ryōichi. *Shizenshugi kenkyū*. Tokyo: Chikuma Shobō, 1957.

Kawamura Minato. *Ikyō no Shōwa bungaku: "Manshū" to kindai Nihon*. Tokyo: Iwanami Shoten, 1990.

Keene, Donald. *Dawn to the West*, vol. 2. New York: Holt, Rinehart, and Winston, 1984.

———. *The Winter Sun Shines In: A Life of Masaoka Shiki*. New York: Columbia University Press, 2013.

Kenmochi Takehiko. "Natsume Sōseki *Sorekara* to Danantsio *Shi no shōri*." In *Sōseki sakuhin ronshūsei*, edited by Ōta Noboru, Kimata Satoshi, and Manda Tsutomu, 6:76–85. Tokyo: Ōfūsha, 1991.

Kikutei Kōsui. *Seiro nikki*. In *Nihon koten bungaku taikei, Meiji hen*, edited by Tanikawa Keiichi et al., 30:1–139. Tokyo: Iwanami Shoten, 2009.

Kim, Kyu Hyun. *The Age of Visions and Arguments: Parliamentarianism and the National Public Sphere in Early Meiji Japan*. Cambridge, MA: Harvard University Asia Center, 2007.

Kinmonth, Earl. *The Self-Made Man in Meiji Japanese Thought*. Berkeley: University of California Press, 1981.

Kishi Noriko. *Tayama Katai sakuhin kenkyū*. Tokyo: Sōbunsha, 2003.

Kleeman, Faye. *Under an Imperial Sun: Japanese Colonial Literature of Taiwan and the South*. Honolulu: University of Hawaii Press, 2003.

Kobayashi Ichirō. *Shizenshugi sakka: Tayama Katai*. Tokyo: Shintensha, 1982.

———. *Tayama Katai*. Tokyo: Sōkensha, 1969.

Komori Yōichi. "Kinsei shōsetsu kara kindai shōsetsu e." In *Iwanammi kōza Nihon bungaku shi*, vol. 11, *Henkakuki no bungaku* 3, edited by Kubota Jun et al., 57–82. Tokyo: Iwanami Shoten, 1996.

———. *Seikimatsu yogensha: Natsume Sōseki*. Tokyo: Kōdansha, 1999.

———. *Shōsetsu to hihyō*. Tokyo: Seori Shobō, 1999.

———. "Sōseki bungaku to shokuminchi shugi." *Kokubungaku: Kaishaku to kyōzai no kenkyū* 46, no. 1 (January 2001): 46–62.

———. "Sōseki no onna-tachi: Imōto-tachi no keifū." *Bungaku* 2, no. 1 (Winter 1991): 27–40.

———. *Sōseki o yominaosu*. Tokyo: Chikuma Shobō, 1995.

Kōno Kensuke. "Sukyandaru jānarizumu to 'hō' no shihai." In *Media, hyōshō, ideorogii*, edited by Komori Yōichi, Takahashi Osamu, and Kōno Kensuke, 21–49. Tokyo: Shin'yōsha, 1997.

Kosugi Tengai. *Hayari uta*. In *Meiji bungaku zenshū*, edited by Itō Sei, 65:77–147. Tokyo: Chikuma Shobō, 1968.

———. *Makaze koikaze*. In *Gendai Nihon bungaku zenshū*, 53:149–350. Tokyo: Kaizōsha, 1930.

Ladin, Jay. "Fleshing Out the Chronotope." In *Critical Essays on Mikhail Bakhtin*, edited by Carly Emerson, 212–36. New York: G. K. Hall, 1999.

Lefebvre, Henri. *The Production of Space*. Translated by Donald Nicholson-Smith. Cambridge, MA: Blackwell, 1991.

Lévi-Strauss, Claude. *Introduction to the Work of Marcel Mauss*. Translated by Felicity Baker. London: Routledge and Kegan Paul, 1987.

Levy, Indra. *Sirens of the Western Shore: The Westernesque Femme Fatale, Translation, and Vernacular Style in Modern Japanese Literature*. New York: Columbia University Press, 2006.

Link, Eric Carl. *The Vast and Terrible Drama: American Literary Naturalism in the Late Nineteenth Century*. Tuscaloosa: University of Alabama Press, 2004.

Maeda Ai. *Kindai dokusha no seiritsu*. Tokyo: Yūseidō, 1973.

———. *Kindai Nihon no bungaku kūkan*. Tokyo: Shin'yōsha, 1983.

———. *Toshi kūkan no naka no bungaku*. Tokyo: Chikuma Shobō, 1982.

Marran, Christine L. *Poison Woman: Figuring Female Trangression in Japanese Culture*. Minneapolis: University of Minnesota Press, 2007.

Masaoka Shiki. "Jojibun." In *Shiki zenshū*, edited by Masaoka Tadamitsu et al., 14:241–49. Tokyo: Kōdansha, 1976.

———. "Kumo." In *Shiki zenshū*, edited by Masaoka Tadamitsu et al., 12:252–53. Tokyo: Kōdansha, 1976.

Matsusaka, Yoshihisa Tak. *The Making of Japanese Manchuria, 1904–1932*. Cambridge, MA: Harvard University Asia Center, 2001.

Mauss, Marcel. *The Gift: The Form and Reason for Exchange in Archaic Societies*. Translated by W. D. Halls. New York: W. W. Norton, 1990.

McClure, John. *Late Imperial Romance*. London: Verso, 1994.

Mertz, John Pierre. *Novel Japan: Spaces of Nationhood in Early Meiji Narrative*. Ann Arbor: Center for Japanese Studies, University of Michigan, 2003.

Midoro Masuichi. *Ninomiya Sontoku: Kinken chochikuhō*. Tokyo: Seikō Zasshi Sha, 1909.

Miller, Laura, and Jan Bardsley, eds. *Bad Girls of Japan*. New York: Palgrave Macmillan, 2005.

Mitani Norimasa. "Takahama Kyoshi no shōsetsu hō: *Chōsen* o megutte." *Kokubungaku: Kaishaku to kanshō* 74, no. 11 (November 2009): 49–56.

Miyauchi Toshisuke. *Tayama Katai ronkō*. Tokyo: Sōbunsha, 2003.

Miyazaki Koshoshi. *Kisei*. In *Shin Nihon koten bungaku taikei, Meiji hen*, edited by Fujii Hidetaka et al., 28:333–479. Tokyo: Iwanami Shoten, 2006.

Miyoshi Yukio. *Sakuhin ron no kokoromi*. Tokyo: Ibundō, 1967.

Mizumura, Minae. "Resisting Women—Reading Sōseki's *Gubijinsō*." In *Studies in Modern Japanese Literature: Essays and Translations in Honor of Edwin McClellan*, edited by Dennis Washburn and Alan Tansman, 23–37. Ann Arbor: Center for Japanese Studies, University of Michigan, 1997.

Mizuno Tatsurō. "'Shasei' no kyōkai: Takahama Kyoshi, *Chōsen* no yōshiki." *Hikaku bungaku* 49 (2009): 21–34.

Moi, Toril. *What Is a Woman? And Other Essays*. Oxford, UK: Oxford University Press, 1999.

Moretti, Franco. *The Way of the World: The Bildungsroman in European Culture*. London: Verso, 1987.

Mori Ōgai. "Maihime." In *Meiji bungaku zenshū*, edited by Karaki Junzō, 27:3–13. Tokyo: Chikuma Shobō, 1965.

Morris, Mark. "Buson and Shiki: Part Two." *Harvard Journal of Asiatic Studies* 45, no. 1 (June 1985): 255–321.

Morris-Suzuki, Tessa. *Re-Inventing Japan: Time, Space, Nation*. Armonk, NY: M. E. Sharpe, 1998.

Morse, Samuel C., ed. *Reinventing Tokyo: Japan's Largest City in the Artistic Imagination*. Amherst, MA: Mead Art Museum, Amherst College, 2012.

Morton, Leith. *Modernism in Practice*. Honolulu: University of Hawaii Press, 2004.

Nagai Kiyotake. "Inaka kyōshi no fukushū." *Nihon kindai bungaku* 74 (May 2006): 108–23.

Nagai, Michiyo. "Herbert Spencer in Early Meiji Japan." *Far Eastern Quarterly* 14, no. 1 (November 1954): 55–64.

Nagamine Shigetoshi. *Dokusho kokumin no tanjō: Meiji 30-nendai no katsuji media to dokusho bunka*. Tokyo: Nihon Editā Sukūru Shuppanbu, 2004.

———. *Zasshi to dokusha no kindai*. Tokyo: Nihon Editā Sukūru Shuppanbu, 1997.

Naitō Chizuko. "Media toshite no *Meian*: Inyō sareta shi no sukyandaru." *Ōtsuma kokubun* 38 (March 2007): 193–209.

———. *Teikoku to ansatsu*. Tokyo: Shin'yōsha, 2010.

Najita, Tetsuo. *Ordinary Economies in Japan: A Historical Perspective, 1750–1950*. Berkeley: University of California Press, 2009.

Nakamura Masanao. *Saikoku risshi hen*. Tokyo: Kōdansha, 1981.

Nakamura Mitsuo. *Fūzoku shōsetsu ron*. Tokyo: Shinchōsha, 1950.

Nakamura Seiko. "Chōsen e, Chōsen kara." *Waseda bungaku* 39 (February 1909): 1–12.

Nakane Takayuki. *"Chōsen" hyōshō no bunkashi*. Tokyo: Shin'yōsha, 2004.

Natsume Sōseki. *And Then*. Translated by Norma Moore Field. Baton Rouge: Louisiana State University Press, 1978.

———. *The Gate*. Translated by William F. Sibley. New York: New York Review of Books, 2013.

———. *Higan sugi made*. In *Sōseki zenshū*, edited by Nakajima Kunihiko, vol. 7. Tokyo: Iwanami Shoten, 1994.

———. *Mon*. In *Sōseki zenshū*, edited by Nakayama Kazuko and Tamai Takuya, 6:345–610. Tokyo: Iwanami Shoten, 1994.

———. *Sanshirō*. In *Sōseki zenshū*, edited by Kōno Kensuke and Yoshida Hirō, 5:271–608. Tokyo: Iwanami Shoten, 1994.

———. *Sanshirō*. Translated by Jay Rubin. London: Penguin Books, 2009.

———. *Sorekara*. In *Sōseki zenshū*, edited by Nakayama Kazuko and Tamai Takuya, 6:1–343. Tokyo: Iwanami Shoten, 1994.

———. *Sōseki zenshū*, 29 vols. Tokyo: Iwanami Shoten, 1993–1999.

———. *To the Spring Equinox and Beyond*. Translated by Kingo Ochiai and Sanford Goldstein. Rutland, VT: Charles E. Tuttle, 1985.

Nijū-seiki Nihonjin jinmei jiten, 2 vols. Tokyo: Nichigai Asoshiētsu, 2004.

Ochi Haruo. *Sōseki shiron*. Tokyo: Kadokawa Shoten, 1971.

Oda [Niwa] Jun'ichirō. *Karyū shunwa*. In *Meiji bungaku zenshū*, edited by Kimura Satoshi, 7:3–109. Tokyo: Chikuma Shobō, 1972.

Ohmann, Richard. *Selling Culture: Magazines, Markets, and Class at the Turn of the Century*. London: Verso, 1996.

Ortabasi, Melek. *The Undiscovered Country: Text, Translation, and Modernity in the Work of Yanagita Kunio*. Cambridge, MA: Harvard University Asia Center, 2014.

Ōtsuki Hisako. *Shinsen Tokyo joshi yūgaku annai*. Osaka: Bungaku Dōshi Kai, 1905.

Partner, Simon. "Peasants into Citizens? The Meiji Village in the Russo-Japanese War." *Monumenta Nipponica* 6, no. 2 (2007): 179–209.

Patessio, Mara. "Readers and Writers: Japanese Women and Magazines in the Late Nineteenth Century." In *The Female as Subject: Reading and Writing in Early Modern Japan*, edited by P. F. Kornicki, Mara Patessio, and G. G. Rowley, 197–204. Ann Arbor: Center for Japanese Studies, University of Michigan, 2010.

Pechey, Graham. *Mikhail Bakhtin: The Word in the World*. London and New York: Routledge, 2007.

Platt, Brian. *Building and Burning: Schooling and State Formation in Japan, 1750–1890*. Cambridge, MA: Harvard University Asia Center, 2004.

Pyle, Kenneth. "The Technology of Japanese Nationalism: The Local Improvement Movement, 1900–1918." *Journal of Asian Studies* 33, no. 1 (November 1973): 51–65.

Reichert, Jim. *In the Company of Men: Representations of Male-Male Sexuality in Meiji Literature*. Stanford, CA: Stanford University Press, 2006.

Reitan, Richard. "Claiming Personality: Reassessing the Dangers of the 'New Woman' in Early Taishō Japan." *Positions* 19, no. 1 (Spring 2011): 83–107.

Robinson, Michael E. *Korea's Twentieth-Century Odyssey: A Short History*. Honolulu: University of Hawaii Press, 2007.

Rubin, Jay. *Injurious to Public Morals: Writers and the Meiji State*. Seattle: University of Washington Press, 1984.

———. "Sanshirō and Sōseki." *Harvard Journal of Asiatic Studies* 36 (1976): 147–80.

Ruskin, John. *Modern Painters*. Edited by David Barrie. New York: Knopf, 1987.

Saeki Junko. *'Iro' to 'ai' no hikaku bunka shi*. Tokyo: Iwanami Shoten, 1998.

Said, Edward. *Culture and Imperialism*. New York: Vintage Books, 1993.

Saitō Hideo. "Shinjū no yubiwa no imi to yakuwari: *Sorekara* no sekai." In *Sōseki sakuhin ronshūsei*, edited by Ōta Noboru, Kimata Satoshi, and Manda Tsutomu, 6:128–40. Tokyo: Ōfūsha, 1991.

Saito, Satoru. *Detective Fiction and the Rise of the Japanese Novel, 1880–1930*. Cambridge: MA: Harvard University Asia Center, 2012.

Sakai Tsutomu. *Tokyo yūgaku annai*. Tokyo: Shūgakudō Shoten, 1903.

Samura Hachirō. *Tōkan no susume*. Tokyo: Rakusesha, 1909.

Sano Yūji. *Jitensha no bunkashi*. Tokyo: Bun'ichi Sōgō Shuppan, 1985.

Schmid, Andre. *Korea between Empires, 1895–1919*. New York: Columbia University Press, 2002.

Seidensticker, Edward. *Low City, High City: Tokyo from Edo to the Earthquake*. New York: Alfred A. Knopf, 1983.

Seki Hajime. *Shinbun shōsetsu no jidai*. Tokyo: Shin'yōsha, 2008.

Shimamura Hōgetsu. "Bungei jō no shizenshugi." In *Kindai bungaku hyōron taikei*, edited by Yoshida Seiichi and Wada Kingō, 3:100–117. Tokyo: Kadokawa Shoten, 1972.

Shimazaki Tōson, *Hakai*. Tokyo: Shinchōsha, 1987.

———. *Ie*. In *Shimazaki Tōson shū. Meiji bungaku zenshū*, edited by Sasabusa Tomokazu, 69:161–349. Tokyo: Chikuma Shobō, 1972.

———. "Kumo." In *Tōson zenshū*, 1:252–64. Tokyo: Chikuma Shobō, 1967.

———. "Shasei." In *Tōson zenshū*, 6:33–34. Tokyo: Chikuma Shobō, 1967.

Shimazu, Naoko. *Japanese Society at War: Death, Memory, and the Russo-Japanese War*. Cambridge, UK: Cambridge University Press, 2009.

Shindō Masahiro. *Besutoserā no yukue: Meiji Taishō no ryūkō shōsetsu*. Tokyo: Kanrin Shobō, 2001.

Shōji Shunsaku. *Kin-gendai Nihon no nōson: Nōsei no genten o saguru*. Tokyo: Yoshikawa Kōbunkan, 2003.

Silverberg, Miriam. "The Modern Girl as Militant." In *Recreating Japanese Women*, edited by Gail Bernstein, 239–66. Berkeley: University of California Press, 1991.

Simmel, Georg. "The Metropolis and Mental Life." In *The Sociology of Georg Simmel*, translated and edited by Kurt H. Wolff, 409–24. Glencoe, IL: The Free Press, 1950.

———. *The Philosophy of Money*. Translated by Tom Bottomore and David Frisby. London: Routledge and Kegan Paul, 1978.

Sōma Tsuneo. *Nihon shizenshugi ron*. Tokyo: Yagi Shoten, 1970.

———. *Nihon shizenshugi saikō*. Tokyo: Yagi Shoten, 1981.

Suehiro Tetchō. *Setchūbai*. In *Meiji bungaku zenshū*, edited by Yanagita Izumi, 6:111–243. Tokyo: Chikuma Shobō, 1966.

Suzuki, Tomi. *Narrating the Self: Fictions of Japanese Modernity*. Stanford, CA: Stanford University Press, 1996.

Takahama Kyoshi. *Chōsen*. In *Gendai Nihon bungaku zenshū*, 40:383–500. Tokyo: Kaizōsha, 1930.

———. "Shōsetsu *Chōsen* jijo." *Hototogisu* 15, no. 4 (January 1912): 5.

Takahashi Kazumi. "Chishikijin no kunō: Natsume Sōseki." In *Sōseki sakuhin ronshūsei*, edited by Ōta Noboru, Kimata Satoshi, and Manda Tsutomu, 6:49–62. Tokyo: Ōfūsha, 1991.

Takai Yūichi. "Tokyo no hikari to kage." In *Sōseki sakuhin ronshūsei*, edited by Tamai Takayuki and Murata Yoshiya, 5:93–98. Tokyo: Ōfūsha, 1991.

Takemori Ten'yū. "Tegami to shisha: *Sorekara* no geki no shinkō." In *Sōseki sakuhin ronshūsei*, edited by Ōta Noboru, Kimata Satoshi, and Manda Tsutomu, 6:242–56. Tokyo: Ōfūsha, 1991.

Takeuchi Yō. *Nihonjin no shussekan*. Tokyo: Gakubunsha, 1978.

———. *Risshin shusse shugi: Nihon no roman to yokubō*. Tokyo: Sekai Shisōsha, 2005.

Tanaka, Stefan. *Japan's Orient: Rendering Pasts into History*. Berkeley: University of California Press, 1993.

———. *New Times in Modern Japan*. Princeton, NJ: Princeton University Press, 2004.

Tayama Katai. *Country Teacher*. Translated by Kenneth Henshall. Honolulu: University of Hawaii Press, 1984.

———. "The End of Juemon." In *The Quilt and Other Stories by Tayama Katai,* translated by Kenneth Henshall, 97–147. Tokyo: University of Tokyo Press, 1981.

———. *Inaka kyōshi*. Tokyo: Shinchōsha, 1998.

———. *Jūemon no saigo*. In *Tayama Katai zenshū*, 14:307–79. Tokyo: Bunsendō Shoten, 1974.

———. "Sakusha no shukan." In *Kindai bungaku hyōron taikei*, edited by Yoshida Seiichi and Wada Kingō, 6:146–50. Tokyo: Kadokawa Shoten, 1971.

———. *Tōkyō no sanjūnen*. Tokyo: Kōdansha, 1998.

Thomas, Julia Adeney. *Reconfiguring Modernity: Concepts of Nature in Japanese Political Ideology*. Berkeley: University of California Press, 2001.

Thornber, Karen. *Empire of Texts in Motion: Chinese, Korean, and Taiwanese Transculturations of Japanese Literature*. Cambridge, MA: Harvard University Asia Center, 2009.

Tokutomi Kenjirō [Roka]. *Footprints in the Snow*. Translated by Kenneth Strong. New York: Pegasus, 1970.

———. *Omoide no ki*. In *Gendai Nihon bungaku taikei*, 9:3–195. Tokyo: Chikuma Shobō, 1968.

Torrance, Richard. *The Fiction of Tokuda Shūsei and the Emergence of Japan's New Middle Class*. Seattle: University of Washington Press, 1994.

Tosa Jun. "*Makaze koikaze* kō: Juyō, zaigen, tekusoto ni tsuite no nōto." *Bungei to shisō* 39 (February 1975): 37–56.

Tsubouchi Shōyō. *Tōsei shosei katagi*. In *Meiji bungaku zenshū*, edited by Inagaki Tatsurō, 16:59–163. Tokyo: Chikuma Shobō, 1969.

Tsubouchi Toshinori. *Masaoka Shiki: Sōzō no kyōdōsei*. Tokyo: Riburopōto, 1991.

Tsutsui, Masao. "The Impact of the Local Improvement Movement on Farmers and Rural Communities." In *Farmers and Village Life in Twentieth-Century Japan*, edited by Ann Waswo and Nishida Yoshiaki. London: Routledge Curzon, 2003.

Tucker, Robert C., ed. *The Marx-Engels Reader*, 2nd ed. New York: W. W. Norton, 1978.

Ubukata Michiko. "Atarashii otoko no shintai: *Sorekara* no Kanōsei." *Seijō kokubungaku* 14 (March 1998): 42–53.

Uchida, Jun. *Brokers of Empire: Japanese Settler Colonialism in Korea, 1876–1945*. Cambridge, MA: Harvard University Asia Center, 2011.

Uchida Michio. *Natsume Sōseki: Meian made*. Tokyo: Ōfūsha, 1998.

Ueda, Atsuko. *The Concealment of Politics, the Politics of Concealment*. Stanford, CA: Stanford University Press, 2007.

Vincent, J. Keith. *Two-Timing Modernity: Homosocial Narrative in Modern Japanese Fiction*. Cambridge, MA: Harvard University Asia Center, 2012.

Wada Atsuhiko. " 'Risshi shōsetsu' no yukue: *Shokumin sekai* to iu dokusho kūkan." In *Disukūru no teikoku*, edited by Kaneko Akio, Takahashi Osamu, and Yoshida Morio, 303–32. Tokyo: Shin'yōsha, 2000.

———. " 'Risshi shōsetsu' to dokusho mōdo: Shinku to iu kairaku." *Nihon bungaku* 48, no. 2 (1999): 24–34.

Walker, Janet. *The Japanese Novel of the Meiji Period and the Ideal of Individualism*. Princeton, NJ: Princeton University Press, 1979.

Walraven, Boudewijn. "The Natives Next Door: Ethnology in Colonial Korea." In *Anthropology and Colonialism in East Asia*, edited by Jan van Bremen and Akitoshi Shimizu, 219–44. Surrey, UK: Curzon, 1999.

Waswo, Ann. "The Transformation of Rural Society, 1900–1950." In *The Cambridge History of Japan*, edited by Peter Duus, 6:541–605. Cambridge, UK: Cambridge University Press, 1988.

Watanabe Kōfū. *Risshi no Tokyo*. Tokyo: Hakuhōdō, 1909.

Watt, Ian. *The Rise of the Novel: Studies in Defoe, Richardson, and Fielding*. Berkeley: University of California Press, 1957.

Wigen, Kären. *The Making of a Japanese Periphery, 1750–1920*. Berkeley: University of California Press, 1995.

———. *Malleable Maps*. Berkeley: University of California Press, 2012.

Yanagita Kunio. "Inaka tai tokai no mondai." In *Teihon Yanagita Kunio shū*, 16:28–50. Tokyo: Chikuma Shobō, 1962.

Yiu, Angela. *Chaos and Order in the Works of Natsume Sōseki*. Honolulu: University of Hawaii Press, 1998.

Yoshida Hirō. "Daisuke no kansei: *Sorekara* no ichimen." In *Sōseki sakuhin ronshūsei*, edited by Ōta Noboru, Kimata Satoshi, and Manda Tsutomu, 6:116–27. Tokyo: Ōfūsha, 1991.

Yoshida Morio, "Hayashi Seizō ni iru fūkei: *Inaka kyōshi* no seisei to hyōgen." *Nihon bungaku* 42, no. 11 (1993): 28–37.

Young, Louise. *Japan's Total Empire: Manchuria and the Culture of Wartime Imperialism*. Berkeley: University of California Press, 1998.

Zwicker, Jonathan E. *Practices of the Sentimental Imagination: Melodrama, the Novel, and the Social Imaginary in Nineteenth-Century Japan*. Cambridge, MA: Harvard University Asia Center, 2008.

Index

Harvard East Asian Monographs
(most recent titles)

351. Michel Mohr, *Buddhism, Unitarianism, and the Meiji Competition for Universality*
352. J. Keith Vincent, *Two-Timing Modernity: Homosocial Narrative in Modern Japanese Fiction*
354. Chong-Bum An and Barry Bosworth, *Income Inequality in Korea: An Analysis of Trends, Causes, and Answers*
355. Jamie L. Newhard, *Knowing the Amorous Man: A History of Scholarship on* Tales of Ise
356. Sho Konishi, *Anarchist Modernity: Cooperatism and Japanese-Russian Intellectual Relations in Modern Japan*
357. Christopher P. Hanscom, *The Real Modern: Literary Modernism and the Crisis of Representation in Colonial Korea*
358. Michael Wert, *Meiji Restoration Losers: Memory and Tokugawa Supporters in Modern Japan*
359. Garret P. S. Olberding, ed., *Facing the Monarch: Modes of Advice in the Early Chinese Court*
360. Xiaojue Wang, *Modernity with a Cold War Face: Reimagining the Nation in Chinese Literature Across the 1949 Divide*
361. David Spafford, *A Sense of Place: The Political Landscape in Late Medieval Japan*
362. Jongryn Mo and Barry Weingast, *Korean Political and Economic Development: Crisis, Security, and Economic Rebalancing*
363. Melek Ortabasi, *The Undiscovered Country: Text, Translation, and Modernity in the Work of Yanagita Kunio*
364. Hiraku Shimoda, *Lost and Found: Recovering Regional Identity in Imperial Japan*
365. Trent E. Maxey, *The "Greatest Problem": Religion and State Formation in Meiji Japan*
366. Gina Cogan, *The Princess Nun: Bunchi, Buddhist Reform, and Gender in Early Edo Japan*
367. Eric C. Han, *Rise of a Japanese Chinatown: Yokohama, 1894–1972*
368. Natasha Heller, *Illusory Abiding: The Cultural Construction of the Chan Monk Zhongfeng Mingben*
369. Paize Keulemans, *Sound Rising from the Paper: Nineteenth-Century Martial Arts Fiction and the Chinese Acoustic Imagination*
370. Simon James Bytheway, *Investing Japan: Foreign Capital, Monetary Standards, and Economic Development, 1859–2011*

371. Sukhee Lee, *Negotiated Power: The State, Elites, and Local Governance in Twelfth-Fourteenth China*
372. Foong Ping, *The Efficacious Landscape: On the Authorities of Painting at the Northern Song Court*
373. Catherine L. Phipps, *Empires on the Waterfront: Japan's Ports and Power, 1858–1899*
374. Sunyoung Park, *The Proletarian Wave: Literature and Leftist Culture in Colonial Korea, 1910–1945*
375. Barry Eichengreen, Wonhyuk Lim, Yung Chul Park, and Dwight H. Perkins, *The Korean Economy: From a Miraculous Past to a Sustainable Future*
376. Heather Blair, *Real and Imagined: The Peak of Gold in Heian Japan*
377. Emer O'Dwyer, *Significant Soil: Settler Colonialism and Japan's Urban Empire in Manchuria*
378. Martina Deuchler, *Under the Ancestors' Eyes: Kinship, Status, and Locality in Premodern Korea*
379. Joseph R. Dennis, *Writing, Publishing, and Reading Local Gazetteers in Imperial China, 1100–1700*
380. Catherine Vance Yeh, *The Chinese Political Novel: Migration of a World Genre*
381. Noell Wilson, *Defensive Positions: The Politics of Maritime Security in Tokugawa Japan*
382. Miri Nakamura, *Monstrous Bodies: The Rise of the Uncanny in Modern Japan*
383. Nara Dillon, *Radical Inequalities: China's Revolutionary Welfare State in Comparative Perspective*
384. Ma Zhao, *Runaway Wives, Urban Crimes, and Survival Tactics in Wartime Beijing, 1937-1949*
385. Mingwei Song, *Young China: National Rejuvenation and the* Bildungsroman, *1900-1959*
386. Christopher Bondy, *Voice, Silence, and Self: Negotiations of Buraku Identity in Contemporary Japan*
387. Seth Jacobowitz, *Writing Technology in Meiji Japan: A Media History of Modern Japanese Literature and Visual Culture*
388. Hilde De Weerdt, *Information, Territory, and Elite Networks: The Crisis and Maintenance of Empire in Song China*
389. Elizabeth Kindall, *Geo-Narratives of a Filial Son: The Paintings and Travel Diaries of Huang Xiangjian (1609–1673)*
390. Matthew Fraleigh, *Plucking Chrysanthemums: Narushima Ryūhoku and Sinitic Literary Traditions in Modern Japan*
391. Hu Ying, *Burying Autumn: Poetry, Friendship, and Loss*
392. Mark E. Byington, *The Ancient State of Puyŏ in Northeast Asia: Archaeology and Historical Memory*
393. Timothy J. Van Compernolle, *Struggling Upward: Worldly Success and the Japanese Novel*
394. Heekyoung Cho, *Translation's Forgotten History: Russian Literature, Japanese Mediation, and the Formation of Modern Korean Literature*
395. Terry Kawashima, *Itineraries of Power: Texts and Traversals in Heian and Medieval Japan*
396. Anna Andreeva, *Assembling Shinto: Buddhist Approaches to Kami Worship in Medieval Japan*